Studies of
War and Peace

Edited by
Øyvind Østerud

Studies of
War and Peace

Edited by
Øyvind Østerud

Norwegian
University Press

Norwegian University Press (Universitetsforlaget AS), 0608 Oslo 6
Distributed world-wide excluding Scandinavia by
Oxford University Press, Walton Street, Oxford OX2 6DP

London   New York   Toronto
Delhi   Bombay   Calcutta   Madras   Karachi
Kuala Lumpur   Singapore   Hong Kong   Tokyo
Nairobi   Dar es Salaam   Cape Town
Melbourne   Auckland

and associated companies in
Beirut   Berlin   Ibadan   Mexico City   Nicosia

© Universitetsforlaget AS 1986

ISBN 82-00-07749-7

British Library Cataloguing in Publication Data
Studies in war and peace
1. War 2. Peace
I. Osterud, Oyvind
327.1 JX1952
Cover design: Harald Gulli

Printed in Denmark
by P. J. Schmidt A/S, Vojens

Contents

Preface

The Nobel Symposium on "The Study of War and Peace—Perspectives on Present Knowledge and Research" was held at Noresund, near Oslo, on 24-28 June 1985. Some distinguished scholars were invited to attend and to reflect upon basic questions in the study of peace and war. The proceedings should illuminate a limited range of important problems. Topics were to be general enough to be of wide interest, and specific enough to make fairly concentrated in-depth discussion possible. This volume presents an Introduction by the editor, the background papers at the Symposium (with minor revisions), comments by the discussants, and a summary of the general discussions. Chapter 7, by Alexander L. George, was commissioned too late for presentation at the Symposium.

The practical and potential relevance of academic scholarship within central disciplines was another of the topics at the Symposium. Different perspectives on crucial issues were examined, and are presented here.

In his opening address, the Chairman of the Norwegian Nobel Committee, Egil Aarvik, stressed the precarious state of the international situation, and the importance of scientific assessment, wisdom and political will.

The Symposium was prepared by a Program Committee comprising the editor (Chairman), Director Jakob Sverdrup, Professor Michael Howard and Director Johan Jørgen Holst. As editor, and on behalf of all participants, I am grateful to this Committee for its support. The Program Committee and the Norwegian Nobel Institute extend their gratitude to authors of the background papers, and to participants who accepted the invitation to contribute to the Symposium.

I express my thanks to the staff of the Norwegian Nobel Institute for their efficient and professional organization of the Symposium, and to Raino Malnes and Helge Pharo who skillfully summarized the discussions while themselves participating at the conference.

Øyvind Østerud

Studies of War and Peace: An Introduction

ØYVIND ØSTERUD

Perspective on Knowledge

Are scholarship, research and academic studies important for illuminating the big questions of peace and war? Scholarly knowledge is like tiny streams in a veritable ocean of popular views, political commitments, insistent agitation and practical decision-making. The role and relevance of systematic research have hardly been properly assessed. It is noticeable that pre-scientific and non-academic views on this topic are one-sided, incomplete or blatantly false. Alas, these features can often also be attributed to the more scholarly contributions in the field. Each discipline and every academic tradition has its own limited view on basic interrelationships and preconditions of war and peace. There is a biologically and a socially oriented psychological position; there are sociological traditions of a systemic, class-oriented, or macro-historical type; there is a wide variety of perspectives within economics, political science and international relations theory; there are also approaches of a more historically individualizing kind, closer to the contextual complexity and specific motivations of the actual situation. Even more confusing, there are unclear frontiers between scholarship and various political and ideological approaches. This problem manifests itself at quite different levels—from the fact that major academic positions might be said to originate from a "deep structure" of ideological dispositions, to the fact that studies concerning peace and war also attract pre-committed missionaries of various kinds. Ideological warfare is even mirrored in some of the value-loaded labels used to characterize specific traditions and networks in the study of war and peace—the fate of "peace research" or "security studies" being cases in point. The constantly precarious difference between analysis and mission becomes even more precarious in times of high tension and strong opinion. The strife for the "relevance" of scholarship is indeed an ambiguous endeavor.

These problems will of course not be adequately resolved in this book, even though most of the contributors have had problems of this kind clearly in mind. It may be asked what contributions academic knowledge really can make; it is quite obvious that insistence on elementary academic standards—openness, systematic scepticism, conclusions from evidence and argued premises—is a necessary basis for any practical relevance.

Still, the contributions of science are, here as always, often indirect and recognizable only in the long term. At best, we recognize them on hindsight. More often, the academic origins of common knowledge, public debate, institutions and problem-solving procedures are forgotten. There are, however, certain problems that research definitely cannot resolve, problems which should tentatively be identified before accusations of lack of relevance are made. Research generally gives few simple answers to the most acute and complex questions concerning peace and war. When scholars do give such answers, they usually act in another respect, politically or in some other way. We might in principle sort out three different sets of situations.

First, the lack of clear-cut research-based solutions is often due to the fact that the questions involved are intrinsically political in nature rather than scientific. It might, for instance, be possible in principle to estimate the risks of war if one particular defense system were adapted. It might also be possible, again in principle if not in practice, to estimate the chances of military occupation at different levels of deterrent strategic posture. Research cannot, in any case, weigh the increasing risk of war against the decreasing chance of successful occupation. This is a question of choice between competing values. Scholarly analysis might help to clarify the dimensions of the dilemma and to make an assessment of the contrasting risks, but the choice itself is a political one. Equally, the evaluation of a smaller risk in the short run against a greater risk in the long run has a definitive non-scientific element. Several questions of peace and war involve uncertainty, with little prospect of a certain answer. It is impossible to be sure whether our opponent is avoiding aggression because of our deterrent posture, or whether he would have done so in any case. The question as to what factors have preserved peace in Europe since the Second World War involves a counterfactual historical hypothesis to which there is no definitive answer. Neither do we know whether the last generation of ballistic missiles will have the accuracy in a hypothetical real war that they show during testing under quite different circumstances. Research might generally supply cues for rational choice under uncertainty; it might explain how vital decisions in the past have actually been made; but it cannot remove uncertainty.

Secondly, there are certain questions to which further research might give the answers, but which are not yet available. Systematic investigations might uncover the quasi-historical myth-making and dubious analogies between past crises and present situations. The decisive mechanisms of the arms race—if "arms race" is an apt characteristic—are not fully understood, although further research might bring vital knowledge. The contextual attributes to decisions of war and peace have in general been only marginally uncovered, although a fairly substantial number of singular historical studies have been produced. The point is that potential academic prospects of this type should be sorted out from the more clearly non-scientific questions in the field.

Thirdly, there are some questions to which systematic research, some of it perhaps not widely circulated, already supplies fairly adequate answers. There is a detailed amount of scholarly knowledge into the conditions of war and peace—more reliable information, extensive data banks, historical insight into past outbreaks of war and into the evolution of present problems, knowledge about decision-making processes, about military doctrines, weapons systems, and swings in public opinion. We also know that many popular ideas about the causes of conflict and war are over-generalized and untenable. The problem is often wrongly posed. The search for a general explanation of war might be similar to the search for a general explanation of disease, or, as Alasdair MacIntyre once sarcastically suggested, a "general theory of holes". The problem is misplaced because there are good reasons for arguing that the word "war" is a common term for a wide variety of phenomena, with a wide variety of "causes" behind them. Scholarly analyses have contributed greatly to the breaking up of exceedingly broad questions into manageable and meaningful portions. Here is a critical and "negative" contribution with rather wide implications. One example is the intensive popular debate between those who believe that peace is preserved by unilateral disarmament, full-scale or piecemeal, and those who believe that preparation for war is the best guarantee of peace. In fact, we do not know under what conditions it is possible to stimulate towards mutual disarmament by means of controlled one-sided rearmament, or whether unilateral arms reductions tend more to move the opponent in the same direction. Since the reactions of political actors are never completely predictable, there are no universally valid answers to such questions.

The contributions to the present volume do not display a full cross-section of contemporary knowledge about peace and war. The presentation concentrates on basic contributions from history and political science, with a few intrusions from related disciplines. These are fairly closely related fields, close enough for a fruitful dialogue; between them they also reflect a substantial amount of tension guaranteeing lively discussion. Dialogue and discussion are displayed in the book. The status of present scholarship is presented not as an authoritative body of knowledge, but rather, more realistically, as a dynamic endeavor with different tendencies and points of view.

The themes of the book are grouped under three main parts.

Causes and Correlates of War

When war is no longer normal, endemic or imminent there is a search for its causes. The widespread modern demand for an explanation of war became an immediate consequence of European events after 28 June 1914. The preceding period of peace had been extraordinarily long, and the questions of responsibility and guilt became politically acute. The origins of the first Great War have thus been studied in minute detail, filling literally thousands of volumes. Later major wars, and War in general, have also been the subject of intensive scrutiny. Yet the question remains unclear and the answers elusive.

Firstly, the notion of war-producing causality is intricate

and ambiguous, from the conscious decisions to the opaque historical forces, or from the triggering events and mechanisms to the wider constellations and deeper tensions. Take the origins of the Great War again. Different explanations were produced in circles emanating from the immediate decisions taken during the mid-summer crisis. Looking for whom to blame, one type of search concentrated on diplomatic maneuvering, military preparations and political decisions taken by the predominant actors. Another searched for historical roots to the crisis—the European alliance configurations from the 1890s, the German imperial heritage from Bismarck, the Balkan wars. Some scholars focused on the nature of the international system—the conditions of international anarchy, the eroding balance of power, the new armaments, the secret diplomacy. One perspective, or rather one group of perspectives, concentrated on socioeconomic forces in Central Europe, the internal dynamics of German society, the declining position of ruling and governing classes, the relics of a semi-feudal ethos, or the internal contradictions of capitalist society as such. The Marxist explanation combined the last point with the war-producing evolution of imperialist rivalry between states. Many commentators also stressed the importance of a specific intellectual and moral climate—like the emotional readiness of the public or the influence of Social Darwinism. Most historical analyses have combined elements from these various modes of explanation, while schools of thought have differed in the relative stress that was put on specific factors.

Pinpointing the "causes of the war" depends on which level attention is focused. A. J. P. Taylor once added complication to an already complex matter by stating that the general factors blamed for the war of 1914—like the secret diplomacy, the balance of power, the great armies—were the same that had given Europe a period of unparalleled peace. What has to be asked is thus not so much what factors caused the outbreak of war, but why factors that had so long preserved peace failed to do so in 1914. And we could perhaps conclude, said Taylor, that diplomacy was not secret enough, that the balance did not balance properly, and that armaments were too small. Here we get a glimpse of the dimensions of the problem, even when we limit the quest to explanations for war in the singular.

Secondly, "war" is a common noun for quite different phenomena. A general causal explanation is likely to be either an abstract platitude or an idiosyncratic declaration. Organized violence between large groups is embedded in the prevalent socio-political conditions. A tribal war, a war of knights, a merchant war, a modern world war, or a war of national liberation have only the most general behavioral characteristics in common. In medieval Europe, war was an integral part of the chivalrous ethos; in the early modern epoch it was ritualized to resemble the military parade; while right up to the Great War of 1914 it was still commonly regarded as quite a normal way of resolving diplomatic tension. There are few likenesses between a war of knights and the war in Vietnam, or between the Falklands war and the First World War. We might be able to explain types of war by grouping them together within specific categories, but we would still lack a convincingly fruitful system of classification: should the types be defined in accordance with different motives (conquest, pre-emption, missionary zeal, etc.), in accordance with international conflict patterns (bipolarity, multipolarity, regional power blocks, etc.), or in chronological order, with specific explanations for war in different epochs? These are still unsettled questions, although the effort is as old as any study of war.

Thirdly, different explanations of war may be partly to the point. At one level, war definitely involves political and military decisions, decisions that are manifestations of more generally recognizable behavior. Thucydides expressed a strikingly modern view in saying that "what made war inevitable was the growth of Athenian power and the fear this caused in Sparta". The motives spring from power and defense, while a shifting balance between contending parties triggers off the conflict. Behavioral parameters are equally central to modern theories of deterrence and crisis resolution. If the decision to go to war involves an element of self-preserving rationality, then the nuclear deterrent has raised the threshold to warfare.

At the macro-level war is embedded in society. Nineteenth-century sociology evolved in the tension between two opposite perspectives on war—an optimistic and evolutionary view of industrial society as alien to militarism and violent conquest, against a pessimistic and cyclical view of modern mass society as more easily inflammable, rootless and belligerent. The more grandiose perspectives on industrialism and war have been specified along three different lines. One is the thesis of international interdependence, originating from early twentieth-century studies of functional internationalism, as a condition of peace. Another line is the idea of Veblen and Schumpeter, which argues that imperialism and militarism are relics of a feudal civilization, contrary to the nature and long-term evolution of modern industrial society—an argument which is elaborated in Arno Mayer's recent study, *The Persistence of the Old Regime*. The third prolongation of the classical macro-sociological tradition is the Marxian view, which states that industrial society is a misleading category covering two fundamentally different social formations—the capitalist one, belligerent and doomed by internal contradictions, and the socialist one, peaceful after the expiation of war-producing tensions. The macro-sociological perspectives are still somewhat trans-historical in character. They can hardly account for war as a specific experience—the origins, outbreak and course of events; the participation and alliance configurations; the dates, dimensions and duration.

The latter characteristics are partly searched from a middle-range perspective, between decision-making and macro-context. This is the quest for the empirical correlates of war. Statistical analyses of numerical data have confirmed the view that war is produced by a combination of various things: there are no simple relationships between state qualities and warfare, nor between international systemic characteristics and the outbreak of war; the hypothesis of a causal relationship between arms races and subsequent war has not been confirmed; the notion of an "arms race" is also somewhat misleading, since factors internal to individual states account for a substantial share of the rearmament.

Important aspects of the decision-making and macro-historical approaches to war and peace are taken up by Michael Howard in his paper, while David Singer extracts from the quantitative study of war. The relative merits of contending approaches are debated in the discussion sections.

Part I of the book also contains explicit perspectives on the three different levels that are often said to classify theories of war—the focus on individual qualities (like the UNESCO declaration in which it is said that war originates in the mind of man), the focus on state qualities (like the Kantian idea that liberal republics don't fight each other), and the focus on inter-state characteristics (like the Hobbesian idea that international society is constantly war-prone because it is an anarchic state of nature). These alternative perspectives, however, also permeate several papers and discussions in Parts II and III.

Strategy and Arms Control

Antagonist states with nuclear weapons and inter-continental delivery systems became a basic challenge to traditional military strategy. The major powers could no longer expect to protect their populations in the event of war. This was mutual deter-rence, with vast civilian populations kept hostage for the sake of non-war. The idea of deterrence seemed to be most tenable and robust at the highest level of violence directly between the superpowers. It appeared to be far more dubious at lower levels of force and at the extended ramifications. How did the superior strategic deterrence affect the use of conventional weapons out-side the mainland of the superpowers? How credible was the nuclear deterrent that was supposed to protect allied countries when the protecting power itself was vulnerable to a devastating second strike? The basic strategic problems have thus changed in the nuclear age. First, there is the problem of credible deter-rence as the basic security issue is transformed from warfare to stability. Second, there is the problem of deciding at which level—below the full-scale exchange of nuclear weapons—war-fare at all can be a usable policy instrument in the nuclear age. This situation requires modes of cooperation between antago-nist powers—by means of arms control and crisis management —that are alien to classical strategy. The situation also implies that strategic doctrines are under permanent challenge: there are no stable and convincing solutions to the problems of extended deterrence and lower level violence. Each generation of doc-trines during the last thirty years—from "massive retaliation" to "mutual assured destruction" to "flexible response" to "seam-less web"—has carried the same basic problems. They have not been resolved, only built into a new formula.

Arms limitation talks between the major powers have been

relatively unproductive—levels of defense spending and technological changes in weaponry have been insignificantly affected;
the concentration on symmetry and verification has brought
meager results; negotiations have themselves been driving forces
in the arms race, for instance by the production of "bargaining
chips" which are never given up; the strategic aims of arms
control have been poorly agreed upon, and stable deterrence
has been defined without specific limitations; there has also
been a dilemma between the aim of reducing the probability of
war and that of reducing destruction should war occur.

Still, there was a strategic *rationale* for arms control efforts
in the 1960s and early 1970s, culminating with the antiballistic
missile (ABM) treaty. This treaty put a brake on technology
and deployment that might have increased the likelihood of an
unwanted war. The prohibition of ABM reduced the incentive
to pre-emptive strike in a crisis, and dampened the drive for
increased offensive capability. But the tendency during the last
dozen years, since Salt I, has been to concentrate on numerical
limitations and quantitative developments rather than on specific improvements and defense systems that might increase the
likelihood of war.

This concentration on numerical deployments now dominates
arms talks as well as public debate. The relationship between
arms negotiations and strategic analysis has thus become even
more confused, with no clear guidelines in front of new technologies and prospects like the cruise missile and the recent "strategic defense initiative". Problems of this kind are forcefully
addressed by Lawrence Freedman and Thomas Schelling in
Part II of this book.

The International System

The international system is an anarchy in a technical sense.
There is no law-enforcing authority above the state units, but
still the inter-state condition is not chaos. There is an element
of hierarchy and domination between great and small powers.
There are—in certain respects—indications of a hegemonic big
power concert. There are also supernational blocks, transna-
tional ideologies, technical and economic interdependence, and
non-state actors in the field above and between states. In short,

the international system is also, as Hedley Bull has called it, an anarchical *society*, where interdependence, power relationships and behavioral norms are preventing chaos. Still, state sovereignty is a basic international condition, and an intricate problem is how peace and order can emanate from this anarchic condition. In this book, the problem is broken up and elaborated in four different directions.

First, there has been a remarkable stability in the central superpower relationship, with forty years without a major war, despite intensive rivalries, permanent dangers and several cold war crises. It seems obvious that the mutual nuclear deterrent has favored some military prudence. The informal global settlement after 1945 was also adapted to the real distribution of post-war power, contrary to the formal peace settlement after the First World War, which called for vigorous revisionist self-assertion in Europe. Tacit rules of the game also seem to have been operative in superpower relationships, e.g. respect for spheres of influence and avoidance of direct military confrontation. Such factors are discussed in post-war historical perspective in John Gaddis's paper, while Alexander George addresses the conditions of crisis management.

Secondly, the rivalry between the superpowers has been far less stable in the geopolitical "gray zones", in Third World areas with no clear-cut dividing lines or no well-established influence relationships. The détente of the late 1960s and early 1970s concealed the lack of a code of conduct in these areas, despite the sketch of a general agreement in 1972. Events in the Middle East from 1973, in Angola in 1975, in the Horn of Africa in 1977-78 and in Afghanistan from 1979 showed that there were basic uncertainties and disagreements about the room for maneuver in the gray zone. This was probably the most remarkable blind spot in détente, with rather fateful consequences for the conception as such. George also touches on this problem in his paper.

Thirdly, there is considerable unrest and warfare in various parts of the Third World, in contrast to the strategic stability between the big powers. Such cases of armed conflict may be indirectly a consequence of past and present influence from the first or the second worlds, sometimes also stimulated by external attempts at destabilization or intervention. The greater powers may, alternatively, be drawn only reluctantly and with confused objectives into a conflict, like the United States in the Falklands war or in the recent Lebanon crisis. The conflict may also be completely generated from local and regional antagonisms, often with origins in pre-colonial conditions, like in South-East Asia or in North-West Africa. There are, however, many ethnic and regional tensions that are produced by the heritage of colonial boundaries. The manifold instability in the Third World is addressed in Soedjatmoko's paper.

Fourthly, there is the problem of reforming the international system towards a more peaceful order. Here, the more radical critique of a sovereign state system, the more extreme anti-state solutions, tend to carry just as many problems as they intend to solve. As dissolving sovereignty requires coordinated action by those same sovereign states, there is undoubtedly a dilemma involved. The radical reformer also implicitly tends to assume that a global authority would reflect the moral and political values of the radical reformer, which is highly unlikely. Finally, transcending the state system might merely imply a verbal transformation of group conflict from inter-state war to civil war within a global organization. Since civil war even today is more common than inter-state war, this would hardly entail a more peaceful world. Michael Walzer, in his paper, is explicitly aware of such prospects, and his major suggestion goes in quite a different direction.

Part One
Causes and Correlates of War

1

The Causes of War

MICHAEL HOWARD

Behind the question "what are the causes of war" there usually lies the assumption that war is an aberration from the norm, a malfunctioning of an organism whose normal condition is one of peace. This was probably the belief of the founders of the Nobel Institute a hundred years ago, and it is one presumably shared by all the participants in this conference. But before we address ourselves to the question as it is posed, it may be useful to examine the assumption itself, and the historical circumstances out of which it developed.

The first thing to notice is that the assumption is rooted in a particular historical culture; one limited, like all cultures, both in time and space. Leaving aside the many war-oriented societies which have existed outside the Western world (of which certain sects of Islam are those most familiar to non-specialists) we cannot claim this irenical approach to war regarding it as abnormal or deviant behavior, to be a traditional feature even of Christian western societies, much less of the Hellenic, Judaic and Roman cultures from which they have developed. Christendom was for a millennium one of the greatest warrior societies in the world, and the Europeans did not extend their sway over the Western hemisphere, let alone Africa and southern Asia, by peaceful persuasion. The vast majority of Christians during the bulk of the Christian era have seen war as an intrinsic part of God's providence for mankind, and fighting as not only a legitimate but an honorable activity.

The irenical philosophy embodied in the aspirations of the Nobel Committee is (if one ignores certain isolated and impotent philosophers and sects such as the early Christian Church) barely two hundred years old, and is part of the *bourgeois* culture which during that 200 years became dominant especially in Northern and Western Europe and North America. In Britain in particular "the Peace Movement" had from its very beginnings a specific correlation to social development and the emergence of a *bourgeois* ideology: liberal intellectuals such as Tom Paine, Jeremy Bentham, and Richard Cobden believed that wars arose simply from the machinations of a feudal-monarchist elite, and was preserved by them as an institution to ensure their class dominance. It was a view which not only became part of the mainstream of the Liberal Movement in nineteenth-century Europe and North America but, *mutatis mutandis*, descended to the Marxists as well. Those thinkers saw and still see war as an aberration, arising out of the unjust ordering of society, and believed that if social relations could be reorganized on a "just" basis, war would no longer exist. The end of feudalism, or later capitalism, would mean the end of war.

This attitude to war has not passed without challenge. "The Peace Movement" was countered in Western Europe at the end of the nineteenth century by a powerful and vociferous "War Movement" which, fueled by Social Darwinism, maintained that war was intrinsic to human development, an activity not only inevitable but essential to the health of mankind, eliminating those societies unfit to survive and ensuring that the future should be inherited by those mentally, physically, and morally best adapted to guide it. Not even the First World War destroyed this philosophy. It emerged in a yet more vehement form in the guise of Fascism; and although it has few reputable adherents in the West today, its existence should be borne in mind, both in considering the validity of our presuppositions and as a factor to be taken into account by all concerned to build a structure of "peace". Few creeds ever disappear for ever: they often adapt themselves to changing circumstances and reappear later or elsewhere with redoubled strength. We would be very rash if we were to assume that our own views represented, and will continue to represent, a common and lasting consensus of mankind.

We do not have to subscribe to the "War Movement" to recognize that most of mankind, throughout much of its history, has lived in a condition approximating more closely to war than to peace. Peace may have been an ideal, but it has rarely been the norm. Nor need we have recourse to psychological theories of "natural" or "innate" aggressiveness to understand that in societies with any degree of complexity conflicts of interest are bound to arise, and that violence will always present itself, to those in a favorable position to use it, as the most direct way of resolving them. The history of the development of organized societies consists very largely in their growing capacity to control and channel armed conflict, and by the formalization of "war" as an activity carried on only by the agents of legitimized authorities. It has indeed been this which has made possible large areas and long periods of "peace". As Weber and others have pointed out, "legitimate" political authorities are those which have achieved a monopoly of the use of armed force within a specified territorial area, so that "war" becomes, not the generalized violence of anarchy but the means by which those political authorities resolve disputes between themselves.

A hundred years ago this process, of the monopolization of civil and military authority, had reached a stage when the control of the entire world appeared to be in the hands of a score of states, of whom only about six—Britain, Germany, Russia, France, the Habsburg and the Ottoman Empires, and the United States—were of any serious significance. The Peace Movement as it then existed saw its function as the prevention or limitation of conflict between these entities, a goal ultimately to be achieved perhaps by a Confederation embracing them all. But even at that time it was clear that the authority, even the existence, of some of those States—the Habsburg and Ottoman Empires immediately, the great colonial empires in the long run—was in itself a source of conflict, pregnant as they were with new nations struggling to be born. Agreements between states over the control of conflict were of little value when their very existence was under challenge from within. The First World War, in the eyes of many of its participants, was fought to decide, not a conflict of interest between Great Powers, but whether one of them, the Habsburg Monarchy, should continue to exist at all.

That was to set the pattern for twentieth-century conflicts, the great majority of which have been fought, not to resolve simple conflicts of interest between states, but to determine whether existing states should survive, whether new ones should come into being, and what the power-relationship between them should be. To this situation the prescriptions of the nineteenth-century Peace Movement, assuming as they did a basically stable relationship between states which were both finite and permanent, have ceased to have very much relevance. Even the very word "war" had to be abandoned by international lawyers, to be replaced by the more comprehensive phrase "armed conflict", which legitimizes the use of violence by non-state actors —the very activity which states came into existence to prevent.

Clausewitz at the beginning of the nineteenth century had sketched out the shape of things to come when he distinguished between the "limited wars" fought by states within the stable framework of eighteenth-century Europe and the "total wars" introduced by the French Revolution, in which the very existence of the state was at stake.[1] This distinction he saw as being more fundamental than the elaborate taxonomy of different "types" of war set out by his rival Jomini and to be elaborated by generations of Peace Researchers down to our own era. Nor did Clausewitz doubt the *utility* of war; something which the Peace Movement has always tended to underrate. After all, by seizing Silesia in 1741 Frederick the Great had enlarged his dominions by a third, doubled their potential wealth, and turned a small, poor principality into a major European power. There was a comparably direct connection between the wealth and power of Great Britain in 1815 and her success in warfare with the French over the previous 150 years. War paid. Comparable examples can be given from more recent eras. By fighting to resist the secession of the Confederacy, the United States prevented the Balkanization of North America and perhaps the indefinite retardation of its emergence as a World Power. By fighting their Arab rivals for the possession of the land of Palestine in 1948-9, the Jews established the state of Israel, which might otherwise have been strangled in its cradle. In these and innumerable other instances, war has been a quite rational act of policy, and the principle of Occam's razor should discourage us from seeking more recondite causes for its existence.

Yet there have been many wars in which the objective has been less clear and the motives less evident: the First World War of course provides the outstanding example. That conflict, with all its terrible consequences, did more than any other to set on foot a search for deeper sociological, psychological and anthropological explanations. There were indeed special circumstances which make any purely "instrumental" explanations of that war incomplete. The secular transformation of European society over the previous century, the resentment of the old feudally-based military elites at the ebbing of their political and social authority, the alarm felt by smaller landowners and a massive petty bourgeoisie at the encroachments both of big capitalism and organized labor, all contributed to a mood of frenetic nationalism which made the "War Movement" a great deal more powerful than the Peace Movement in 1914. But none of the innumerable studies of the crisis of July 1914 have revealed a moment when popular nationalistic pressures were overtly and directly influencing decision-makers, even in Germany. No doubt all these feelings were present in their own breasts, deeply internalized; "unspoken assumptions", as they have been termed by Professor James Joll.[2] The statesmen of 1914 were as "patriotic" as the peoples they led. But the calculations, both long-term and short-term, which led them to opt for war rather than to remain at peace in July 1914 were based on much the same considerations of *Realpolitik* as had inspired their predecessors in the eighteenth century and would continue to operate throughout the twentieth. If they did *not* fight, they calculated, the power of their adversaries might be so enhanced that their own nation-state would survive, at best as a power of the second rank, at worst as a client at the mercy of an alien hegemony. This the British and the French feared with respect to the Germans; this the Germans with respect to the Russians. All fought, as they saw it, for "freedom"; and this belief unleashed the immensely powerful dynamic of patriotic sentiment in all sections of society which kept the war going for so long and made it so difficult to reach a compromise peace. The particular characteristics of capitalistic industrial societies at the beginning of this century certainly gave both to the war itself and the crises which led to it a specific form; but the structure of fears and rivalries which directly precipitated the conflict was little different from that which had characterized wars in the pre-industrial age or are likely to threaten the stability of post-industrial societies, whatever their internal political systems may be.

This structure has of course been self-reinforcing. A millennium of endemic warfare in the West after the collapse of the Roman Empire did produce an elite for whom war was a preferred way of life, and whose conflicts were at least as much agonistic as instrumental. It was a class, as Professor Arno Mayer has reminded us, whose dominance persisted in Central and Eastern Europe until 1914, and whose war-oriented values continued, in those societies, to be highly influential.[3] The same class maintained its ascendancy in Japan until the Second World War. But in Britain, and France in the twentieth century their influence has been barely significant; in the United States and the Soviet Union they do not exist at all. The disappearance of feudal elites and the advent of industrialism meant that war ceased to be agonistic, but it did not wither away as the nineteenth-century positivists, St. Simon and Herbert Spencer, had expected that it would. Industrial society, whether pluralistic or totalitarian, developed its own civilian war leaders, its own bureaucratic defense mechanisms and its own military professionals to deal with problems of security which appeared no less pressing than before. In perspective it is clear that the problem of security creates military elites; not vice versa. At most, the relationship is reciprocal.

The task therefore which faces good *bourgeois* liberals like ourselves is not the elimination or "cure" of war, as if that were a condition that could be isolated and treated like a disease. It is the building of a global society in which groups, large or small, do not regard one another as alien and as threats to their own value-systems; the creation and maintenance on a world scale of that social and political consensus which characterizes communities wherein the State does effectively enjoy a monopoly of violence, and conflicts can be habitually settled by peaceful means; the development, in short, of a globally acceptable political order.

This is a problem which far transcends the creation of acceptable relations between governments, whether through the largely informal conventions of diplomacy, the institutionalization of intercourse through Leagues or Unions of Nations or the establishment of norms of behavior through international law. The incremental value of all these processes is not to be underestimated. But even on the most optimistic assessment it cannot be said that the international community has done more than barely maintain the standard of orderly relationships which characterized the Concert of European Powers during the nineteenth century—if it has even done that. Indeed the growth of self-awareness among peoples, which was so largely responsible for destroying the European Concert, works ever more powerfully to disrupt the global community; not simply by continually creating new crisis-points on the international scene, but often by calling into question the legitimacy of the governments which claim to speak for them.

Yet the framework of order which these institutions have created, incomplete as it is, is the best that we can reasonably expect. The "unspoken assumption" of the founders of the United Nations, as of the founders of the League of Nations, was that it would institutionalize the hegemony of the wealthy liberal *bourgeois* societies of the West and their value-systems over the rest of the world. Even if the cleavage between the Communist East and the pluralistic West had not destroyed that possibility from the outset—itself a cleavage far more cultural than ideological—the global multicultural explosion which has characterized the second half of the twentieth century and which is itself largely a reaction against white *bourgeois* domination has made any such assumption quite anachronistic. But without the existence, and more important *the acceptance*, of a single dominant culture, any expectations of moving towards any centrally-directed world community commanding universal consensus, "World Peace through World Law", will continue to be vain.

Is it inevitable that this "anarchical society", as Professor Hedley Bull has so aptly termed it, will necessarily be a warlike society?[4] Must the inevitable conflicts which arise within it continue to be settled by violence? Even within this imperfect framework, can not alternative and preferable means of conflict-resolution be developed?

We must base our answers to these questions, not on our own moral preferences, but, so far as we can, on objective analysis—itself, unfortunately, a cultural phenomenon. My own conclusions are that, at the margins, the use of violence to solve political problems can never be totally eliminated, any more than it can be eliminated from social life. There will always be the desperate, the fanatical, or those generally oriented towards violent solutions, and however successfully alternative means of conflict-resolution may be developed, these groups will continue to prefer direct action. The British problem in Northern Ireland, at the heart of the most "civilized" and orderly community in the world, is a sad case in point; to say nothing of the persistence of terrorism in other developed countries. The problem is how to keep this violence at the margins, in international as in domestic societies; and prevent it from encroaching on the central structure of world order.

Alternative and peaceful means of resolving conflicts are only likely to be effective if there is a disposition to use them, and the cultivation of such a disposition is no less important than the development of the means. "Bellicism", as I have termed the cultural orientation towards war,[5] is now rare in industrial societies, whether they be totalitarian or pluralist; although "bellicosity" as a mood may surface unexpectedly (as it did in Britain over the recent Falklands Islands crisis) and complicate crisis management. "Peace education", the deliberate indoctrination of the public through education and propaganda to "renounce war", a policy advocated by the Peace Movement throughout this century, is an attractive option, and certainly one to be encouraged. But it has two drawbacks. The first is that, unless such a policy is universally implemented, it can be dangerously destabilizing and produce the contrary effects to those which it intends. The experience of the 1930s cannot be totally ignored. Societies which cannot or will not defend themselves or their interests offer attractive opportunities, not only to bellicist rivals, but to governments which are unconstrained by public opinion and have few scruples about using force to achieve their objectives if they think they can get away with it. Again, the Falklands affair is relevant: in 1982 the use of force appeared to the Argentinian government a highly effective means of achieving an objective of national policy in the absence of any likely reaction by the British, and it is not surprising that they had recourse to it.

The Falklands crisis, however, is relevant also to the second problem of "peace indoctrination". Within the Peace Movement there has been, ever since its origins, a tension between those whose concept of "peace" is based on the maintenance of the status quo in international and internal politics, and those who would seek it through the elimination of perceived "injustices". In the pre-revolutionary era such "injustices" usually consisted in the wrongful possession or alienation of territory. The Argentinian claim to the Malvinas is one such example; the claims of the Peoples' Republic of China on the Soviet Union for territories alienated under the "unequal treaties" is another. But over the past century and a half, the "injustices" which have given rise to most concern have derived from the perceived oppression of subject peoples by an alien hegemony; the situation which the British feared might arise if the Malvinas, with their British population, were to be repossessed by Argentina. And to this dilemma, "peace education" has little to contribute.

The obvious solution to such conflicts is that they should be resolved by the mechanisms of arbitration, negotiation and peaceful change. But this is possible only when the territories or the peoples concerned are seen by their rulers as *expendable*; as being marginal to the security and survival of their own political entities. The hard cases are those in which they are not so perceived, and it is over such cases that wars are usually fought. The rulers of the Habsburg Monarchy (especially those in Budapest) believed that if they relaxed their control over the South Slav peoples within their territories their entire Empire would disintegrate. They were in fact probably right; and they were prepared to fight a war in order to prevent it. In our own day we see the same attitude adopted by the white minority government of South Africa towards its Black populations: to yield to their demands would involve, it believes, the dissolution of their entire political and social order. Again, they are probably right; and again, they are prepared to fight rather than peacefully acquiesce in their own destruction. A slightly different category of such "necessary injustices" are those involving the control of territories deemed vital by governments to their national security. Into this falls the Soviet hegemony over Eastern Europe; the United States' determination to dominate Central America; and the continuing presence of Israel on the West Bank of the Jordan. These are areas whose control the hegemonial power regards as non-negotiable, and whose possession they are determined to retain, even at the cost of war.

This leads us to two further reflections. The first is that one of the conditions of peace may unavoidably be the acceptance of situations widely perceived as unjust. There are always likely to be disputes over territorial or population control which the incumbent authority considers to be non-negotiable and which it is prepared to use any necessary force to defend. Peace in Europe between 1815 and 1859 depended on the continued acceptance of Austrian hegemony over Italy. Between 1871 and 1914 it depended on French acquiescence in the alienation of Alsace and Lorraine, and Russian acceptance of Austro-Hungarian dominance over Slavic territories. Between 1919 and 1939 peace depended on German acceptance of the loss of her eastern lands to Poland. Since 1945 it has depended on the acceptance of Soviet hegemony over Eastern Europe. Peace lasted, in fact, for as long as the power of the incumbent authority and its allies appeared so great that it could not be effectively challenged by force, and the irredentists were in consequence driven to the political margins. Once the international balance of forces shifted they again became influential and pressure for a "just war" increased. It is not to be wondered at that, although many in the West see the Soviet oppression of Western Europe as a constant provocation if not indeed a justification for war, the Soviets themselves see their presence in these areas as a guarantee of continuing peace; an argument once used by the British to justify their imperial presence in India and the Middle East. This has been the justification for imperial rule throughout the ages, and it is a hard question to answer, whether peace based on this kind of imperial order is morally preferable to the turmoil which usually follows the dissolution of imperial rule.

The second reflection is that major wars are caused, not by the kind of disputes which are justiciable, and which almost by definition are marginal to the interests of the powers concerned, but by conflicts in which states believe that their very existence—their power, that is, to control their environment and defend their values—is at stake; conflicts which no amount of arbitration can mitigate. These conflicts are less likely to develop out of any sudden dramatic confrontation than from a perception of a gradual change in the balance of forces, the incremental development of a hostile power to a point where, if it is not challenged, it might become dominant. In such situations, the decision as to what constitutes a *casus belli* may be quite arbitrary, and states may decide to go to war over matters which in themselves are not very significant. The French decision to challenge Prussia in 1870; the Austrian government's decision to fight Serbia over the Sarajevo assassination in 1914; the British decision to offer, and implement, a guarantee to Poland —a nation with whom the British had no ties of interest or culture–in 1939; these were taken in the belief that if hostile power was not checked now, it would soon be too late. It is a perception which has led states to embrace allies and causes with which they have little in common, and fight in places where they would much rather not be. It has led them to enter into wars which they dread and which they know may well be catastrophic; but they do so because they fear that the consequences of *not* fighting may be even worse.

This is the central problem which must be addressed by all those concerned with the abolition of war. It is one very familiar to practitioners of international politics. A whole web of conventions has grown up in international intercourse to formalize and constrain power relationships; by which states define and communicate those "interests" which they believe to be "vital" to their integrity and existence, if possible avoid conflicts over issues known to be critical, and defuse crises if they do arise. The amount of effective peacekeeping and crisis-management which goes on continually in the normal course of diplomacy is seldom appreciated by non-specialists, and between states sharing common "core values" it is normally quite effective. It fails usually only when one or more of the participants *want* it to fail; either because they have determined on war as the best solution to their problem (as Austria certainly and Germany probably did in 1914) or because, like revolutionary France, Nazi Germany or contemporary Iran and Libya, they are hostile to the whole system and wish to destroy it.

States build up armaments, both to insure against the failure of such peacekeeping mechanisms, and to give themselves greater bargaining power in the process of protecting their interests. The size of their armaments is taken as an index of their power; it may promote acquiescence in their demands, or competition, or both. This competitive arming is popularly and inaccurately referred to as the "arms race", and is also popularly and in my view inaccurately believed in itself to be a major cause of wars. Another assumption of the Peace Movement over the past hundred years is that the checking of the "arms race" would in itself prevent international rivalries and promote peace, and this assumption also needs to be critically scrutinized.

"Arms races" are a feature peculiarly of industrial societies, and one example among many of the competitive modernization which has characterized those societies ever since their origin early in the nineteenth century. It is a competition as much internal as external, and takes place as much between friendly as between rival states. American and French and British firms compete with one another as much as they do with the Soviet Union. Whether such competition is seen as a threat to the security of the state depends on the political relationships of the powers concerned. Britain saw French naval armaments as such a threat before the *Entente Cordiale* in 1904 but not thereafter. She then saw German naval armament as a threat because she judged, quite accurately, that it signaled a revisionist intention to challenge the hegemonial position at sea which the British considered to be vital to their national security; and they signaled their intention of maintaining that position by entering into a competitive building program. This rivalry was indeed a contributory factor to the British decision to enter into the First World War, but it was German power and ambition *as such* that Britain feared; not just the weapons being forged to give effect to it. When a few years later the United States signaled comparable aspirations to world power by the naval building program she undertook in 1916, the British acquiesced with a better grace. They did not enter into a race against the United States, partly because they did not have the resources, but even more because they did not see in America the kind of threat to their security and their values that was quite explicitly posed by the Second and even more by the Third Reich. Indeed, had the United States been seen as posing such a threat, the resources to counter it might perhaps have been found.

There was an intensive *quantitative* arms competition between the continental powers of Europe on the eve of the First World War, as both alliances strained to make available every man to fight in the conflict which after 1911 was generally seen to be inevitable. But that is the point: it *was* now seen to be inevitable. It was the imminent prospect of war that fueled the arms race and not vice versa. Much the same was to happen in the mid-1930s when the revelation of Hitler's full revisionist ambitions forced Britain into a crash rearmament program intended, first as a deterrent but, after 1938, to equip her for a war now seen as inevitable. Again, it was not Germany's arms as such which provoked the British reaction: it was the fear of what she intended to do with them.

For all these reasons, I do not accept the conventional wisdom that arms races, or armaments in themselves, are significant causes of wars. Arms races may precede wars, but they can also precede long periods of peace such as that which has prevailed between Britain and France for the past eighty years. Fears of being outdistanced in an arms race may be a factor in determining the moment when a state decides to challenge its rivals, as fear of growing Russian power was almost certainly a consideration in the minds of German decision-makers in Berlin in 1914; but at any level of armament there will be some moments that appear more propitious for war than others. It was fear not so much of Russian armaments as such as of the huge potential that lay behind them, and all that the development of Russian power might mean for German security, that haunted the mind of Bethmann-Hollweg and his colleagues in the years before 1914.

One might summarize a highly complex situation by suggesting that wars fall into two categories. There are those where the use of force appears the most effective means of obtaining a specific national objective, whether it be national liberation, the acquisition of territory, or the general improvement of status in the international system; and those when, in the short or long run, the very existence of the state appears to be imperiled by the growth of hostile and revisionist power. The former normally fall into the category of limited wars, the latter of total. The former are usually begun by statesmen who believe that the benefits of going to war will outweigh the costs; the latter by those who fear that the costs of remaining at peace will outweigh the benefits. In the nuclear age the entire basis on which these calculations rest has been transformed, but since we have yet to see a war between nuclear powers it is not possible to say how far we can legitimately extrapolate from the experiences of the pre-nuclear age. But those who propose nuclear disarmament as a means of creating a more peaceful world need to consider whether such a measure would not eliminate one of the most effective disincentives to war, whether limited or total, that the world has yet seen.

DISCUSSIONS

Kenneth N. Waltz

At the end of his stimulating paper, Michael Howard asks how far we can extrapolate in calculating the expected benefits and costs of using force when nuclear weapons have transformed the military world. Only insofar as the world is not transformed can we extrapolate at all. In one sense we continue to act in a conventional world. Wars have frequently been fought since 1945 and always with conventional weapons. Where only conventional weapons are used, nuclear weapons have seemingly not changed the basis of extrapolation. Wars in the last forty years have continued to be fought for the two principal reasons that Michael Howard identifies. The use of force sometimes promises benefits; the failure to use force may threaten disaster. Thus in 1939 when Germany attacked Poland, Britain and France intervened fearing that "if hostile power was not checked now, it would soon be too late". Anthony Eden in Egypt, Dean Rusk and Henry Kissinger in Vietnam, Ronald Reagan in Central America applied the old logic.

In the three later cases, extrapolation was faulty; but this was not because nuclear weapons changed the basis of calculation. Guided by the domino theory, and motivated by the related concern to maintain credibility, many American leaders have profoundly misunderstood international politics. In the world of states, winning ordinarily leads not to more winning but to losing. If states are free to choose, they do not jump on the bandwagon of a winner, but instead seek safety through balancing behavior. When the growing power of one or of some states threatens others, they work singly and together to increase their strength in order to avoid domination. This is both the lesson of history and the message of international-political theory. When Henry Kissinger, thinking of Vietnam, suggested that "if leaders around the world ... assume that the U. S. lacked either the forces or the will ... they will accommodate themselves to the dominant trend", he described precisely how states do *not* behave.[1] Thus, to add one example to the many familiar ones, in May of 1954 Dien Bien Phu fell; in September, SEATO was formed to promote cooperation among Southeast Asian nations in order to contain the growing power of North Vietnam.

The lesson of the 1930s was not that all aggression should be promptly opposed. States need to act in haste to counter an aggressor's gains only when they would make him dangerously strong. Imbalances of power in one's favor make prompt response to threats unnecessary. Moreover, without destroying all continuities, the presence of nuclear weapons does make important differences. Earlier, states of comparable capability had reason to fear that major territorial gains by some states would make them dangerously strong. Nuclear states can score only minor gains because scoring large ones risks retaliation. The accumulation of significant power through conquest, even if only conventional weapons are used, is no longer possible in the world of nuclear powers. Nuclear weapons have banished war from the center of international politics. The world has enjoyed more years of peace since 1945 than had been known in the nineteenth or the twentieth centuries—if peace is defined as the absence of war between great powers and of general war among the major ones. Making war has increasingly become the privilege of the weak.

Michael Howard suggests an additional reason for our recent good fortune. Centuries of warfare produced an elite in Central and Eastern Europe and in Japan "for whom warfare was a preferred way of life". Neither in the United States nor in the

Soviet Union does such a class exist. The United States and the Soviet Union are not militarist societies as Thorstein Veblen and Joseph Schumpeter defined them. Now "the problem of security creates military elites; not vice versa". Moreover, it is not arms racing that leads to war; instead insecurity causes competitive arming.

There is much to this, but also much is omitted. The old militarism, borne by a social class, is dead. Yet one wonders whether nations can for decades maintain large military forces without promoting militarist attitudes in much of society. All the more so when technology changes rapidly, military and civilian interests begin to fuse. Business, science, and the academy are drawn into military affairs. Such effects must reach even farther in the Soviet Union since it spends perhaps twice as large a proportion of its smaller Gross National Product on its military forces than the United States does. One worries not that military leaders and their supporters will seek occasions for war as military interests permeate society. Military men are often more reluctant to go to war than civilians are. Instead the dangers lie especially in two tendencies fostered. The first is increasing militarization of international politics. Relations between the United States and the Soviet Union, and among some other countries as well, have come to be defined and conducted largely in a single dimension, the military one. The second is the growing inclination to equate security with larger and more powerful military forces. The caution and conservatism of military officers easily leads them to exaggerate the adversary's strength and to underestimate their own. As Lord Salisbury wrote to Lord Lytton: "If you believe the doctors, nothing is wholesome: if you believe the theologians, nothing is innocent: if you believe the soldiers, nothing is safe."[2]

The likelihood of war varies not only with weaponry but also with doctrine. Military organizations, uncomfortable with deterrence, have succeeded in redefining the concept. Deterrence, contrary to the original notion of dissuading an enemy from attacking through fear of retaliation, is now said to require defensive and war-fighting capabilities as well. Pernicious results have followed. One of them is the creation of a need for stronger conventional forces, which will presumably enable NATO to sustain a longer war in Europe at higher levels of violence. At some moment in a major, protracted war, however, one side or the other—or perhaps both—will believe itself to be losing. The temptation to resort to nuclear weapons may then prove irresistible, and they will be fired in the chaos of defeat with little chance of limited and discriminant use. In a nuclear world, a war-fighting strategy is the worst possible one, more dangerous than a strategy of relying heavily on nuclear deterrence by threat of retaliation.

Emphasizing conventional forces diminishes the role of nuclear weapons. President Reagan's Star-Wars defense would further the effect. Large-scale wars at the center of international politics can "safely" be fought only if nuclear weapons are negated. If the unimaginable near-perfect defense against strategic nuclear weapons were achieved, such wars would again become possible. World War III, should it come, might then look like World War II, except that conventional weapons have become greatly more destructive in the meantime. A strategic defense could serve as the shield that would make the sword usable. President Reagan's Strategic Defense Initiative is mistitled. It should be called the Strategic Offense Initiative. As French Ambassador, Bernard Vernier-Palliez said, when interviewed at the end of his Washington tour: "Twenty centuries of history have taught us that conventional deterrence [i.e., defense] does not work.... It would be very dangerous if this country lost its belief in nuclear deterrence."[3]

To solve the problem of war may require development of "a globally acceptable political order", but as Michael Howard adds, expectations of achieving it are vain. The perpetuation of peace among nuclear states is an easier problem to solve, although necessarily with less than full assurances of success. Peace requires negating the two principal causes of war. Relatively small numbers of nuclear weapons are sufficient for the task if they are geared to a deterrent strategy, rather than to strategies of defense and war fighting. A deterrent force protects countries and perpetuates peace better than conventional forces have done. Surely Michael Howard is right in suggesting at the close of his paper that nuclear weapons have been "one of the most effective disincentives to war ... that the world has yet seen". The solution nuclear weapons offer is the best we have, and so far the best has been very good.

Karl W. Deutsch

In his important paper, Professor Michael Howard has proposed a cognitive theory of war, which is intended to be general. To discuss it, let me define my terms. By "war" I mean not just any kind of deadly violence, but the *large-scale* killing of at least 1,000 persons in battle, *organized* and prepared by a state or quasi-state and *legitimized* by it. By "cause" I mean any condition or process that substantially increases or maintains the probability of the occurrence of such a war or of its continuation.

For centuries, as Michael Howard reminds us, such wars have been widely perceived as "normal"; they have been often heard of and widely reported, but they have been rare as actual events. According to carefully prepared data by David Singer and his associates, such a war has occurred since 1815 about once every eighteen months somewhere within the international system or at its boundaries. Death in battle in such wars, or in civil wars, together with directly war-related civilian deaths from bombardments, fires, famine or disease account for less than 3 percent of all deaths between 1816 and the present. Of the world's 160-odd states, less than one-half have ever been at war—in part, of course, also because they came into existence only after 1945. For most people, war is a "normal" part of what they hear or read about, and fear, but not a normal part of direct personal experience.

Ordinarily, war has been feared, not liked. Michael Howard makes the valuable point that though there has been a "Peace Movement" since the late eighteenth century, there was also a "War Movement" in the late nineteenth and early twentieth century, ascribing to war a major value in itself. This War Movement lasted in most of the industrial countries not much more than two generations, roughly from the 1850s to a peak about 1914 and then petering out in the mid-1920s. In Italy, Germany, and Japan it lasted through the 1930s and ended only after 1945.

The main causes of war, according to Howard, are not primarily emotional nor instinctive, but cognitive. Rulers and decision-makers start a war, in his view, because they see it as a rational instrument to gain some limited political result, or else because they see it as necessary to defend the existence of the state by preventing a much worse outcome of some processes of change in the world around them. Referring to Clausewitz, Howard calls the first kind of wars "instrumental", limited in aims and methods and based on calculations of costs and gains; the second type he sees as wars of "survival", likely to become total, and based on calculations of what will happen if the state does *not* go to war now or soon. Both types of war decisions thus appear based on general and rational rules of government behavior.

What implications can we draw from this scheme, and what modifications might be worth exploring?

How Rational are States that Go to War?

Decisions to initiate an instrumental war usually are *formally rational* in the sense that they are based on processes of reasoning that can be retraced step-by-step, but their *substantive rationality*—the likelihood that they will suggest behavior that will lead to the intended outcomes—has been changing in the course of history. From 1816 through 1911, those states that started a war—in the sense of first sending substantial organized forces across a currently existing international boundary against large-scale armed resistance—won this war on the average in about 80 percent of all cases. The initiators lost the war they had started on the average in about one in every five cases, that is, they incurred the cost of war but failed to gain any of their major objectives, as previously announced or laid down in internal government communications or inferred by reputable historians.

After 1911, these proportions changed strikingly. The average rate of successes for war initiators from 1912 to 1978—and it seems also through 1984—dropped to 40 percent, one-half of what it had been in the earlier period, and the rate of failures trebled to 60 percent against the mere 20 percent before 1911. Such cases of unsuccessful war initiations wars included the First World War, in which the principal initiators Austria-Hungary, Russia and Germany all lost; the Second World War started primarily by Germany, Italy and Japan, all of whom lost; the 1950 attack of Communist North Korea on South

Korea; India's initiation in 1962 of the Himalaya War against China and Pakistan's attack on India in 1964 over Kashmir; and such recent cases as the United States' massive entry into Vietnam in 1965 and its "incursion" into Cambodia in 1970; the Soviet intervention in Afghanistan in 1978; the attack of Iraq on Iran in 1980; the Argentine attack on the Falkland Islands in 1982, and the Israeli incursion into Lebanon in the same year.

This list says nothing about the legal or moral justification—or lack of it—for any of these wars. It does remind us that quite often after 1911, wars were undertaken for what seemed to be rational purposes to the relevant decision-makers but with results that were very different from what they had expected. It would not have been new that rulers could err. What was new was that after 1911 they erred so frequently.

Is this rising rate of errors an accident, or is it corroborated by some reasons in theory? We may put aside any general notion that the judgment of statesmen has declined; I know of no independent evidence for it. But there seem to be some reasons in the theory of communications. Since 1911, the number of states and quasi-state movements has steadily increased and by now has more than trebled. Shipping and aircraft have in many ways reduced the effective distance between them; communication and mass media have multiplied the flow of messages; and social mobilization, including the spread of mass literacy and mass politics, have greatly increased the importance and urgency of politics within each country.

Yet the day of each ruler still has no more than twenty-four hours in it. The result is *decision overload*, and neither individual rulers nor entire governments have so far found any very good way to cope with it. The usual ways of dealing with too many messages in too little time all have their costs: turning off one's attention, skipping or selecting items haphazardly, setting rigid priorities in advance of changing and unforeseen developments, bundling different events and messages into a few categories by means of prejudice, or simply accepting a much higher frequency of errors in one's own decisions—all these make decisions much less rational than they would be expected by believers in simple "rational choice". In matters of foreign policy the factor of cognitive and communicative overload and the responses of inattention, delay, prejudice, and frequent error are becoming increasingly relevant. This has an implication for the future. Truly rational, "instrumental" wars will become less and less frequent, but the words may remain in use to cover some exercises of governments in self-deception.

Another tendency is working in the same direction. As the world's population keeps becoming more numerous and more active, technology is becoming more powerful. Our decisions are setting larger forces in motion—larger in terms of mass, energy, and manpower. The larger the decisions in this sense, the larger are ordinarily their consequences, not only the immediate and direct ones, but also their remote and indirect results, including the results of significantly large interactions with other decisions by the same or other actors. These indirect and/or delayed consequences cannot be ignored except at rising costs. This leads to a paradox: the more powerful an actor becomes, the more he risks being ignorant of some of the consequences of what he is doing and encountering unpleasant surprises. Power tends to make blind and to the blind all things are sudden. And powerful actors who try to avoid this trap by making greater cognitive efforts, risk incurring a still greater overload of information and decisions.

Through all these processes, the age of more powerful states and more powerful technologies may tend to become one of greater and more frequent errors.

These considerations should cast some doubt on the old image of "instrumental wars". Ever more rarely will the initiation of war turn out to be a rational instrument for almost any political purpose. For a time, it may remain practicable among minor powers, where the expectable scale of its consequences may be smaller, and even there the choice for war may prove increasingly often to have been made in error.

The risk of an increasing frequency of errors applies even more to those alleged "survival" wars that are fought—or claimed to be fought—for the very existence of the state or for its presumed "vital interests". Professor Howard shows the ominous elasticity of these notions when he writes of "conflicts in which states believe that their very existence—their power, that is, to control their environment and defend their values—is at stake" (p. 26). How many states have had this "power to control their environment" outside their borders? Out of today's 160-odd states less than a dozen; yet all the others obviously exist and the power of even the very largest and most heavily armed states to control events at greater distance from their borders is limited indeed.

In matters of mental health, psychiatrists must try to make sure whether a patient is hallucinating or whether his fears and perceptions correspond to reality. The same concern for a "reality principle" should apply to the mental health of nations and to the responsibility of social scientists who study their behavior in international affairs. From this point of view, much of the history of the twentieth century to date has been shot through with periods of unawareness, when the governments and elites of nations did not know what they were doing and failed to foresee the consequences of their actions.

Most often, their errors were not random but systematic. A number of errors are typical and repetitive and may be listed under seven headings:

1. *The costs of war are underestimated.* The coming of nuclear weapons, which is likely to be irreversible, has intensified this danger.
2. *The costs of peace are overestimated*, and so are the dangers of a continuation of some present trends, foreign or domestic. This fear of peace and of an unfavorable future includes the ignorance or underestimation of countervailing trends.
3. There is a general *overestimation of one's power to predict* events and developments, particularly across geographic, cultural and social distances.
4. There is an overestimation and *inflation of supposed "vital interests"* preceding a war or a near-war crisis.

Thus Bosnia was overestimated in its importance by both Serbia and Austria-Hungary in 1914, Constantinople by Russia and Trieste by Austria in 1915, respectively, Algeria by France in 1954, the Suez Canal by Britain in 1956, Vietnam by the United States in 1965, Afghanistan by the Soviet Union in 1978, the Malvinan-Falkland Islands by Argentina in 1982, and Lebanon by Israel in 1982. The loss of non-acquisition of control over these territories was survived by these "vitally" con-

cerned nations in each case—though not always by their governments of the day—with the sole exception of Austria-Hungary.
That empire, perished not for the loss of a province or seaport
but as the result of a war intended to keep them at a cost that
proved to be intolerable to some of that empire's component
nations.

Nevertheless, some "vital interests" may be historical and
psychological realities. Their core territories and their daily lives
will be so perceived by large majorities of most peoples for a
long time to come, in contrast to the artificial "vital national
interests" drummed up by some passing government to
strengthen the lacking popularity of some risky foreign policy.

5. The *overestimation of one's material national power* over one's
   international environment, requiring only a firm "national
   will", with no other perceived limits.
6. *Overreliance on one's own power* to control or stop large
   international developments. A classic image is the British
   story of the Danish King Canute and the tide.
7. *Underestimation of one's own capacities to adapt, reform and
   cope with changes*, while preserving the essential features of
   one's own cultural and political identity.

As this list suggests, I agree with Michael Howard's theory
of the cognitive bases of most wars. This theory should be
supplemented, however, by analyses of the breeding grounds of
these recurrent cognitive errors. Such breeding grounds include
mass media, elites, institutions, and military-industrial com-
plexes of interests in armaments.

What implications can we derive from this scheme, and what
critical modifications might be worth exploring?

Professor Howard's scheme presents wars as *instrumental*,
and that throughout the nineteenth and twentieth centuries.
That is to say, he suggests that wars are undertaken rationally
for the purpose of attaining some intended goal of policy. This
view is not entirely confirmed by empirical data. If we define
winning a war as attaining a major goal of policy, publicly
announced or clearly inferred by competent historians, usually
on the basis of documents, then it is indeed true that about 80
percent of all substantial wars between 1816 and 1910 were won

by the countries that *initiated* them by sending their organized forces across some widely recognized international boundary in the face of organized resistance by a government on the other side of that border. Only 20 percent of such wars were lost, in the sense that the initiating country was either defeated or at least failed to reach any of its major territorial or political objectives after having incurred the costs of war in blood and treasure. The consequences of starting a war between 1816 and 1910 were to a considerable extent calculable and predictable, although even then Cavour and Bismarck were better at this game than was Napoleon III.

But this favorable general ratio of successes to failures of war initiation changed drastically in the twentieth century. Between 1911 and 1985, about 60 percent of all wars were lost by the governments that started them, about three times as large a share as in the nineteenth century. In only 40 percent of the cases did the attackers succeed, only in one-half the proportion of the earlier epoch. Major examples of the unsuccessful sending of troops into another country include the First and Second World Wars, Japan's invasion of China in 1937, the North Korean invasion of South Korea in 1950, the Suez War of 1956, the Indian effort to reconquer disputed territories in the Himalaya War of 1962, the United States interaction in Vietnam, in 1965-75, the Soviet intervention in Afghanistan since 1978, Iraq's attack on Iran in 1980, Argentina's invasion of the Falkland Islands in 1982, and Israel's invasion of Lebanon in the same year. The rarer cases of political success include the Soviet intervention in Hungary in 1956, Israel's "6-day-war" of 1967, Egypt's Sinai War of 1973, and Tanzania's intervention in Uganda in 1978-79. For the entire period of 1911-85 the errors clearly outweigh the successes.

What has happened? Are the statesmen of the post-1911 period more stupid, or haven't they rather become overloaded by the mounting pressures of domestic politics and the increasing complexity of the international system? The latter seems more plausible. The governments of all major powers are endangered by an overload of communications and decisions with a consequent decline of rationality.

This irrationality is not randomly distributed. Time and again it tends toward confrontations and collisions and toward their escalation to the brink of war. The recurrent errors, listed earlier in this statement for the most part tend in this direction toward collision courses in international politics. What are the breeding grounds of these persistent bellicose errors? Some of them are inherent in the processes of perception and cognition. All cognition depends on two kinds of feedback—on feedback to the actor from the outside world, telling him some of the results of his own actions, and on feedback of information stored in the actor's memory (or memories) to his decision-making centers. These feedback processes are vulnerable to distortion.

Fast and prominent feedback signals most often outweigh slower and less prominent ones in processes of decision, even if the slower processes have larger payoffs attached to them. Perceptions and memories are reinforced or weakened by quick rewards or penalties. Reality perceptions are often accepted or rejected, depending on their consonance or dissonance with an actor's perception of his own role in a bureaucracy or social group, or with the "life lie" of his self-image, or with his image of the audience that he will have to face. In all these ways, cognitive corruption and distortion enters into an actor's definition of the current situation and his interpretation of subsequent messages.

The strength and prominence of messages is reinforced by the selective effects of interest groups and institutions. Together, this plurality of sources of cognitive distortion may help to account for the cognitive causes of war which are at the heart of Professor Michael Howard's theory.

What can be done to weaken these causes? The expectable costs of war, and particularly of nuclear war, are steadily becoming larger and more prominent. Even frequently repeated errors can be identified and exposed, so as to lose at least part of their power to deceive. The cultural and institutional breeding grounds of warlike sentiments can be reduced, and so can some of the short-run reward mechanisms; warlike perceptions focus attention less on the initiation of a conflict, but rather on any significant step towards its escalation. Governments, peoples, and international organizations may aim at the marginalization of war. War may be ineradicable for some time among small, poor, and militarily weak rivals, remote on the world's periphery, but we may concentrate all efforts on opposing any war among the world's more powerful or more centrally located nations, or, in second place, any war involving a highly industrialized nation, even if only on one side. In time it may then become possible to push large-scale war—like cannibalism and chattel slavery—entirely out of the field of politically expectable actions.

General discussion

The first issue that comes up for debate is how to define "war": are we to conceive it as some kind of unitary phenomenon, or as a class of highly diverse entities? Recognizing diversity implies that the quest for the "causes of war" has to be divided into separate studies concerning the causes behind various *kinds* of war. This raises the question of how wars should be classified. One may rely either on an a priori typology, classifying wars by, e.g., the objectives of the actors, or wait for a typology to emerge from the research findings. The latter strategy could be the one to yield the criteria by which types of wars may be differentiated, but an a priori typology would still be needed to get the research started.

One way to look for the causes of war is in the *decision-making processes* which issue in the initiation of armed conflict. These processes presumably involve *cost-cost calculations* of a peculiar kind: while the costs of going to war can be estimated in a manner that minimize wishful thinking, they are nonetheless liable to be outweighed by the costs of *not* going to war. These are often very immediate and very important in domestic political terms, as the decision of Great Britain in the Falklands crisis illustrates.

It is argued that there are growing *inhibitions* among states as regards the use of force. It is very costly today to keep another population or territory under occupation or control, as the experiences of the two superpowers in Vietnam and Afghanistan bear out. This marks an important difference from the situation in nineteenth century Europe, and indicates that war is thought about today less often as an instrument of policy. It is suggested that the difficulty of maintaining occupation also stems from self-deterrence on the part of the occupiers. Moral considerations may play a role in this, as states now seem to hold somewhat different standards with regard to the use of force.

Doubt is raised about the adequacy of the decision-making analysis in the study of war. There is a need to move beyond cognitive processes to *"fundamental"* causes. For instance, the importance of ideology in producing distorted images of the self and the opponent has to be recognized. Moreover, modern military technology is a possible predisposing condition of war, in particular in relations between the US and the USSR. There are many ways in which military expenditure may cause increased insecurity, and thwart the improvement of political relations. The last 40 years of military build-up has focused attention in superpower politics on the issues of arms and arms control, relegating everything else to second place.

The distinction between causes of war at various levels—from underlying, predisposing forces to the decisions that immediately precede hostilities—brings up the question of *research priorities*. It is pointed out that the time when different modes of explanation were thought to be exclusive of each other has gone. However, the current inclination to multilevel and multi-theoretical research is not without its problems. To the extent we have a normative interest in thinking of ways in which the risk of war may be reduced—if, that is, we are concerned with policy—we should perhaps not devote too much attention to basic causes, but instead look for things which are malleable. Policy-makers tend to write off factors which do not lend themselves to change at relatively short notice, concentrating instead on elements which can be changed.

2

Research, Policy, and the Correlates of War

J. DAVID SINGER

In the formulation of national policies, what is the role of the scholarly community? In making decisions in the national security sector, what contributions can be expected from those of us who conduct research into matters of war and peace? Are we primarily there to write learned essays on the wisdom and virtue of our own foreign policy elites? Conversely, is it to provide lively polemics, questioning that wisdom and challenging that virtue? Or, alternatively, is it our mission to identify and advocate options other than those likely to emanate from the decisional apparatus?

Readers of the scholarly journals and books in many parts of the world could be forgiven for inferring that most of us do little more than speak either for the elites, the counter-elites, or for some third force in our respective nations. To the extent that these impressions are correct—and they seem all too correct to me—we may well be failing in our mission and derelict in our duty. Is there a different way to define the scholar's mission in the field of war and peace? Might our countrymen not expect more from us than the role of cheerleader, critic, or pundit? I suspect that there *is* a different mission, and will address it in the introductory section before turning to matters more substantive.

The Roles for Research in National Security Policy

Explanatory and Correlational Knowledge

Perhaps the dominant role is that of generating explanatory knowledge such that the dangerously high error rate in the policy process might be reduced. As our knowledge regarding the regularities and patterns of international conflict dynamics becomes more cumulative and more integrated, we should increasingly be able to identify the key characteristics of the case at hand, classify it into the proper and more general class of historical cases to which it belongs, and indicate which behavior patterns on the part of which protagonists led to which particular outcomes, and why, given the contextual conditions that characterize that class of cases. This is, of course, a tall order, and one that we are unlikely to satisfy until our research becomes far more systematic, theoretically coherent, and methodologically reproducible.

This is not, however, the only contribution that we might make in our efforts to reduce the menacingly high frequency with which governments make incorrect predictions as to the consequences of their conflict behavior. A *second* task, somewhat more modest and quite appropriate to the current stage of development in our discipline, is that of generating correlational-predictive knowledge resting on empirical evidence. To generate predictions in which we can have high confidence, resting on a solid mix of both explanatory and correlational knowledge, may still be some years into the future. But to generate more limited knowledge which can be used not only for making contingent forecasts, but for debunking the folk wisdom of the moment and indicating that certain propositions are *not* historically accurate, or are accurate only for an earlier epoch, a different region of the world, or another class of cases, can be quite helpful.[1] Foreign policy elites and their apologists are very fond of invoking the "lessons of history" but it will require a great deal of assistance from the research community before they begin to draw the correct lessons with greater frequency. As May reminds us, most policy-makers "use history badly. When resorting to an analogy they tend to seize upon the first that comes to mind. They do not search more widely. Nor do they pause to analyze the case, test its fitness, or even ask in what ways it might be misleading."[2]

A few illustrations should suffice. First, there has been this tendency to ransack the historical record or personal memory in search of the self-serving analogy. One of the more egregious cases was that of the US foreign minister, Dean Rusk, who argued that the situation facing the democratic powers in Indochina twenty years ago was highly similar to that which faced us at the time of the Munich crisis. Nor was he effectively challenged as to the class of cases to which it belonged, the distinguishing characteristics of that class of cases, the other cases in that class, and the extent to which the alleged policy consequences obtained in that population of cases. The same may be said of Anthony Eden's equation of the Suez crisis of 1956 with Munich, leading to equally unfortunate results. Then there is the recurrent phenomenon to which Ray alludes, in which successive generations of policy-makers learn the "opposite mistake" lesson.[3] Persuaded, for example, that the First World War was virtually guaranteed by the ubiquitous defense pact commitments in the European system (88 percent of the major powers were so committed from 1903 to 1914), statesmen consciously avoided them during most of the inter-war period (with none at all until 1935), and then persuaded that it was the *absence* of such pacts that brought us the Second World War, the post-war generation turned to alliance making with a vengeance, such that all major powers were in one or more defense pacts by 1950.[4]

Conceptual Precision and Operational Indicators

Yet a third role for the research community is that of demanding, encouraging, and providing conceptual precision. While obvious to the point of embarrassment, it nevertheless seems necessary to not only emphasize the importance of such precision but to note its relatively infrequent appearance. Whether describing the putative priorites of one's own or another nation, comparing their capabilities, characterizing systemic conditions or trends, or classifying the behavior of a given regime, there is considerable room for improvement.

The researcher in this field can, of course, do more than call attention to lapses in precision and suggest more accurate verbal labeling. He or she can also devise, test, and apply operational indicators of many of the concepts used in international intercourse.[5] For example, there are several extant indicators in the literature by which we can more precisely measure the polarity, alliance aggregation, capability concentration, or structural clarity, of the international system or its regional subsystems.[6] Similarly, we can distinguish among—and then enumerate the frequency of—militarized disputes, civil wars, inter-state wars, etc., after which we can describe such events in terms of their magnitude, severity, intensity, and so forth.[7] Other indicators that come to mind are political integration, economic interdependence, international tension, and inter-state behavior patterns.[8] These efforts at the construction of indicators that can validly capture and reliably measure some of our more widely-used concepts are, then, not only essential to the development of a body of cumulative evidence, but to greater clarity and lower error rates in the description and prediction of international phenomena.

Broadened Horizons in Time and Space

Then there is a role for the research community that is as much an ethical as it is a scientific one. Reference is to the need for a broader and longer perspective on the nations' foreign policies. It is all too natural that political elites will tend towards a relatively short-run outlook, giving much greater emphasis to the time horizon that more or less coincides with their expected tenure in office, and less to the consequences that may unfold later on. "Not on *my* watch" is often the focus, and scholars could be helpful by identifying and making more salient the middle- and long-run implications of policy, even when the forecasts rest on a less than solid scientific foundation.

Equally natural is the tendency toward geographical myopia, cultural chauvinism, and xenophobic interpretations of world affairs. Even when foreign and defense ministries are partially isolated from domestic politics, those who shape the larger policy orientation are preoccupied with the need for support from a variety of interest groups, regions, professions, and social strata, and thus give close attention to how a policy will sit with the army and "how it will play" in Marseilles, Manchester, and Middletown. While recognizing the fact that elites must operate in both the domestic and the global contexts, researchers can remind us that the keys to success in these two settings are often incompatible, and that "bashing" another government will not only cause difficulties with those foreigners but will also reinforce exactly those domestic tendencies that set such devastating constraints on foreign policy rationality the next time around. By reminding the elites, the counter-elites, and the opinion-makers that, to the citizens of each nation all the others are foreigners, and that their perceptions and priorities may well be different than ours, the scholar might play yet another constructive role.

Data-based Research for Policy Purposes

Needless to say, several of the intellectual tasks outlined in the previous section need not be assigned to the research community alone; several of them might well be taken on or shared by a variety of world affairs specialists. But there is one task that can only be assumed by scholarly researchers, and unfortunately, only a small fraction of that small community. While scholars from a range of methodological orientations can play (and already have played) a valuable ancillary role, the bulk of this task must fall to that lamentably limited sub-set of researchers who work in the explicitly scientific mode. Without the more traditional scholars, our conceptual repertoire would be less rich, our mastery of historical detail less complete, and our range of explanatory hypotheses far less adequate. Having been trained in that tradition long before the scientific orientation re-surfaced in the world politics field—and I say re-surfaced in deference to the monumental pioneering efforts of Bloch, Richardson, Sorokin, and Wright—I take second place to no one in my appreciation of the value of traditional scholarship.[9] But honesty requires me to distinguish between the necessary and the sufficient. As Deutsch and others have reminded us, without concepts we cannot recognize patterns and organize facts, and without the historical facts we cannot even begin to search for regularities and explanations.[10] But as necessary as these activities may be, they are not and never will be sufficient if we aim to describe, predict, and explain with an adequate degree of competence.

All too many years ago, several of us began to exchange views on the relative merits of the "classical" and the "behavioral" orientations, and in the years since have merely agreed to disagree.[11] Were we students of art history or comparative literature, or even of molecular biology or astrophysics, it would be quite seemly for advocates of different epistemologies to carry on a genteel academic debate, full of tolerance and good humor. Not very much is really at stake, and whether a certain pigment came to Verona from the Moors or the Persians, or whether Tolstoy or Dostoyevskii best captures the Russian culture, or even whether DNA really contains the essence of the genetic code, or whether the "big bang" model best explains the origins of our universe is not central to the survival of the human race. These are exciting, important, and engaging controversies, and it would be satisfying to arrive at answers. But if it takes another decade or another century to do so is of minor consequence to most of the inhabitants of the global village.

On the other hand, it matters greatly whether major powers typically back down or escalate under certain classes of threat, or whether negotiations are more likely to succeed when the agenda is a broad or a narrow one. More specifically, it matters greatly that we—those of us who make or shape policy—*know* which of these pairs of hunches is more correct; it is not merely a matter of academic interest, individual hunch, or idle curiosity. For example, American national security elites believe that the way to deal with confrontations vis-à-vis their major rival is— time after time—to stand firm, hang tough, and pursue escalation dominance while providing the Soviets with a face-saving capitulation, when the evidence is that this strategy only works—and not as well as believed—for the first two or three confrontations.[12] Acting on this ill-founded proposition, we could lay waste to most of the Northern Hemisphere in less than a day.

In other words, strategies of world politics are so pregnant with real consequence that we just cannot afford to continue treating such questions as "matters of opinion". To use a crude analogy, if a scuba diver subscribes to—and acts upon—the belief that a high calcium diet permits him to ascend at more than the prescribed number of meters per minute, he will die or spend the rest of his life as a vegetable. Or if, to go further back in history, a surgeon believes that 200 leeches will cure a certain infection, he will kill a good many patients, or if (to take a recent example), an engineer believes that 5/32″ steel plates will hold the girders of a bridge together, dozens of motorists will die in disconfirming his belief. To put it bluntly, it is time for us to get serious, turn professional, and begin to treat matters of war and peace as if human survival—rather than mere academic reputation—is at stake.

Having argued, perhaps too energetically, for "the importance of being scientific", let me reiterate the need to be modest about our accomplishments to date. Given the complexity of the problem, the mulitiplicity of rival models, the paucity of the data base, and the difficulty of validly measuring our concepts—not to mention the limited number of scientifically educated scholars and the inadequate resources that go to this small band—it comes as no surprise that nothing worthy of the name has yet emerged in the way of a compelling theory of war. Space limitations preclude any effort here to describe, compare, or evaluate some of the contenders (and pretenders), but one can, in my judgment, indicate certain of the characteristics of what that theory will most probably look like.

First, its central variables will almost certainly be those already used by the many scholars and practitioners who work, explicitly or otherwise, with one or another version of the *real-politik* model. Over-stated, our theory will revolve around capabilities, commitments, and contiguities, and the ways in which these three sets of phenomena both drive and constrain those who act—and have acted since the Napoleonic Wars—on behalf of the territorial state. But, second, our theory will be far more attentive to the internal-external interface and the processes by which the external interactions of nations impinge on domestic politics, shape the internal configurations of power and of beliefs, and thus help to modify and/or reinforce external behavior in relatively long cycles of policy orientation. And, third, our theory will give greater emphasis to the role of extra-rational (as distinct from ir-rational) considerations in that messy, multilevel, cross-pressured process that passes for foreign policy decision-making.[13]

Fourth, and not surprising in light of the above observations, such a theory will postulate a high degree of uniformity in the internal-external relationship, downgrading the putative importance of political-economic regime type and national culture while recognizing the role of material capabilities and the fluctuating levels of militarization and economic activity in the respective societies. Another way to express this theoretical orientation is to point out the remarkable—and alarming—similarity in the national security/foreign policy decision rules of such dissimilar societies as Russia, America, and Israel in today's world, or England and Germany at the beginning of the century. This theoretical model and the inductive and deductive premises behind it will be spelled out in greater detail in a later work.

If it is correct to say that we have no adequate theory as yet, what sorts of advances *have* we made? Let me devote the balance of this essay to an illustrative summary of two sets of empirical findings from the Correlates of War project, accompanied by a cursory overview of their implications for the policies of nations as they stagger—like the three Norwegian trolls with only one eye among them[14]—along the highways and byways of the international system, often managing to reconcile and coordinate their policies, but all too frequently getting themselves trapped into dysfunctional interaction patterns that bring them again and again to the brink of war.

System Properties and the Incidence of War

Let me begin with a discussion of what we call the "structural clarity" model, in which it is postulated that the vertical and horizontal configurations of the international system impinge on the decisional elites in such a way as to increase or decrease their ability to predict changes and continuities in the environment in which a given rivalry occurs. On the *horizontal* dimension are those inter-nation bonds and links that affect governments' ability to predict who will line up with whom if a rivalry or conflict approaches the brink of war: alliances, diplomatic recognition, shared memberships in international organizations, trade, and geographical contiguities. On the *vertical* dimension are the indicators that reflect the capabilities of the relevant nations in the system: industrial, military, demographic, and diplomatic. Looking out on the systemic setting, these two sets of indicators should enhance or reduce the elites' capacity to predict who will be on which side in a "crunch" and with how much "clout".

At this juncture, however, we find two contradictory models. One says that war will be less likely if there is a high degree of vertical and horizontal *clarity* in the system structure, on the premise that such clarity makes it relatively easy to predict the outcome of a militarized dispute or war. As the cliché has it, the weaker coalition *dare* not fight, and the stronger side *need* not; such predictability is said to preclude the need to go to, or over, the brink of war since the outcome is almost foreordained. There is also a counter-hypothesis, equally plausible. This is that war will be less likely under conditions of *ambiguity*, inasmuch as elites tend to be more cautious and prudent when it is difficult to predict the commitment-capability lineup. Unsure of the configuration, they will be reluctant to press the adversary for concessions and will be more amenable to compromise.

Faced with these incompatible models—each finding considerable support in the classical literature—of the consequences of structural clarity, it seemed worthwhile to construct the relevant indicators, generate the appropriate data sets, and then go on to examine the resulting evidence. Given the modest tone in my evaluation of our research findings to date, one need not be astonished to hear that the results were far from complete or consistent. As in any scientific enterprise during its very early stages, results will initially be inconsistent and inconclusive; this does not justify a sense of failure, but rather a realization that much remains to be done.

Returning to the matter at hand, what *did* turn up? We found that neither model was successful in post-dicting the incidence of war for the century and a half from 1816 to 1965, and this led us in turn to see whether one or the other model offered a strong fit to the historical data for one or more of the familiar epochs during the full period. Interestingly enough, the conventional inter-century division did produce the best fit, but with divergent results. That is, for the current century, war was consistently less frequent and/or less severe following periods of *high* structural clarity, but for the nineteenth century, *low* levels of clarity (i.e. high ambiguity) led to a diminished incidence of war.[15]

While we have yet to follow up these anomalies in a systematic way, despite the excellent suggestions of Zinnes and others, several other studies tend to point in the same direction.[16] For example, one might look at a more limited aspect of structural clarity such as the extent to which military and industrial capabilities are highly concentrated in the hands of one or two of the major powers or more equally distributed among all of them. Interpreting high concentration as one indicator of structural clarity, we found even stronger confirmation of the inter-century difference. That is, for the nineteenth century, fluctuations in the concentration indicators alone accounted for as much as 73 percent of the variance in war, with low concentration scores making for less war, whereas the relationship was a negative one in the twentieth century. Not only did *high* concentration make for less war in this epoch, but less clearly so, with no more than 46 percent of the variance attributable to these systemic properties, suggesting that the *realpolitik* variables are, in general, less dominant in recent decades than during the earlier ones.[17]

National Attributes, Behavior, and the Incidence of War

Moving abruptly from a couple of studies designed to tell us what sorts of configurations in the *system* tend to make war more probable, and thus prudence in the conduct of disputes more crucial, let me turn briefly to some tentatively ascertained effects of *national* attributes and behavior on the incidence of militarized disputes and war. While most major wars tend to settle certain structural ambiguities and to produce a fairly clear vertical hierarchy among the major powers, this pattern of status consistency rarely endures. As the nations at the top begin to decline (objectively and subjectively) on various capabilities or influence dimensions, they typically try to correct that decline by looking to their alliances and by increasing their military allocation ratios. The trouble with this recurrent strategy is that it tends to make them more likely to get into militarized disputes. Our data show unambiguous positive relationships between military capabilities and dispute-proneness for the major powers since 1815; 17 percent of the nation-years with high military expenditures and personnel were followed by militarized disputes, as opposed to only 10 percent for the medium scorers and 7 percent for those in the lowest grouping.[18]

Not quite as compelling, but equally suggestive, is the effect (statistically speaking) of the military allocation ratio, calculated by dividing each major power's percentage share of the subsystem's combined industrial capabilities each year into its share of the military expenditures. Here we see that the very high nation-year allocations have as low a frequency of dispute involvement as the very low ones (6 percent), whereas the medium range ratios are five times more likely (31 percent) to be followed by involvement in a militarized dispute. We have not yet examined the effect of the *rate* of increase or decrease, but one plausible inference from the results is that the most dispute-prone phase occurs as major powers gain momentum in their efforts to put larger and larger shares of their resources into preparedness programs. Perhaps it is in this phase that they are allocating too little to deter but more than enough to provoke their rivals.

But this propensity to become *involved* in militarized disputes is only part of this menacing scenario. Our next set of findings is considerably more dramatic and points to the sort of misreading of the lessons of history that May warns against.[19] Shifting from the propensity to become embroiled in militarized disputes to that of being able to "prevail" and walk away with more gains than losses while avoiding war, we find that the major power whose military expenditures are *lower* than the protagonist's prevail in 39 percent of the disputes, while the higher prevails only 21 percent of the time; in terms of military personnel, the figures are 39 percent and 27 percent. What helps to accentuate these figures is that they are virtually reversed when *industrial* capabilities are examined. Here we find that the stronger power prevails 39 percent of the time as opposed to only 20 percent for the weaker, using iron and steel production as the indicator, and nearly identical figures of 29 percent and 19 percent emerge when industrial energy consumption is the indicator of industrial strength.

If this is not enough to make us look again at the conventional wisdom, let us turn now from capabilities to allocation ratios. Once again the relationship between "strength" and success is a negative one, but even more so. Whereas the major power whose military expenditure to industrial capacity (iron/steel and energy combined) ratio is higher prevails only 18 percent of the time, the putatively under-prepared protagonist comes away successful in 36 percent of the militarized disputes since 1816.[20]

While there is no reproducible evidence to date, one plausible interpretation of those findings might be drawn from the works of Schumpeter and Lasswell dealing with the idea of the militarized society and the garrison state.[21] As a society begins to allocate resources to the military sector above and beyond some "normal" threshold, we can expect that those who advocate and stand to gain by that allocation will indeed become slightly more numerous and influential than prior to that allocation, and as the process continues, that influence will expand.[22] Necessarily believing that the military instrument is there to be used, and that it will be effective, elites with such orientations will tend to bring their nations into militarized disputes more frequently.[23] Moreover, as this process goes forward, the tendency will not only be to escalate from mild to militarized disputes more often, but to manage them less skillfully; belief in the efficacy of the more blunt instruments of international intercourse leads to a narrowing of the diplomatic repertoire, while the more appropriate instruments tend to be neglected.

Thus, we find a self-amplifying process in which higher allocations to the military are followed by increases in the frequency of involvement in these brink-of-war disputes, additional increases to the military, further militarization of the nation's foreign policy, more failures in the management of the disputes, and yet additional resource allocation. If force, and the threat of force, was not successful, perhaps it was because there was an insufficient level; like those addicted to gambling or alcohol, one more iteration should make things turn out better next time!

The historical evidence suggests otherwise. In an earlier study, we found for the period 1816-1964 strong positive correlations (from 0.51 to 0.63) between the military capabilities of nations and their tendency to become involved in—and to initiate—war.[24] Looking only at the major powers, this same pattern holds, with the nation-years of high capabilities followed by war three times more frequently (0.035 to 0.013) than the low capabilities years. Less dramatically, but in the same direction, the high allocators among the major powers are also more war-prone than those at the low end of the military allocation scale, with comparisons of 0.018 to 0.013, 0.018 to 0.016, 0.027 to 0.013, and 0.018 to 0.010, depending on the indicators used.

Just to add to the evidence, it is worth noting that victory in war, when it comes, is indeed associated with higher military capabilities, but much more influential in determining that outcome are the industrial capabilities of the opposing sides. Military expenditure "superiority" led to victory by 57 percent to 36 percent, whereas higher steel production led to victory by 74 percent to 29 percent. But when it comes to allocation ratios, the earlier pattern obtains, with the low allocators winning their wars 70 percent of the time while the high allocators emerged triumphant in only 50 percent of their war experiences.[25]

These, then, are just a few of the data-based historical investigations from a single research team on the extent to which we can account for, if not fully explain, variations in the incidence and outcome of militarized disputes and international war. The literature is of course considerably larger, suggesting that we are at least on the way to being able to show which conditions and events have in the past, and might in the future, lead toward or away from bloody confrontation.

Conclusion

Enough has been said to suggest that the social science community may already be far from irrelevant to the policy process and the ways in which the nations navigate the murky waters between war and peace. While it remains true, in my judgment, that foreign policy elites are still likely to do better relying on intuitive judgments than on data-based research alone for making their contingent forecasts in the national security sector, a prudent mix would probably be better than either by itself.

But as already indicated, the research community has *several* roles to play and contributions to make while we move—all too haltingly—toward development of the sort of data-based and deductively tight theories from which predictions of high reliability (but not total certainty) could be expected. First, there is the simple post-dictive/pre-dictive contribution, in which we can make reasonably solid predictions, but only the most tentative explanation as to *why* a given sequence of events in a given type of context culminates in a certain outcome with great regularity. Hence the interim importance of early warning indicators.[26]

Then there is the ability to move toward increasing verbal

and quantitative precision in our descriptions of events and conditions that affect outcomes and determine destinies, and considerable progress has already been registered. And, third, because of our familiarity with a long historical span, a wide geographical area, a complex variety of cases, and an awareness of the findings of related disciplines, we should be able to help the decisional elites see their problems in a more complete context: less parochial, self-righteous, and short-sighted.

All of these could be—and to a very modest extent, already have been—of considerable help in reducing the error rate in the international security field. Without denying for a moment the significance of all those other factors—a badly organized international system, a weak sense of global ethics, centuries of accumulated bad habits, the destabilizing effects of technological innovation, the unsettling impact of non-state groups, the incompatibility of internal and external incentives, and of course, the genuine clash of security interests—ignorance must nevertheless be recognized as a critical variable in the onset and escalation of disputes and wars. Rigorous social science research can help to ameliorate the effects of that ignorance.[27]

But even if the members of the scientific community were to increase their number by ten-fold, their creativity by twenty-fold, and their resources by a hundred-fold, the policy impact could remain marginal. Those who make, shape, modify, evaluate, and execute policy in national agencies, legislatures, international organizations and secretariats, private institutions, and the media, may have a great many conflicting interests and incompatible priorities. Yet, in light of the current weapons technology, they do have one strong interest in common: reducing the frequency of civil or international war. Even the most Clausewitzean bureaucrats in the most revisionist of nations must recognize that armed conflict at that level of violence is ultimately disadvantageous to their interests and far from the most functional of outcomes for their nations. And if, as this analysis suggests, war is more often than not a consequence of faulty diagnosis and erroneous prediction, the practitioner should also have a preference for greater rigor in the analysis of international politics.

Thus, the practitioner must also become more sophisticated in both the substantive and methodological sense. To make use of research results, the practitioner needs to be equipped to identify, comprehend, and evaluate the quality and relevance of those results, yet few of them are so equipped to date. Whereas medical and legal practitioners in most societies receive three or four years of professional training after university, foreign policy and national security specialists rarely do. And when such post-graduate training *is* utilized, it is far less rigorous than it needs to be, looking all too similar to that offered to teachers, journalists, or social workers.

Post-graduate preparation of high quality is, of course, not enough; intellectual preparation needs to begin at the undergraduate level, or better still, in secondary school. The more adequately prepared the advanced student is, the more rigorous and sophisticated the later training can be, and if, as at present in the West (and elsewhere, one suspects), much of the post-graduate program is devoted to "remedial" work in logic, philosophy of science, statistics, and measurement, there is less opportunity for the student to move on to more challenging work in which substance and method are brought together.

Another obstacle here is the questionable notion that since the potential world affairs specialist will not be expected to *conduct* scientific research, there is no need for that to be included in the curriculum. Whether the premise is correct or not, it strikes me as irrelevant. If the practitioner is to read, comprehend, and apply scientific research findings, he/she must know how it is, and should be, done; there are all too many examples of decision-makers looking at incompetent studies that rest on inappropriate analyses of invalid indicators, and then making destructively inept policy judgments (such as in the US Department of Defense during the Vietnam War). And as the unhappy practice of contract research by "beltway bandits" for federal agencies in America (and perhaps elsewhere) continues, we can expect more examples of counter-productive policy decisions emanating from inadequate understanding of research results.

Finally, even if both the scholarly community and the policy elites do begin to move toward the generation and application of first-rate research, a serious problem would still remain. That is, the journalists who report and interpret the news, as well as the citizens who ultimately acquiesce in or endorse certain policy decisions (and the arguments in support of them) can continue to do great mischief. Hence the above suggestion that a systematic and scientific approach to matters of public policy needs to begin in the undergraduate university curriculum, if not earlier.

In sum, the sort of research—and teaching, and consulting— that is reflected in the Correlates of War project and others like it needs to be more carefully examined, considered, and perhaps emulated. To reiterate, there is more involved than academic curiosity or the desirability of scholarly tolerance and open-mindedness. The physical and biological sciences no longer operate on the assumption that one person's opinion is as good as another's; there are procedural standards and there are stringent criteria for the evaluation of evidence. And given how much more is at stake in the area of international politics, continued acquiescence in pre-scientific analysis and shifting intellectual fashions may well qualify as the ultimate in war crimes, not only because of the destruction it may visit on humanity, but also because it would take so little to correct our ways!

DISCUSSIONS

Dina A. Zinnes

David Singer's paper makes three general points. First, he puts forth the proposition that policy and science not only can, but to assure good policy, must go hand in hand. He supports this argument by providing examples of policy-makers who drew lessons from the past in an ad hoc rather than scientific way and shows how this led to incorrect conclusions and disastrous policy consequences. Singer's second major point is a proposal for a training and monitoring institute. If science can service policy then a more direct connection should be established between the two. A third part of the paper demonstrates the importance of scientifically generated results about international conflict. Illustrative examples of findings from the

Correlates of War project are described. I will react in turn to each of these three points.

That policy and science have important interdependent links is a proposition that I support, but with some qualifications. On the positive side, there is no question that one cannot change, control or manipulate a phenomenon unless one understands it. And from my perspective there is no question that understanding comes best from a scientific approach. By scientific I mean explicit definitions, the statement of specific hypotheses, the systematic and objective collection of data and the use of established procedures to evaluate the hypotheses and draw conclusions. Such understanding is "best" for two very important reasons. First, it makes the entire knowledge process open to scrutiny allowing others the opportunity to challenge, revise or extend. Second, the systematic and objective collection and evaluation of evidence minimizes the probability of error when drawing conclusions about one's beliefs concerning the world. The scientific approach, as I am using that term here, very simply means openness and honesty about one's propositions and the way in which one has evaluated those propositions.

If policy is the implementation of certain procedures to achieve goals, then clearly the extent to which one understands the links between procedures and goals is the extent to which one will be successful. For this reason I support the idea that science can be a significant contributor to policy. But that it can be does not necessarily mean that it will be. I have two worries. The first concerns both the reliability and validity of the findings that we have to date. The second concerns the capacity of policy-makers to use such information appropriately. The scientific study of international politics generally and conflict and war more particularly is a very young field, no more than 40 years old. We have become increasingly sophisticated and have learned a great deal not only about international politics but of perhaps even more importance, about how to do good scientific work in this field. But to say that we have come a long way is not to say that our results are ready for dissemination. Our findings are tentative and typically embedded in the specific environment in which they were generated. Consequently, results must be understood within the context of how the hypotheses were formulated, how the data were collected, what measures were used to operationalize the concepts, and the specific assumptions that underlay the statistical analyses.

Of equal concern is the policy-maker's lack of training in social science methodology. Singer highlights the consequences of decisions based on generalizations drawn from the wrong set of historical cases. This problem is only alleviated by scientific research when the context within which the research results were generated are understood. For example, a recent study shows that democratic countries are less war prone than countries having other forms of government. Any foreign policy decision based on this result could lead to as disastrous results as those noted by Singer, unless the decision-maker were aware of such important methodological issues as (1) the operational definition used for "democracy", (2) the time period over which the analysis was done, (3) the countries used in the study, (4) the type of statistical design employed to process the data and generate the conclusions. Taken out of context our research results could produce the same type of disastrous consequences that Singer notes with his reference to "self-serving" case analogies. Indeed, christened with the label of "scientific" the harm that might be done could well be even more severe. The problem is not so much whether results should be made available to decision-makers, but when this should occur and under what conditions.

These twin worries are in fact two sides of the same coin. To the extent to which we gain confidence in our results we need worry less about misinterpretation and misgeneralization on the part of policy-makers. And to the extent to which policy-makers are trained to understand the methods and approaches underlying the research findings we need be less concerned about the misuse of findings in policy decisions. The problem is that neither of these two conditions currently exist. Our results are still tentative and policy-makers are inadequately trained to understand the nuances and limitations of this form of research. From my admittedly conservative perspective, we have not reached the "when" stage.

The discussion thus far, as it is in Singer's paper, has focused only on one direction of the arrow relating science and policy; the arrow from science to policy. There is, however, another direction worth noting which is not mentioned in Singer's paper: the arrow from policy to science. Much research in the United States is funded by mission agencies—bureaucractic branches of the government—with very particular problems to solve. These agencies send out RFPs (requests for proposals) with incredibly short time fuses and a narrowness of research focus as to stifle most creativity and much that is admirable in science. Since the bucks are often big the lure, particularly for the inadequately funded social scientist, is almost undeniable. The consequence is that policy problems drive science in unfortunate and oftentimes counterproductive ways. While there is no question that decision-making problems can pose interesting and challenging questions for science, the need to find specific and immediate answers can drive science in the wrong direction.

Let me turn next to Singer's proposal for a training and monitoring institute. The foregoing should provide the rationale for my reactions here. For all of the reasons cited above I do not believe that analytical and empirical research in international relations is far enough along to develop a reliable and valid monitoring program nor do I feel that either researchers or policy-makers have sufficient understanding of international processes to know what should be done with such a monitoring system. What will be monitored, how will it be measured, who will interpret the results? I cannot, therefore, support the monitoring component of Singer's proposal. The training of policy-makers, however, is another issue. Policy-makers should be made aware of the existing methodologies, hypotheses, and results. They should be trained to understand how research questions are formulated and the procedures used to obtain answers. This will sensitize them to what is available and how best to interpret and use the results. It may also make them more sympathetic to research and possibly more supportive of the research enterprise. But while I would favor the training of policy-makers, I am not convinced that this could best be done in a separate institute, as advocated by Singer. My own sense is that the intellectual and technical capabilities of a university setting are far better suited for this type of study.

I come then to the third part of Singer's paper: the results from the Correlates of War project. In my earlier comments I was concerned that results might be taken out of context, misinterpreted and thus incorrectly used for decision-making. In my concluding comments I want to offset a possible misunderstanding of those remarks. I want to emphasize a point I made earlier: we have come a long way in only a very few years. While I do not feel that we are ready to give answers to policymakers, I don't want to leave the impression that our findings are minimal or unimportant. Indeed, my concern with Singer's discussion of the results of the Correlates of War findings is that it does not go far enough. It leaves the impression of a few scattered and sometimes incompatible or even contradictory results when in fact the picture is far more exciting, far more positive. In the brief space here it is only possible to broadly sketch these results.

Our knowledge in the general field of quantitative international politics is of two types: (1) substantive facts about international processes, conflict, crisis, and war, and (2) an understanding of how to do scientific research in a field in which experiments are not possible, so that "theory", "test", and "data" take on different meanings. Let me turn first to the substantive realm. We have accumulated and are accumulating increasingly more sophisticated data sets that document the attributes and activities of nations in ever finer detail. Singer's Correlates of War data sets are a prime example, covering as they do all wars, major militarized disputes, alliances, between nations for the nineteenth and twentieth centuries, together with numerous national attributes for the same period such as diplomatic recognition status, power, governmental structure. These data sets have been extended by others to cover earlier time periods and to provide finer detail on events that precede major crises and wars. There are, in addition, two other broad types of data sets in existence. One begun by Karl Deutsch and subsequently continued by Bruce Russett and Charles Taylor and supplemented by Ted Gurr, contains extensive information on a vast array of attributes of countries, including measures of domestic unrest. A third type of data set has come to be known as "event data". Collected by at least three different research teams—Charles McClelland, Edward Azar, and Charles Hermann—these data sets contain the systematic and daily coding from public sources of all interactions between nations. These are but a few of the more major data sets that have emerged in recent years, but they should demonstrate one form of research activity.

In addition to data sets, we have accumulated a number of pieces of evidence concerning conflict and war. The picture is by no means complete, but it is beginning to take shape. To a large extent we are discovering that maxims that have been thought to be true (and often used in policy-making) don't hold water when systematic evidence is brought to bear. National attributes such as power cannot be shown to make a nation more or less war prone. A country's internal difficulties also do not make it more or less likely to engage in conflict. Arms expenditures tend, on the other hand, to be positively related to the amount of war engaged in; a strong military defense does not seem to keep one out of war. Arms races don't seem to produce wars, and indeed it is difficult to show that arms races—accelerating military expenditures in the face of a potential enemy who is doing likewise—even exist, as the domestic setting can be shown to account for military expenditures far more clearly than the international context. Relative power, particularly between bordering nations, is a factor which enhances the probability for war, but contrary to the theory of the balance of power, wars are most likely between equal rather than unequal nations. One's intuitive feeling that wars are typically the consequence of accumulative, escalatory hostile interactions cannot be documented through numerous post world war crises and wars. These are but a few of the results that have emerged. They should not be considered exhaustive but only illustrative. My purpose has simply been to augment the various results noted by Singer and to demonstrate the array of questions and research programs that currently exist.

But while data sets and results are accumulating to provide a better understanding of international conflict, perhaps the most important consequence of scientific work in this area has been the increased understanding of how research must be done. We have learned how to formulate and express theoretical ideas in ways which generate deductions that are empirically testable. We have learned how to define key concepts in measureable ways, how to evaluate sources for data collection purposes, how to collect and code data. We have learned how to adopt and extend indicators to provide ways that translate raw data into measures that capture basic concepts, such as power, inequality. We have learned how to use and modify statistics to be applicable to problems where issues like sampling and experiment have a different meaning. In short we have learned what maxims can be taken from other sciences and what procedures must be modified and extended to allow us to do research in this area.

I don't want to sound as if all is done. We have a long way to go. But I do believe the ground work has been prepared and that we are now in a position to move ahead in a dramatic way.

F. H. Hinsley

The aims of this paper are clearly set out: to generate explanatory and predictive knowledge with a view to producing lower error rates in description and prediction. We must all applaud them. I do not doubt, moreover, that progress towards them can be made by adopting a scientific approach to the evidence. I cannot raise much enthusiasm, however, for the results the paper offers us.

In the first place, the results are disappointing in themselves. We are told that there are two contradictory structural models; that when put to the test of historical evidence neither gives consistent readings; but that if we refine them by distinguishing the nineteenth century from the twentieth century the odds favoring the view that ambiguity (not clarity) in the perceptions of governments produces restraint drop—and that only on evidence studied after the event—only from 73 percent to 46 percent. There are other differences between the nineteenth and twentieth centuries which, though not so easily measurable, are vastly greater than this. Even smaller divergencies emerge when the propensity to quarrel is tested against various criteria of armaments expenditure; by one criterion, indeed, we learn that very high and very low expenditure has produced no divergency whatever. Horses frequently win races at odds that are worse than any of the figures that are produced.

Secondly, even if the results were more pointed—even if, for example, they produced a much stronger correlation between the level of military capacity and the tendency to be involved in war—they would still do nothing to advance, or to enable scholars to advance, the ability of governments to forecast developments and predict crises, and thus handle them more sensibly. The paper goes some way to conceding this by saying (p. 24) that foreign policy elites are still likely to do better by relying on intuitive judgments for their forecasts than by relying on data-based researches alone. But it does not recognize that the main reason for this is that the discontinuity of conditions as between recent times and either the nineteenth century or the twentieth century up to the 1960s is far greater than any discontinuity between the nineteenth century and the twentieth century. In particular, it does not recognize that calculations in relation to war that were rational or reasonable in the nineteenth century or even in the twentieth century up to the 1960s are no longer so.

If this oversight merely reflected the perceptions of today's policy elites, it would be bad enough. But things are worse than that. The paper emphasizes "the dangerously high error rate in the policy process", claims that "the frequency with which governments make incorrect predictions is ... menacingly high", suggests that in the political-security sector the lack of expert institutions is "ominous", and pleads the need for more adequate theory "in circumstances which bring the states again and again to the brink of war". But the fact is that although the elites of today may be anxious, frightened, even paranoiac, those in the developed states know that they are not being brought "again and again to the brink of war".

What has cried out for correction in the past 20 years is a situation in which these states have finally lost their belief in the efficiency of armaments, at least for the purposes of war, and yet remain no more skilled in the management of their disputes than they were in the nineteenth century, if not less so. And why is this so? It is not because they are poorly informed about how to detect the onset of disputes; this is not a difficult task and it is one by which they are absorbed to an unhealthy extent. It is because they are inadequately aware of the extent to which fundamental changes in the international system permit and require them to revise their perception of international problems other than the danger of inter-state war.

These other problems are merely listed in the paper (p. 25):

> a badly organized international system; a weak sense of global ethics; centuries of accumulated bad habits; the destablilizing effects of technological innovation; the unsettling impact of non-state groups; the incompatibility of internal and external incentives, and of course, the genuine clash of security interests.

Some of them have greatly declined in recent years while others have enormously increased. It is to the further analysis of such problems—of the reasons why some have eased and of the means by which others could be brought under control—that rigorous social science should now be directing its attention.

General discussion

The discussion dwells largely on possible limitations of the approach followed in the *Correlates of War* project. The prime value of correlative knowledge, if the correlations are powerful enough, lies in *prediction*: prediction can alert policy-makers, to avoid spurious courses of action. But correlations are not in themselves, of course, evidence of *causal* relationships, and predictive models have no claim to explanatory value. For explanatory purposes, correlations have to be interpreted by means of *theoretical* models. And so there is a need to link this kind of research more explicitly with the variety of theories developed in the field. This underscores how the increasing preoccupation with statistical studies of war must not overshadow the significance of elaborating and refining theoretical models—making them more precise, assessing the assumptions on which they rest, and spelling out the expectations they engender concerning national decision-making and inter-state interaction.

It is asked whether there is a theoretical *bias* in the quantitative methods employed in correlative research. Through their use of indicators, quantitative methods focus largely on factors like interactions, capabilities, alliances, etc. This tends to favor the structural mode of explanation, as opposed to institutional and cultural modes. There is therefore a danger of these methods diverting attention away from the need to at least supplement structural models with considerations of institutional variations and cultural specificities. It is arguable whether comparative research, rather than generalizations about global patterns, may be the more effective way of accumulating knowledge.

It is suggested that more effort should be made to subject correlational findings to the test of *case studies*: is there a link, through intervening causal processes, between the independent structural variables and the outcome of particular courses of events? It would be advisable, in general, to move back and forth between statistical research and carefully chosen historical studies.

Doubt is aired about Singer's proposal for a *training institute*, the purposes of which would be to teach policy-makers and diplomats how to think more systematically about international conflict, and to equip them to read and evaluate research in the field. It is questioned, in general, whether foreign policy might not be better if decision-makers were to listen more to scholars and researchers. A problem here is the tendency of academics to exaggerate the importance of the phenomena they are studying. Another problem is how to make scientific results available to policy-makers. These results are mostly used in disputes by proponents of opposing views; science is essentially ammunition which hopefully favours the right side. Moreover, most academics—perhaps all those who do not actually become participants in the policy-making process—know too little about international conflict to be able to make intellectual contact with decision-makers. The upshot of all this may be that scholars will have to content themselves with making their input on policy as part of the democratic debate, and expect no more privileged access than anybody else to the policy-making elites.

Part Two
Strategy and Arms Control

3

Nuclear Weapons and Strategy

LAWRENCE FREEDMAN

I

For the last forty years something called "nuclear strategy" has been discussed extensively in official circles and beyond, and in a variety of languages. Nuclear strategy ostensibly covers the ways and means by which nuclear weapons can be used to achieve the ends of policy. The nature and extent of the literature surrounding this issue suggests something that is infinitely rich and complex: the product of an interaction between a dynamic technology and a changing political order; the analysis of circumstances that are by definition dramatically different from those that obtain at the moment.

Yet the argument can also be heard that much of what passes for nuclear strategy is in a fundamental sense utterly besides the point. The carefully constructed scenarios designed to show how a nuclear war might start are artificial, and thus provide us with few clues as to the political context in which the really hard decisions concerning nuclear threats, or even employments, would have to be taken. The discussions of what might happen after the first nuclear volleys are even more fanciful. It is hard to avoid the conclusion that whatever the nuclear strategists may propose in terms of deliberate moves up a well-defined escalation ladder, the manifold uncertainties connected with this sort of high-intensity warfare renders its course almost impossible to predict and any attempts at intellectual or even organizational preparations for the moment of truth even harder.

One school of strategy has fought hard against such negativism arguing that despite the uncertainties and the complexities it is possible to anticipate at least some of the critical factors that will determine the outcome of a future war, and that the attempt must be made because if we fail to come up with *any* intelligent ideas as to what to do should deterrence fail, then the whole basis of the West's policy of deterrence is revealed to be the most gigantic bluff, with the revelation itself making it even more likely that the bluff will be called.

Others, while less convinced that serious strategies can be divined for actually fighting a nuclear war, are less despondent about the implications of this limitation for deterrence. Deterrence, it can be argued, does not depend on anybody's deliberate strategy at all: just on the recognition that in the fraught and chaotic circumstances that would accompany the collapse of the current international order, somebody, somewhere, in a position of authority, will think that there is a strategy that in the circumstances would be worth a try.

This line of argument suggests that nuclear strategy, as it is practised under current conditions, can involve little more than drawing the attention of the world's statesmen to something that by and large they seem able to work out for themselves: that the existence of large stockpiles of nuclear weapons argues for great caution in the event of any major international crisis.

In the 1940s and 1950s, as the two great alliances of the post-war world took shape and adjusted to the new logic of the nuclear age, at times it did appear as if fear of nuclear war was not sufficient to prevent a fight, or that the arms race was one that might be "won" with some sort of decisive advantage. With the growth of the nuclear stockpiles, and the Berlin and Cuban crises of the early 1960s, the two sides cured themselves of any illusions about the nature of power politics in the nuclear age. For the last two decades there have been plenty of harsh words, the occasional pointed reference to nuclear capabilties, and even one low-level nuclear alert, but the two superpowers have never come close to blows. Whatever is to be decided between East and West, neither side has shown itself inclined to decide it by force of nuclear arms.

Though most strategic analysts prefer not to notice, the actual conduct of international affairs bears no relation to their models which tend to magnify the importance of every nuance or asymmetry in the strategic balance. Because nuclear weapons play such an overbearing role in international relations it is assumed that the details of the nuclear arsenals must be important. Much doctrinal debate and arms control activity proceeds on this assumption. It is arguable that the opposing proposition is closer to the truth: nuclear weapons are *so* overbearing that they have the same political effects within remarkably wide quantitative and qualitative limits.

Nuclear strategy would therefore only come into its own at the point when the situation was close to breakdown or in the process of breaking down. What then might nuclear strategy have to offer? There are three possibilities. First, it might be possible to prevent such a breakdown by helping to construct a strategic balance with features irrelevant to the current relatively relaxed conditions, but vital when it comes to withstanding the stresses and strains of a major crisis. Second, they might be able to propose strategies of crisis management that do more than simply avoid war but are also able to use this situation to secure a more satisfactory political position; third, and much more ambitious, it might be possible to develop operational strategies for the employment of nuclear weapons to ensure that any nuclear hostilities that did break out could be terminated on tolerably favorable terms.

The disposition among professional strategists (rather than academic dabblers) is to assume that the third requirement is the key. Should a convincing operational strategy be devised by the United States then the Soviet Union will be less tempted to challenge Western interests, would back off in a major crisis, and would not be able to prevail should war occur. A failure to develop such a strategy will make the two prior tasks all the more difficult. Against this it is argued that few things are likely to undermine a stable strategic balance more than just the appearance—never mind the reality—of a successful operational strategy (usually described pejoratively as "war-fighting"). Either way, the first question to be asked is: Can there be a nuclear strategy in the active sense, of employment of nuclear weapons to gain a military victory through which political objectives would be secured?

II

The most familiar concepts of nuclear strategy revolve around the terms first and second strike. It is generally agreed that the minimum objective of a nuclear arsenal is to deter a nuclear attack. Some would argue that this is the only realistic and tolerable objective for a nuclear arsenal and might then, in a resigned manner, admit that such deterrence will be a continuing strategic task given that neither nuclear weapons nor international antagonism can be wholly eliminated. President Reagan has raised the possibility of an alternative involving the application of the most futuristic defense technologies, but this thought need not detain us for long as even his advisors have found it prudent to describe this concept as a "vision" and have admitted that there is no practical way by which the United States, never mind its allies, could render itself invulnerable to a nuclear attack.

For the forseeable future this task of minimum deterrence will be handled by ensuring that any nuclear aggression will trigger a response in kind. Both sides have worked to protect their means of retaliation from a first strike by the other and to the extent that they have succeeded we can talk of a *condition* of mutual assured destruction. This is to be distinguished from a *strategy* of assured destruction which implies (though it was never actually adopted in this form) that the most appropriate nuclear employment will in all cases be the utter destruction of the enemy's society, economy, and political structure.

One of the reasons why it seemed appropriate in the past to stress the potential for mutual assured destruction was that whatever the assumptions about less horrific outcomes with which a belligerent might enter nuclear hostilities, this would be the most likely result. Another reason was that the only sort of nuclear employment that might make sense would be a first strike that could remove the enemy's means of retaliation, and that prospect might alarm the enemy into doing something rash and pre-emptive while the weapons were still available. Any employment which could not disarm the enemy would be inviting retaliation and so would be quite foolish.

The conclusion that second-strike capabilities are likely to continue to be the most impressive features of nuclear arsenals for some time to come encourages confidence that these weapons can continue to meet their basic strategic objective of deterring each other. But it also throws into relief the problem that has in practice been the source of the great dilemmas of strategic thought in the nuclear age. The more profound the disincentives against going on to the nuclear offensive the weaker, at least in theory, extended deterrence.

The US nuclear guarantee to Europe depended initially on an *imbalance* of power which would make it plausible that if faced with Soviet aggression against Western Europe, even if only at the conventional level, the US would set in motion nuclear exchanges. The promise to do such a thing has now become institutionalized and embodied in the security policies of many nations and the orthodoxy of a supranational organization.

If such a guarantee were suggested now, under conditions far less favorable than those of the early days of NATO, then the very idea would no doubt be deemed preposterous. As the Soviet Union developed its retaliatory capability, the US nuclear guarantee suffered a loss of credibility that it has never been able to recover despite the sterling efforts of at least two generations of nuclear strategists. To restore this lost credibility, some way has been sought to create either a cast of mind or a physical condition that would make it conceivable an American President would authorize a nuclear strike of one sort or another. He might believe that the use of short-range weapons tucked away on a German hillside would be less inflammatory than the use of longer-range weapons on submarines lurking under the Atlantic Ocean, or that an attack on military targets might induce comparable restraint and so spare cities, or that releasing just a few kilotons would be seen at worst as a stern warning.

The difficulty with all these options is that their success depends on them being received in the right way by the other side so that the response is at worst comparably mild and at best surrender. The difficulty for the strategists is that they cannot show with any certainty or confidence why this should be so. It would only be if the other side could be physically prevented from mounting an effective form of retaliation that a nuclear offensive would make any sense. This explains the continual hankering after a first-strike capability or at least some technical fix to the problem of controlling the consequences of first nuclear use. Hence the continuing sense that secure second-strike capabilities are both welcomed for the constraints they impose on the adversary but resented for the resulting limitations on the West's freedom of maneuver and the doubts cast over the credibility and thus the durability of the US nuclear guarantee.

III

Until there is some breakthrough in anti-submarine warfare capabilities that would render ballistic- and cruise-missile carrying submarines vulnerable to a coordinated and decisive attack (rather than just steady attrition), then a genuine first-strike capability can be ruled out. Even if such a breakthrough were achieved, a successful first strike would involve a quality of target acquisition, weapons reliability and performance, timing and tactics that has eluded generals in the past attempting much more modest military operations, and seems implausible with untried weapons in wholly unique circumstances. It is inconceivable that a serious military planner in the coming decades will be able to inform his political masters with sufficiently high confidence that an available mix of offensive and defensive systems and tactics can remove the possibility of a devastating nuclear retaliation to either zero or as near as makes no difference (and that would have to be very near).

A variety of schemes have been suggested for strategic nuclear exchanges in which the relevant weapons are directed against each other or at least substantial military targets, rather than civil targets. The main difficulty here is that a large number of the relevant military targets are found within or close to populated areas. Another approach also assuming that one can render nuclear strategy more moral by attacking weapons rather than people is President Reagan's Strategic Defense Initiative, which is often discussed (in its less ambitious guise) as a means of denying the enemy access to certain high-value military targets (but not the country as a whole) by attacking offensive weapons *en route* to these targets. However, the point remains that unless success in either counterforce or strategic defensive operations is total or that the war has been terminated while they are underway, once the non-assured destruction strategies are exhausted the condition of and potential for mutual assured destruction remains.

Arguments in favor of partial first strikes depend very largely on a political judgment concerning the likely reactions of the enemy leaders to a strike directed against military targets but which has also destroyed some 10 percent or more of the population and left large areas devastated: will they be paralyzed with fear and recognize that a response against the enemy will only make things worse, or be so furious that they unleash a devastating riposte? The fact that the question can be posed indicates that there might be such a thing as a successful partial first strike. However, the fact that the enemy is left with such a choice indicates the enormous risks that would have to be taken in launching such a strike. Nuclear strategy in peacetime and in war therefore appears to be essentially political in nature—with success in the end determined by the effects on the perceptions and attitudes as much as the capabilities of the adversary.

IV

This point is reinforced when an alternative approach to nuclear strategy is considered, based on using these weapons almost as if they were conventional weapons in order to turn the tide of a land war in Europe. If nuclear weapons are to conform to the dictates of traditional strategy then it can be argued that the features which they share most with traditional weapons must be accentuated while those features which are distinctly "nuclear"—such as radiation and massive destructive effects—need to be correspondingly reduced. To some extent this has been made more possible with steady improvements in warhead technology (which allow for some effects to be enhanced at the expense of others) and weapon accuracy which mean that, to destroy a given target, far lower explosive yields are required thus reducing the risk of collateral damage. In principle this process could develop to the point whereby nuclear weapons were little more than a higher form of artillery and all connection with instruments of mass destruction were lost. In which case there would be nothing special about nuclear strategy; it would just be another branch of conventional strategy.

There are limits on this sort of development. The basic difficulty is that not *all* nuclear weapons can be expected to take this form. So long as nuclear weapons that are essentially instruments of mass destruction are still deployed in large numbers, then it is they rather than the less awesome types that will set the tone of nuclear strategy. Strategies based on integrating battlefield nuclear munitions with general purpose forces depend on the possibility of nuclear use being contained at this level and not escalating to something more generally destructive and less "controllable". This depends on the relevant weapons being accepted as more akin to conventional weapons than those other nuclear weapons which are still understood as instruments of mass destruction.

The proposition that any nuclear employment could be restricted to these new precision/low yield/low collateral damage types has been challenged on a number of grounds. To start at the most mundane level, enemy efforts at the passive and active protection of targets, or the need to attack a variety of dispersed and mobile targets, may push up the requirements for the numbers of weapons to be employed to a point where the cumulative effect approaches the most fearful consequences of older generations of weapons. Another problem is that the enemy may respond to an attack involving limited numbers of precise and clean nuclear weapons being used in a selective manner with an undiscriminating attack involving large numbers of crude and dirty bombs of their own. If restrictions are to be sustained then both sides must honor them and, in the conditions in which use was being contemplated, that would be unlikely.

Whether or not such a strategy would be possible, NATO has shied away from adopting it. In its statements and procedures NATO has made it clear it recognizes that nuclear weapons are quite different from other types of weapons, that any use would be the result of the most careful and considered political decision. In fact the procedures that have been established for this decision ensure that the most opportune moment for use would have passed by the time authorization for nuclear release had been obtained by the military commanders. If nuclear weapons are to be employed *as if* they were conventional weapons, then they need to be available from the start with conventional weapons—when the enemy is making its initial thrust and may be providing just the sort of concentrated targets for which super-artillery might be deemed especially appropriate. The longer the wait before authorization the more likely that nuclear use will simply be an act of desperation.

The connection with mass destruction ensures that release would only be imaginable in the most extreme circumstances. This prospect of nuclear use only as a last resort is in fact the prospect which NATO seeks to convey to the Soviet Union. The strategy does not revolve so much around the actual employment of the weapons, but the creation of circumstances sufficiently extreme for employment to be even considered. Nuclear weapons are still seen in this concept to have their greatest strategic effect by scaring the enemy into restraint or hesitation. Again they cannot enforce such restraints or hesitations or even withdrawals on the other side by straightforward *force majeure*. Again whatever positive strategic effects that they produce depend on the perceptions and responses of enemy decision-makers who will still retain a substantial freedom of maneuver.

So both nuclear deterrence and nuclear war-fighting depend on the quality of the political assessments used to support them. A judgment has to be formed on such matters as the likely responses to nuclear threats or indeed nuclear strikes as well as lesser threats and inducements; the ability of one's own society and political structure to cope with such challenges; and of the likely cohesion of alliances in such stressful circumstances. Relevant to such judgments will be the actual issues which prompted the confrontation in the first place. It will not be enough to assess the matter in terms of the crude categories of will and resolve with which these matters are often discussed let alone the personalities of the national leaders involved (tough, soft, unpredictable, cautious, robust, impetuous, etc.). So it cannot be said that a moderately non-Pyrrhic nuclear victory is an impossibility. Only that it could be achieved through an enormous and desperate gamble that is likely to appear reckless and suicidal when proposed.

V

This leads to the proposition that there can be no peacetime calculation that could offer even high confidence of prevailing in a nuclear war, even though it cannot be wholly ruled out that one side might actually prevail. Thus a strategy which depends on a threat of nuclear first use to deter an attack with conventional forces must be inherently suspect. It is doubtful that any further bursts of ingenuity in strategic studies can remove these risks (and with the Reagan Administration the profession has now probably shot this particular bolt). But this argument represents no sudden revelation or insight. The limitations of a first-use strategy have been acknowledged since the problem of a strategic stalemate first arose. So the real question is why has not extended deterrence already failed?

Part of the answer has already been mentioned. The propensities among national leaders to take enormous risks are not as high as strategists often assume. The circumstances in which the relevant decisions on nuclear use would be taken would hardly be conducive to rational (or for that matter moral) decision-making and so all sorts of terrible things could well happen even if they could not be forecast beforehand. The leaders of East and West have been wary of getting involved in any military confrontation with each other, even at the lowest rungs of the escalation ladder, which does not suggest enormous confidence in the promise of escalation dominance.

The second point is that the respect for the consequences of any confrontation has encouraged the two sides to consolidate the political status quo (at least in Europe) rather than maintain the option of mounting a serious challenge at some point. Extended deterrence is now easier than it ought to be because the state of the nuclear balance does not single-handedly shape all other basic international relationships.

At this point it is worth considering the conventional view that there is a close and positive relationship between a military balance and political stability. The first point is that political instability can have many causes other than self-evidently destabilizing military developments. Political change is a constant. As individuals, peoples and nations act on their grievances and aspirations they come into conflict with others. This provides the dynamic to international life.

Political relationships can break down and lead to war even when the military relationship is stable and the high commands on all sides lack confidence. This was more or less what happen-ned in 1939. In the nuclear age we tend to assume, and hope, that the point at which a severe breakdown could lead to war has been pushed back further because the risks of war are so drastic and obvious. However, the point remains that even an ultra-stable military relationship might still be overcome by a ferocious political dynamic. Stability in the nuclear age, as in previous ages, still requires attention to political as well as military dynamics.

Nor are the effects of military instability on political stability self-evident. A military imbalance need not in itself create political instability. Nations can live perfectly amicably beside one another despite great disparities in military capabilities without threatening violence. It did not need the nuclear age to turn war into a matter of last resort. Nor does it become attractive just because of a favorable balance of forces. Even the exercise of superior force involves blood and treasure and military commanders are aware that things can go wrong.

At most military instability might exacerbate political instability rather than create it. The idea that a certain configuration of forces might force the pace of a crisis lies behind the concept of crisis stability, which has always been very influential in arms control theory. According to this concept the tempo of diplomacy and the search for a political settlement should not be driven mercilessly by the tempo of military preparations and the fear of pre-emptive attack, as was assumed to be the case in August 1914. Instability in this sense is synonymous with any incentive to initiate hostilities or possibly to raise the profile of military preparations.

Crisis stability therefore concerns anything that might make it impossible to leave the military option as the last resort and force it into play before the diplomatic possibilities have been exhausted. It is not synonymous with equality or balance. A relationship in which one country is decisively superior to another will generate its own political logic (normally hegemony) and can so be extremely stable. Instability only becomes a problem when the identity of the victor is in doubt and is thus as likely to result from a true balance as any other type of relationship. This is despite the fact that the major powers often claim that they are doing some tense region a favor by helping to create a military balance.

Three forms of crisis instability might be identified:

(a) The transition from one military relationship to another, in which one side sees its position worsening. There is an incentive to act while the position is relatively favorable.

(b) A condition in which there is a clear premium attached to getting in the first blow. When the nation that takes the military initiative can alter its position decisively in its favor, both sides are nervous about waiting for diplomacy to take its course. There are two variants of this:

  (i) At any given time and whatever the stage of mobilization, the first strike can make a significant or even decisive difference.

  (ii) The implementation of crisis and war plans imposes its own momentum. Once mobilization begins it will take time to halt or reverse it. The build-up of front line forces increases the threat to the other side which is tempted to attack before the process is completed. Alternatively, plans are based on forward movement and once the motion has begun it is difficult to stop.

(c) The likely outcome of a war is sufficiently unclear for both sides to feel that they have a good chance of prevailing. Neither side therefore feels obliged to back down or make concessions to facilitate diplomacy.

Of these only (a) is wholly dependent on a particular relationship of forces. It became argued in the concern over the reciprocal fear of surprise attack concept that two sides with the same set of forces could find themselves nervous lest the other move first. At issue in (b) is the availability of, or dependence on, a particular strategic move which, if implemented, could disadvantage the other side. Involved in (c) are judgments over technical skill, tactical prowess and physical adaptability as well as assessments of force levels.

It is also noteworthy that with these three types the degree of instability depends on the perceptions of the belligerents. It is what political and military leaders believe to be the case that can matter more than what an objective observer (should such a body exist) knows it to be. Unfortunately recognition of this factor has been overdone and has allowed too great a tolerance for subjectivism. If it is "all in the mind" then anything can be disturbing and strategy becomes either impossible or an exercise in speculative psychology. It is suggested out of respect for perceptions that perhaps we ought to use weapons to engineer a particular view of the balance, by emphasizing sheer size or numbers of warheads or somesuch. It is doubtful that those truly obsessed are impressed by the evidence, or that even those who care moderately are influenced by much more than a broad sense of the other's power rather than the detail. (Quick exercise: write down the numbers of nuclear delivery vehicles and warheads available to the US and USSR: no peeping at *The Military Balance*.) Furthermore, if nuclear arsenals come to be interpreted in a particularly distorted way then the sources of distortion will as likely as not be in the manner of the interpretation (which might involve bureaucratic, cultural, and political factors) as much as presentation. If nuclear strategy is about presentation, then it would have to be said that far more attention is given by both sides, though in quite different ways, to the impression that is created on a domestic audience than on the potential adversary. The concern about perceptions never seems to be backed up with much market research!

In fact in the case of Europe there are fewer grounds for misperception than there might be with other potential troublespots. It is one of the features of the East-West relationship that the military balance is a continual preoccupation, even an obsession. In other periods, countries might not worry about the "balance" from one crisis to the next. For the two great alliances there would be no excuse for either side to be shocked or surprised at the state of affairs at a time of crisis. This one can argue is a positive source of stability.

In practice the most profound source of crisis instability is likely to take the form of the disintegration and formation of alliances, which would appear to individual countries as questions of neutrality or commitment. If one is going to war it is a natural objective to limit the number of enemies to be faced, and if one wishes to deter war then it makes sense to put together as powerful a coalition as possible of states enjoying at least a temporary coincidence of interests.

All this leads to the conclusion that the cohesion of the alliance system in Europe is as vital for the stability of East-West relations as is the particular hardware at the disposal of the two alliances. The greater the doubts about the willingness of individual states to follow a superpower leader, the greater the temptation for the aggressor to adopt a strong and adventurous approach in a crisis in order to sow divisions among its potential enemies. It is the very rigidity of the alliance system and the consequent lack of fluidity in the fundamental political arrangements that makes it so difficult (thankfully) to think of plausible scenarios for the outbreak of a war on the continent.

It is also for this reason that much nuclear strategy has as its political objectives not so much deterrence of the adversary but the cohesion of the alliance. Key questions of nuclear policy are as often as not about sustaining a set of understandings within the alliance as to each member's rights and duties. Opponents of US bases in Europe may feel that there is a sufficiency of nuclear capability facing the USSR from the other side of the Atlantic. But the real issues concern the political consequences of the link between the US nuclear arsenal and the defense of Europe becoming severely attenuated: the effect on European policy of the US being seen as a pushy, unpredictable, and high-risk protector or on American policy of the Europeans appearing unwilling to share the risks of the nuclear guarantee that has been generously proferred by the United States.

As a result an objective of NATO policy has been described as *coupling* the two halves of the alliance together. Unfortunately there are few precise guidelines on exactly what serves to couple. According to one point of view the more nuclear weapons in US bases in Europe the greater the commitment to its defense that has been demonstrated. Another point of view argues that these bases serve to endorse and even create doubts as to the credibility of the US guarantee. The point is that nuclear policy in the end is not so much an independent variable in alliance relations as shaped itself by broad economic and political factors. If alliance cohesion is a function of much more than a military relationship then it should be more resilient in a crisis. This still leaves nuclear strategy as being less important than the nuclear strategists would like to think.

VI

This paper has reflected the view of those who suspect that the current nuclear relationship is extraordinarily stable and can therefore accommodate all manner of variations in current plans and armaments—upwards, downwards, and sidewards —without it making a great deal of difference to the calculations of military risk in a crisis. The fundamental feature of the nuclear age is the unavoidable risk of horrific devastation. Unless a way can be found of removing that risk war will remain an unacceptable option. The basic questions that need continual attention are the sources of tension between East and West and within the two alliances. Nuclear policy is as often as not directed towards these tensions, so that the weapons themselves serve as political symbols either in arms control negotiations or in affirmations of the US nuclear guarantee. The real challenge for nuclear strategy will come when this relationship between nuclear policies and political relationships is more immediate and urgent and less routine than it is at the moment. The Great East-West Crisis serves as the focal point for all nuclear strategy, but often only in the sense that the character of the nuclear relationship will determine the basic outcome. The challenge in such a crisis however would be to match any military, including nuclear, moves to a developing political situation. The preoccupations of the nuclear strategists with the detail of force structure and highly stylized nuclear exchanges have left their political leaders ill-equipped for such a task.

DISCUSSIONS

Kiichi Saeki

Generally speaking, Professor Freedman's papers are quite excellent, sophisticated and well elaborated. At the same time they are very abstractly described. His criticism of the military strategist's arguments is very sharp but he is rather reluctant to recommend an alternative strategy.

I would like to point out that I have great respect for Professor Freedman's views. I was intellectually stimulated. I received insights which I continue to think about today. In particular, his remarks about the great dilemma of strategic thought in the nuclear age related to extended deterrence, and his acute arguments on the relationship between military balance and political stability are quite enlightening.

With respect to extended deterrence, he emphasized that: "The more profound the disincentives against going on to the nuclear offensive the weaker, at least in theory, extended deterrence." And he raised the consequent question: "Why has not extended deterrence already failed?" His response to this question was quite attractive, but yet not persuasive enough. I think his first statement is, "the propensities among national leaders to take enormous risks are not so high as strategists often assume". Second, "the respect for the consequences of any confrontation has encouraged the two sides to consolidate the political status quo (at least in Europe) rather than maintain the option of mounting a serious challenge at some point". I wonder how long such reasoning will hold. Referring to the relationship between a military balance and political stability he made clear three points. Those are the following:

1. Political relationships can break down and lead to war even when the military relationship is stable and the high commands on all sides lack confidence.
2. The effects of military instability on political stability are not self-evident. A military imbalance need not in itself create political instability.
3. At most, military instability might exacerbate political instability rather than create it.

He stressed five important points concerning crisis stability.

1. Degree of crisis instability depends on the perceptions of the belligerents.
2. Most profound source of crisis instability is likely to take the form of the disintegration and formation of alliances.

3. The cohesion of the alliance system in Europe is as vital for the stability of East-West relations as is the particular hardware at the disposal of the two alliances.
4. Much nuclear strategy has as its political objectives not so much deterrence of the adversary but the cohesion of the alliance.
5. Nuclear policy is not so much an independent variable in alliance relations as shaped itself by broad economic and political factors.

I quite agree with these views as well as the main ideas of his conclusion. Those are as follows:

1. Nuclear strategy is less important than the nuclear strategist would like to think.
2. Current nuclear relationship is extraordinarily stable.
3. The fundamental feature of the nuclear age is the unavoidable risk of horrific devastation. Unless a way can be found of removing that risk, wars will remain an unacceptable option.
4. The basic questions that need continual attention are the sources of tension between East and West and within the two alliances.
5. The real challenge for nuclear strategy will come when this relationship between nuclear policies and political relationships is more immediate and urgent and less routine than it is at the moment.

The important questions that are not clearly addressed in the paper concern particularly the specific sources of tension between East and West, the importance of an accurate assessment of East-West military balance, the relative importance of political relationships between the military alliances, and the implications of the recent Strategic Defence Initiative. These issues deserve further consideration.

General discussion

The discussion largely revolves around the questions of crisis instability and crisis management. There is wide agreement that the nuclear situation is sufficiently stable to ensure against a surprise attack during a period of low tension. Discussants are mainly concerned with possible developments during an escalatory situation. Changing weapons technology is also considered likely to complicate the process of handling crisis situations. It is very strongly emphasized that although crisis situations have been successfully handled in the past, there is no guarantee that this will always be the case.

There is thus considerable agreement that the idea of a stable nuclear situation has to be challenged. Most discussants are in agreement that there is little chance of an accidental war, but some raise the problem of technological error. Furthermore, the problem of considering the state as a unitary actor is also taken up in this context. Yet the debate focusses largely on the question of inadvertant war, the possibility of stumbling into war when a crisis situation is entered. It is emphasized that certain sets of beliefs could lead the superpowers into war if they came together during the crisis. A combination of fear of meeting a crisis where management could break down, and the idea that war was becoming inevitable, that one would be better off going first, could lead to a confrontation. In tense situations, there could be doubt as to the rules of the game. In such a situation, of course, the fact that states are not necessarily unitary actors might seriously aggravate the problem of crisis management.

It seems to be widely agreed that the acquisition of new weapons by the West might considerably aggravate this already existing uncertainty. The policies of the West in this respect might lead to strengthen the hand of the most reckless on the other side.

On several occasions during discussions the possibility of a conventional build-up in Europe is mentioned as a most likely destabilizing factor. The crisis in deterrence and in crisis management to many discussants makes it imperative to focus on the problem of conventional war. A crisis would most likely originate with a conventional war, and nothing could be more dangerous than such a drawn-out struggle. Accordingly, it also seems necessary to pay close attention to US-European relationships and the problem of reassuring the Europeans.

Most discussants distinguish between the problems of military stability and political stability. Political instability might easily break through a stable military situation. Accordingly it seems mandatory that more attention has to be paid to the domestic political situations and the problems of states as co-alitions of actors rather than unitary actors: As one discussant puts it, states could be considered federations of warring tribes. Military stability could not be considered a sufficient barrier against a crisis situation.

Historically, political and military stability coincided for a considerable period during the post-war era. It could be maintained that general stability would prevail within a context of either military or political stability. Dangerous situations would occur when both instabilities coincided, such as with new weapons technology and instability in Europe. Historically, however, it could reasonably be argued that inadvertent wars rarely occur. Certainly very few present-day historians would consider the outbreak of war—possibly the most popular case—in 1914 inadvertent. Historians would not on that basis preclude the possibility of inadvertant nuclear war. The task for strategists would be to make sure it could not happen. The relationship between the developed world and the Third World is also touched upon. Some discussants maintain that while the military balance between the superpowers might seem reasonably stable, stability might not be easily maintained within the non-European world. There were possibilities that the superpowers could get involved in a nuclear war between regional powers, or one could conceive of the possibility of nuclear strikes if local trouble-makers were to acquire the bomb.

While the discussion as a whole centers on the problems of avoiding crisis and on crisis management, some dissenting voices profoundly doubt the possibility of basing national security on threats rather than cooperative behavior. They find nuclear armaments morally unacceptable, and point to the dilemma—which is generally recognized—on acquiring for political use weapons which are generally accepted as militarily useless. How could it then be possible to create a stable balance. The dissenting voices are also much preoccupied with the technological dangers inherent in the nuclear balance.

4

What Went Wrong with Arms Control?

THOMAS C. SCHELLING

Arms control, at least where strategic weapons are concerned, has certainly gotten off the tracks. Not only is it going nowhere, what are called arms negotiations have become little but a public exchange of accusations. If genuine arms control has to reflect a perceived common interest in the avoidance of a war that neither side wants, there is little evidence that any common interest is perceived at the levels of government where negotiating policy is determined. It sometimes looks as if it is arms negotiations that drive the arms race.

Maybe the inflammatory public debate about armaments is independent of the forum in which it takes place, and is unaffected by the pretense that either side is serious. But it is hard to escape the impression that the planned procurement (at latest count) of fifty MX missiles, a weapon whose military utility hardly anybody avers, has been an obligation imposed by a doctrine that the end justifies the means—the end something called arms control, and the means a demonstration that the United States does not lack (or appear to lack) determination to match or exceed the Soviets in every category of weapons.

And the latest episode, the Strategic Defense Initiative (SDI), is sufficiently amorphous that it has been variously characterized by administration spokesmen as a potential joint strategic effort based on shared technology to make nuclear offensive missiles obsolete, a substitution of brute-strength (albeit high technology) self-defense for mutual restraint based on mutual deterrence, a potentially negotiable bargaining chip, and, finally, as a modest way to make fixed-site land-based missiles like the MX less vulnerable to attack.

Despite the inflamed state of rhetorical relations on the subject of strategic weapons, there does not seem to be much substance behind the spate of ill will that followed détente. Nobody seriously believes that either side's capacity to retaliate horrendously after receiving a nuclear attack is, or will be, in sufficient doubt to make pre-emption a preferred strategy in any crisis that can be imagined. Détente survived a US war against a Communist ally of the Soviet Union in Southeast Asia; it didn't survive the vicious Soviet war against the people of Afghanistan, but the reprisals to Afghanistan were little more than an attempt to deny athletes, bread grain, and pipeline equipment to the Soviet Union, of which one attempt failed and a second was reversed for the benefit of American farmers.

Poland became, and continues to be, a theater of contention between East and West, but of all the possible Soviet responses to what must have been for the Soviets (and the Polish government) an unacceptable condition in Poland, the one that ensued was probably the gentlest that anyone could seriously have anticipated, in absolute contrast to Hungary in 1956 or Czechoslovakia in 1968.

There is little sign that the Soviets would wish or even know how to create a crisis in Central America comparable to Cuba in 1962 or Berlin before that.

Furthermore, we have what ought to be an important source of reassurance, a "confidence-building experience". We have forty years of nuclear weapons without nuclear war. That should be a sufficient demonstration that nuclear war is not inevitable. This is a conclusion that some advocates of disarmament do not like voiced, afraid it may lead to complacency. But I like the idea that national leaders in a crisis may be complacent in the knowledge that nuclear war is so unlikely that initiating it is never prudent. I am not so complacent as to believe that strategic arms decisions do not matter; I take seriously that we may have accomplished the forty years without nuclear war in part because of some correct decisions on strategic weapons.

I see no reason to believe, as the Palme Commission wrote two years ago, that the likelihood of nuclear war has been increasing fearsomely in recent years. I can see that if peace depended on mutual respect between adversaries and confidence of each other's abhorrence of violence the current situation would not look good. At least, it would not sound good. I know of no way to reassure the people who disagree with me on that; but I do think that there is no prudential wisdom in exaggerating the danger of nuclear war by an order of magnitude, and both sides of the political spectrum in the United States appear to have been doing that for several years.

With those remarks as prelude, I want to turn to my own historical interpretation of what has happened with strategic arms control during the past thirty years. To anticipate, I shall argue that the thinking on arms control was on the right track, and was effective, from the late fifties to the early seventies, culminating in the ABM treaty of 1972, and that things have substantially unraveled since then. Maybe the loss of direction in the past dozen years was natural and expectable, even inevitable. Even so I think it is worth examining what went wrong.

I date the modern era of strategic arms control from the late 1950s. In 1957 the Gaither Committee (named for its chairman, C. Rowan Gaither) conducted a searching examination into the adequacy of US strategic weapons and their deployment and became alarmed at the vulnerability of the retaliatory force to surprise attack. Bombers capable of carrying immense destructive power transcontinentally were clustered, unprotected, on a small number of bases. Studies done at the RAND Corporation persuasively argued that Soviet bombers, too few to be identified by the Distant Early Warning Line, might be sufficient to visit the bases and destroy or disable the fragile aircraft, eliminating the prospect of the reprisal that was supposed to deter the Soviet attack in the first place. Announcement in 1957 of the Soviet flight test of a potentially intercontinental ballistic missile capable of carrying a hydrogen warhead further dramatized the vulnerability of a retaliatory force that offered only a small number of soft targets to a surprise attack.

The seriousness with which this bomber-vulnerability problem was taken by the Eisenhower administration was evidenced by the institution of a limited airborne alert in the last years of that administration, a procedure intended to keep at least a small bomber force safely in the air at all times, capable of proceeding on a retaliatory mission in the event of attack on the bomber bases.

It was in 1958 that President Eisenhower and Chairman

Krushchev, at the Summit, agreed to initiate east-west talks on "measures to safeguard against surprise attack". It was not clear what they had in mind. There had been an earlier initiative by Harold Stassen, for a time the president's disarmament adviser, that became known as the "open skies" proposal. It was to make East and West German airspace, or perhaps a larger territory, accessible to reconnaisance flights from both sides, to prevent undetected military build-ups that might give an attacker the advantage of surprise. It was not clear how this idea might generalize to intercontinental warfare.

With a commitment to negotiations the US government had to collect its thoughts on the subject of surprise attack. A high (Assistant Secretary) level planning group in the government met regularly and ultimately educated itself, with some help from people at RAND and elsewhere, that the surprise attack problem was the strategic-force vulnerability problem. If a retaliatory force that was intended to deter by the prospect of reprisal could itself be destroyed in the attack that it was supposed to deter, it could not deter; it invited attack; and surprise was precisely the element that might make it vulnerable, incapable of retaliating, incapable of deterring.

The Geneva negotiations were to involve five participants from the West and five from the East; representatives of Canada, the UK, France and the Federal Republic met in Washington in the fall of 1958 to prepare for the negotiations. By the time the negotiating team went to Geneva after a few weeks of Washington consultation, the identification of strategic-retaliatory-force vulnerability as the essence of the surprise-attack problem, and indeed as the essence of the problem of potential nuclear war, had become widely shared.

An intellectual milestone was the publication, in January, 1949, of Albert Wohlstetter's "Delicate Balance of Terror" in *Foreign Affairs*. The manuscript had been available to the Surprise Attack negotiating team. My own "Surprise Attack and Disarmament", in the *Bulletin of the Atomic Scientists* that same year and in *Survival* in early 1960, explicitly identifying arms control with reciprocally reduced strategic-force vulnerability, came out of those negotiating preparations.

Nothing directly came of the negotiations on surprise attack. But the occasion was crucial in identifying on the Western side, and probably in the Soviet Union, what was to become pivotal in arms negotiations for the next decade and, perhaps more important, in the design of strategic forces.

In addition to the airborn alert that was instituted by President Eisenhower, there was the abandonment of the large, above-ground, soft, slow-to-fuel Atlas missile in favor of a missile dubbed Minuteman for its ability to fly instantly on warning; and the Navy's strategic future was assured with the development of the untargetable Polaris system.

Within the first year of the Kennedy administration, 1961, strategic-force vulnerability had become identified with the entire problem of "war by accident, miscalculation, and surprise attack", those being the only conditions considered capable of generating nuclear war. The idea of "accidental war" had come to be viewed as this same problem: nuclear accidents might not be a function of strategic-force vulnerability, but the likelihood that an accident of some sort, or an unauthorized act, or a strategic miscalculation, could actually lead to nuclear war was seen to inhere in the importance, in the event of war, of striking first, or if not first to be a close second, and launching if in doubt. Secure, survivable forces were identified with what came to be called "strategic stability".

The idea that both sides could have an interest in each other's strategic-force security was dramatized by Secretary McNamara's testimony to Congress that he would prefer to see the Soviet Union invest in secure, hardened underground missiles rather than soft missiles above ground, because the latter both invited and threatened pre-emptive attack and the former would be conducive to Soviet patience in a crisis.

In the end, the vulnerability problem was temporarily solved by unilaterial action without any boost from explicit arms control. (A number of ideas for resolving anxiety in a crisis were considered, of which the hotline is the best known example to have been adopted.) Reciprocal measures to safeguard against surprise attack proved unnecessary with the advent of the missile technology of the early 1960s, although measures to safeguard against misapprehension in a crisis were considered worth pursuing nevertheless.

Two developments of the 1960s came along to endanger the strategic-force stability that had been achieved through the procurement of systems of very low vulnerability. One was ABM, the other MIRV. ABM was seen by arms theorists and the US Office of the Secretary of Defense as potentially destabilizing. ABM at that time was seen primarily as the area defense of populations, not as the defense of military hard targets. The destabilization seemed to have two dimensions. The most worrisome was that ABM might provide a strong advantage to the first strike. The idea was that ABM would be effective but not terribly effective, might work better when alert than when taken by surprise, might work poorly against a prepared attack but well against a damaged retaliatory force.

The second dimension was sometimes called "arms-race instability" and was the prospect that to maintain a good retaliatory capability against burgeoning active defenses would require indefinite enlargement of the offensive retaliatory force. It was therefore thought that ABM would make pre-emptively initiated war more likely and the arms race more expensive. It was this conviction that led the Johnson administration to seek a treaty to forestall the deployment of ballistic missile defenses.

This notion, that protecting people from retaliatory attack is bad, that mutual deterrence is good (or at least the best situation achievable), that populations should be naked hostages to peace, was of course an anomaly by traditional standards according to which defensive weapons were less ugly than offensive. The concept of mutual deterrence was institutionalized in the negotiations for an ABM treaty.

The treaty had a characteristic that was importantly incompatible with its own philosophy, but that I judged to have been probably a political necessity. The treaty can be thought of as designed to protect the efficacy of retaliatory forces, to keep them from being degraded by enemy active defenses. It treated human and economic resources as hostages to be left unprotected. But ballistic missile defenses could also be used to protect military hard targets, indeed were generally thought much superior in that mode of deployment. Land-based fixed-site missiles might be difficult and expensive to protect passively, by hardening, and active defenses against ballistic missile attack might have been cost-effective and would have been compatible with the philosophy of the treaty as long as there was a clear distinction between the technology of defending military targets and the technology pertinent to an area defense of human and economic resources. (This possibility was acknowledged in the provision for a very limited local active defense, a provision that in the end the United States chose not to take advantage of.)

I have always supposed that the failure to make provision for local hard point defense was partly the difficulty of guarding against upgrading, surreptitiously or upon denunciation of the treaty, but partly also for political simplicity. It might have been hard to get the American public, which may have had its own reasons for disliking ABM, to believe that exceptions should be made for Air Force assets and not for urban residents.

The other development of the sixties that threatened to destabilize the strategic balance was MIRV. A missile with ten independently targetable warheads is a kind of replica of an air base with many aircraft. If it takes one weapon to destroy ten, two or three weapons to destroy it with confidence, MIRVed but targetable forces equal in size are reciprocally vulnerable to an attack by 20 or 30 percent of an enemy force. (For retaliatory forces that cannot be targeted, things that are hidden or mobile and cannot be found on short notice, MIRV is merely an economical way of packaging warheads.)

There was no serious effort to constrain MIRV until more than a decade after the ABM ban became a US policy objective. The SALT II treaty attempted to limit not only numbers of missiles but numbers allowed to be MIRVed.

I find that fifteen-year period, from 1957 to 1972, to be a remarkable story of intellectual achievement transformed into successsful policy. Three books appeared in 1961 that epitomized an emerging consensus on what strategic arms control should be about. Each represented a group effort and stimulated discussion even while being written. During the summer of 1960, Hedley Bull's manuscript, *The Control of the Arms Race*, was circulated by the Institute for Strategic Studies in preparation for the second annual conference of that Institute, held at Worcester College, Oxford, in September. That same summer a study group sponsored by the Twentieth Century Fund met on the outskirts of Boston, and Morton H. Halperin and I produced a little book, discussed at numerous meetings of the Harvard-MIT Arms Control Faculty Seminar during the fall, reflecting what we took to be a consensus, one that was wholly consistent with the ideas that developed around Hedley Bull's manuscript at the ISS. And during the spring of 1960 Donald G. Brennan organized a conference under the auspices of the American Academy of Arts and Sciences that generated an issue of *Daedalus* devoted to arms control and a somewhat larger book, *Arms Control, Disarmament, and National Security* that appeared in 1961. Together those efforts were a substantial intellectually creative achievement; and a number of participants in the Harvard-MIT Seminar took important positions in the Kennedy adminstration in the White House, the Department of State, and the Department of Defense; others from RAND and elsewhere, who had been part of this intellectual movement, moved into those two departments. So, although it is surprising it is not completely surprising that those ideas became the basis for US policy and ultimately were successfully implemented in the ABM treaty. I consider the culmination of fifteen years of progress not merely the high point but the end point. (Others would tell the story with more attention to a local summit achieved in 1963 with the signing and ratification of the nuclear test treaty or a local summit in 1970 with the coming into force of the nuclear non-proliferation treaty. These were indeed important achievements but independent of any body of strategic theory.)

Since 1972 the control of strategic weapons has made little or no progress and the effort on our side has not seemed to be informed by any consistent theory of what arms control is supposed to accomplish. Maybe there is nothing for it to accomplish right now. But I would argue that there has been retrogression in the doctrine.

There is a qualification to this judgment that nothing constructive has happened. The interim agreement governing strategic offensive weapons that was part of the SALT package was succeeded by the treaty that was still unratified at the invasion of Afghanistan and never had a chance after that. Both sides have so far avoided going expressly beyond the limits contained in a draft treaty that has no formal standing. This is a powerful demonstration that restraints can be reciprocated without formal obligation. Indeed, since treaties can be renounced upon notice, there is not much formal difference between a tacit moratorium that each side abides by only on condition that the other side do too, each side free to break out without a moment's notice, and a formal treaty that requires a moment's notice. There is probably a lesson here. Possibly overt departures from the non-binding understanding could be informally communicated and responded to, in a process of continuous informal "negotiation", with the outcome not much different from a formal treaty as far as the weapons are concerned. (Popular satisfaction with the outcome may be a different thing.)

One development since 1972 may have been a hardening of the belief, both among diplomatists and in the public, that arms control has to be embedded in treaties. I used to believe, in the early and middle 1960s, that a tacit understanding might be arrived at regarding ballistic missile defenses, namely, that the United States would have to proceed at full speed unless the Soviets stopped in their tracks, but the United States would happily forgo the cost of ABM if the Russians did stop in their tracks. I saw no advantage in a treaty. I later came to believe that the advantage of the treaty was to put the quietus on ABM in this country, especially in the military services and in the Congress. But in principle I still think that reciprocated restraint may often be as good as formal negotiations and treaties, sometimes better, and that this idea was better understood up until a dozen years ago than it has been during the past dozen years. I was interested to see Mr. Adelman, the director of the Arms Control and Disarmament Agency, resurrecting the notion that not all arms restraint has to be formalized.

I'll give a favorite example, to illustrate not only how something that deserves to be identified as arms control can come about quite informally, but even how it may not be recognized as arms control by the participants. This is the apparent understanding that a war in Europe should be kept non-nuclear if possible, and that efforts should be made to keep it non-nuclear. Secretary McNamara began in 1962 an aggressive campaign for building up conventional defenses in Europe on grounds that nuclear weapons certainly shouldn't be used and possibly wouldn't be used. (The no-first-use idea emerged as a reflection of the same principle.) Throughout the 1960s the official Soviet

line was to deny the possibility of non-nuclear engagement in
Europe, even to deny as well that any nuclear war could be
kept limited. There has never been overt acknowledgment that
both sides contemplate an anti-nuclear limit on warfare itself
in Europe.

Yet the Soviets have spent enormous amounts of money
developing non-nuclear capabilities in Europe, especially aircraft capable of delivering and fighting with conventional
weapons. This capability is not only expensive but utterly
useless in the event of any war that is nuclear from the outset.
It can only reflect a Soviet acknowledgment that both sides are
capable of non-nuclear war and interested in keeping war non-
nuclear. If arms control includes expensive restraints on the
potential *use* of weapons as well as on their deployment, this
reciprocated investment in non-nuclear capability has to be
considered a remarkable instance of unacknowledged but reciprocated arms restraint. (And it reminds us that the inhibitions
on "first-use" may be just as strong without declarations as
with them.)

Until the recent emergence of a Strategic Defense Initiative
(SDI), on which I shall comment later, the arms-control attention to strategic weapons has been on offensive weapons for
the last thirteen years. (I am not going to discuss the issues
surrounding deployment of Pershing II and cruise missiles in
Europe and their Soviet counterparts.) What I will argue is that
proposals and negotiations on strategic offensive weapons have
been mostly mindless, without a guiding philosophy, and what
guiding philosophy there used to be has got lost along the way.

The main difference between the pre-1971 and post-1972 eras
has been a shift from an interest in the *character* of strategic
weapons to an interest in *numbers*. In the United States, this is
the common interest that has joined left and right with almost
no room between them. The proposals of the Carter and Reagan
administrations have been for reduced numbers. Simultaneously
the unilateral *programs* of the Carter and Reagan administrations have been to match numbers. (This is matching in each
category, not merely in some aggregate index of firepower.)
Sophisticates in the freeze movement could talk privately about
second-strike and first-strike weapons, about vulnerability and

survivability, but the simple public goal was freezing numbers and looking toward reduction. The last two administrations appeared intent on matching hard-target capabilities, number for number, almost without regard to whether *denying* strategic-weapon *targets* to the enemy was a superior alternative to matching hard-target capability.

There are two things here to be discussed. One is the interest that everybody seems to claim in ultimately reducing numbers through arms control. The other is the interest, in these last two administrations, in matching enemy capabilities whether we like them or not.

First the "arms control" interest in reducing numbers. I think there are two pertinent observations about the interest in reducing numbers. One is that nobody ever offers a reason for preferring smaller numbers. I may exaggerate: saving money is a legitimate reason, and whether or not smaller numbers would cost less, people may be excused for thinking so. And occasionally people think that with fewer weapons there is less likelihood that one will fall into mischievous hands or be launched by mechanical error; this I think is incorrect, but may not be worth refuting because nobody believes it strongly enough for it to be a main motivation. For the most part, people simply think that smaller numbers are better than bigger ones. For those who believe that we already have ten times what we need, it is not clear why having merely five times as many is any better. If people really believe that zero is the ultimate goal, then it is easy to see that they would believe that downward is the direction in which to seek the goal. But except for President Reagan, who has a dream about making nuclear weapons obsolete a couple of generations hence, hardly anybody who takes arms control seriously seems to believe that zero is the goal.

Furthermore, political and even professional discussion, to say nothing of editorials and popular discussion, appear to be poor at knowing what numbers matter. I am always surprised at how few intelligent laymen, and even how few people who concern themselves seriously with arms control, are aware that the sheer explosive energy in American strategic weapons, the megatonnage of alert warheads, was at least five times greater twenty years ago than it is now. I don't mean that gross megatonnage is the important measure; my point is merely that this is not an uninteresting datum, and people who are unacquainted with it may be people who really don't know (or don't care) what numbers they ought to be interested in. Secretary Laird in the Nixon administration used to be good at representing his military services on the Hill by showing charts of Soviet and American throw-weight, to make the claim for more and better US weapons, while including at the bottom of the chart the comparision of Soviet and American numbers of "alert warheads", which reassured the Congressmen that things were not in bad shape.

In 1962 Lieutenant-General (then Colonel) Glenn Kent published an Occasional Paper of the Harvard Center for International Affairs in which he looked at the question, if we were to have a limit of some kind on strategic nuclear missiles, what would be the limit that made the most sense. He argued that we wanted both sides to be free to proliferate weapons in whatever dimension might reduce their own vulnerability without increasing the other side's vulnerability to pre-emptive attack. In those days accuracies were poor, megatonnage mattered more than today, big explosives were less efficient than small explosives because target destruction would be proportionate to the ground area covered by a lethal overpressure while the yield of a bomb determined the volume with a given overpressure. He concluded that the correct magnitude to limit was the sum of the lethal areal covered by all the warheads in the inventory, which would be summed by using the two-thirds power of the yield of each weapons. Each party would then be free to proliferate smaller and smaller warheads on more and more missiles, becoming less and less vulnerable without achieving any enhanced pre-emptive capability. He further calculated that the weight-to-yield ratio went up as warheads got smaller, that the weight of the warheads would be roughly proportionate to the two-thirds power of the yields, and that no matter how many warheads were on a given missile the physical volume of the missile would be approximately proportionate to that calculated index of lethality. And you could calculate the volume by looking at a missile from a distance, so that monitoring would be easy.

Kent's specific formula may be somewhat obsolete technologically, but it continues to display the virtue that it attempts to answer the question, if you were to limit something, what would you want to limit?

My point in recalling Kent's nifty little paper is that this is a question that does not get the attention it deserves. In a very crude way the distinction between MIRVed and unMIRVed weapons moves in that direction; and the Scowcroft Commission's advertisement for a single-warhead missile to substitute ultimately for the MIRVed MX reflects a tardy and halting return to some kind of inexplicit criterion in the spirit of Kent's philosophy.

The SALT procedure tends to deal not only with numbers but with numbers and fixed categories. And the categories relate to things like land, sea, and air, not strategic characteristics like susceptibility to pre-emption or capability for pre-emption, nor even relevant ingredients like warheads per target point, readiness, speed of delivery, accuracy, recallability after launch, etc. The result has been that as fixed-site ground-based missiles have become more and more susceptible to successful attack (unless fired on warning), and as the limits on MIRVed missiles invite building up to those limits, things have moved exactly opposite to the direction that the Kent formulation pointed to.

What has been lost is the earlier emphasis on the *character* of weapons, and what has taken its place is emphasis on *numbers*, and specifically numbers within *fixed categories*, the categories having nothing to do with the weapon characteristics that most deserve attention.

The rigidity of the emphasis on defined categories can be illustrated by the MX controversy. The Scowcroft Commission was in a quandary: it apparently found no military virtue in the MX but felt it necessary to demonstrate, to the Soviet government and to allied governments, that the United States was determined to spend money to overcome any strategic-weapon deficiency compared with the Soviet Union, and specifically an apparent deficiency in large multiple-warhead missiles. The MX was alleged to be the only missile ready for procurement, and since procurement of something was essential, the Commission recommended procurement of a hundred MX, somewhat longingly wishing that an economical single-warhead missile were ready for procurement. Bemused by the SALT tradition, their horizon in searching for appropriate weapons to procure was short of the oceans, and they appear not to have considered as an alternative the scheduling of some equivalent number of Trident submarines. Perhaps Tridents were not considered quite equivalent militarily to the MX; but since the object was a demonstration of resolve to procure and not the particular characteristics of the MX anyhow, and because the Trident system solved the basing problem that had perplexed the Carter and Reagan administrations for most of eight years, the Trident solution at least ought to have been considered. But—one may object—five or six additional Trident boats (enough, say, to provide one hundred D-5 missiles continuously on station) would have been in violation of the informally observed SALT treaty; such an alternative was impermissible and would have been objected to by Senators and Congressmen interested in arms control even more than they objected to the MX.

What a strange result of an arms agreement—to constrain the United States to purchase one of the least attractive weapon systems (in terms of what arms control is intended to bring about) and preclude the procurement instead of a secure, non-targetable undersea system. What a lost opportunity to announce that the United States would stay within the *spirit* rather than the letter of an agreement that had proved itself technologically obsolete through the perfection of MIRV and the improvement of accuracy. This is truly arms control for its own sake, not for the sake of peace and confidence.

Arms control for its own sake seems to be similarly involved in the widespread abhorrence of submarine based cruise missiles capable of reaching targets in the Soviet Union. The cruise missile as advertised is an economical retaliatory weapon, too slow for use in pre-emptive attack, difficult to defend against as it penetrates Soviet air space, impossible to locate on station because it can be based on nuclear powered submarines. It might seem to be a splendid answer to the problem of vulnerability in the retaliatory force. The widely voiced objection is a simple one. It is easy to hide; its production may be easy to hide; it can be got surreptitiously on board submarines; because it can be fired from a torpedo tube and each submarine can have a re-load capability, and because there are many more attack submarines capable of carrying cruise missiles than any treaty limitation on the missiles would allow, there is no satisfactory way to monitor a limitation on numbers. The logic is that if you cannot find them you cannot count them, if you cannot count them you cannot have verifiable limits, if limits cannot be verified you cannot have arms control.

But who needs arms control if economical and reliable retaliatory weapons are available that are neither susceptible to preemption nor capable of pre-emption? There may be an answer to this question, but it hasn't been given. Again arms control appears to get in the way of reaching its own intended objective.

There is a somewhat separate development that I have to weave into my story. It was about ten years ago, late in the Nixon administration, that the Secretary of Defense began to pronounce a new doctrine for the selection of strategic weapons. This doctrine entailed a much more comprehensive target system than would have been compatible with the McNamara doctrine. Its philosophical basis was that the President, if a war occurred, should have some alternative to mutual destruction. The alternative proposed was a counterforce capability that could be operated purposively in a wartime environment, susceptible to control. And there was a new strategic element: the threat of destroying a large part of the Soviet population and industrial capacity might not deter Soviet leaders, whose affection was for their own leadership and not for the people they served, and the only effective deterrent threat might be the destruction of their entire military power base, including ground and naval forces. This required, of course, enhanced target destruction capabilities for our forces and even something like armed reconnaisance with a new generation of bombers. The philosophy underlying the ABM agreement came under attack as the mad notion that the only alternative to peace was mutual obliteration, and the name of the strategy was abbreviated, and the abbreviated acronym, MAD, has been brandished as a slogan. I had thought that since 1964 the name of the strategy was "assured capability for mutual destruction", not "assured mutual destruction", the difference being that the capability did not have to be ineluctably exercised to capacity at the outbreak of even an intercontinental nuclear war. The three crucial elements were an assured capability, restrained targeting, and some capacity for war termination.

What has happened is that a capacity to maintain control of the war has been identified with a vigorous and extended counterforce campaign while retaliatory targeting has been identified with what Herman Kahn used to call "spasm". If you draw a 2 x 2 matrix and label the rows "controlled" and "uncontrolled", and the columns "values" and "forces", the choice is presented as one between controlled counterforce (upper right) and uncontrolled countervalue (lower left). I find it more plausible that the actual choice is between the two opposite cells in the matrix. A controlled countervalue capability (upper left) seems to me supremely important, as these things go, and probably achievable, at least if somewhat reciprocated on the other side, but it seems to me unlikely that counterforce warfare on the scale typically envisioned could be sustained all the way to a termination that left populations and their economic assets substantially intact, and lower right is what you get.

But as long as the extended counterforce doctrine is governing, it will indeed be hard to impose a reciprocal denial of substantial pre-emptive capabilities, since hard target destruction, publicly eschewed by McNamara, may now have become central to the target doctrine. Just how this doctrine can be squared with arms control has never been clear to me, but it perhaps explains why the current arms control framework has become the one within which the numerical arms race is driven.

I should note briefly that the bargaining chip idea has again become brazenly transparent. The US administration, the Scowcroft Commission, and even Democratic Congressman Les Aspin have all publicly averred that an initial MX program was essential to drive the Soviets to the bargaining table. No one has given a quantitative estimate of the likelihood of successful disarmament negotiations in the presence of MX and in its absence; if the prospect were 10 percent without MX and 30 percent with it—a differential I find high—it could still be a bad bargain if MX is not the weapon we want. The administration has never been altogether clear whether the MX itself is a definitive program whose completion will lead to arms control or is a contingent program whose abandonment is up for discussion. The idea of publicly acknowledging that Soviet intransigence can oblige the United States to procure an expensive weapon of admittedly little or negative military utility is embarrassing.

Another debating strategy that attempts to make things better by first making them worse is publicizing the argument that any perceived inadequacy of US strategic weaponry vis-à-vis the Soviet Union's, or even a perceived lack of competitive determination on the part of the United States, would invite the Soviets to press hard in the next confrontation in the confident belief that the United States must back down, much as Krushchev did in 1962; and in the face of Soviet hubris based on strategic superiority, the United States will have no choice but to back down—a situation that invites confrontation. This may be a good argument on condition that Americans believe it and Russians don't. It is dangerous if Russians believe it and believe Americans do too. I find no logic in the argument, but it is one of those that could be self-fulfilling in a dangerous way. The argument might easily have been neutered by an administration that saw the danger in it and that did not itself rely on such arguments to bolster political support for its programs. I just hope the Russians are not beguiled by this fatuousness.

What I have written explains why I think arms control, in theory and practice, made progress for fifteen years and has become progressively disorderly during the past dozen. I feel even that my account of it is altogether coherent regarding those first fifteen years and without order with respect to the past dozen. And I am less sure of my diagnosis than of my description.

Possibly there is some imperative in the nature of arms control to do something about offensive weapons, even when there is nothing constructive to do, so something was done that couldn't be very constructive, and the result is confusion or worse. Possibly the first SALT treaty became a compelling model for formal negotiations and limitations; Secretary Laird, returning from the signing of SALT, referred to it immediately as "SALT I" and looked forward to SALT II, freezing a procedural pattern. Perhaps the US Arms Control and Disarmament Agency nurtures itself on formal negotiations and ratified treaties, and lost any subtlety that it might have had. (Adelman's *Foreign Affairs* article is at least a hint at the possibility of a less heavy-handed approach.) Perhaps an administration with no genuine interest in arms limitation finds in arms control the best pulpit from which to preach arms competition.

Finally we come to SDI, the Strategic Defense Initiative, President Reagan's dream of harnessing the technology of the near future to provide impregnable defenses against ballistic missiles sometime in the farther future, thus making nuclear weapons obsolete and permitting nuclear disarmament. How it can be thought that space-based defenses against intercontinental ballistic missiles can completely deny the delivery of nuclear explosives to the proximity of US population centers by land, sea, and air, I do not know, but I'll excuse the idea as an extravagance and try to see how the concept fits into arms control.

There is an easy way to fit it into arms control, even into the philosophy of the ABM treaty, but it is an interpretation that rather denigrates the President's dream and is nowhere near commensurate with the attention the proposal gets. That is that defending targetable US missiles, like the MX, against pre-emptive attack, through high-technology active defenses, is attractive and unobjectionable. It was a flaw in the ABM treaty that "good" ABM was disallowed along with the "bad", and in consequence there was no way to protect the MX against attack; and a partial reversal of the ABM ban permitting defense of retaliatory weapons would be back in the McNamara spirit. This is a line taken by many defenders of SDI, although it is not clear to me whether it is an opportunistic rescue of ground-base missiles under the SDI umbrella, a minimally defensible foot in the door for SDI, a fillip to advanced research or merely an effort to rescue the President's image by showing that the concept of SDI, though perhaps overblown and oversold, is not altogether empty.

There is of course the technical question whether defenses good at protecting ground-based missiles are sufficiently distinguishable from defenses that are good (but not very good) at defending population centers, and rather than repairing the ABM treaty by making an important exception to it we should be choosing whether or not to abandon it. There are so many interested parties with different interests that it is hard to find common ground even among those who share a common enthusiasm.

As I said, I shall leave aside the fact that the population of Boston, in which I include myself, is soft, immobile, unconcealable and I believe unprotectable, no matter how successfully ballistic missiles may be fended off, there being such a multitude of alternative means of wartime delivery or pre-war pre-positioning available. What I would like to raise is the question whether the President's dream is a proper dream.

He dreams of no longer depending on deterrence but of being unilaterally able to nullify any Soviet nuclear attack. Would we prefer to rely on defense, which is unilateral, or on deterrence, which is contingent and reciprocal? (I am still assuming that the strategic defenses envisaged in the President's program would not be too pre-emptively oriented. That is, I am assuming that unlike the ballistic missile defenses disallowed by the 1972 treaty, they would not provide too great an advantage to a coordinated attack against an unprepared missile response.) My question is whether we should wish away deterrence as the foundation of peace.

I call to your attention a new publication, *Policies for Common Security* (Taylor and Francis, London and Philadelphia, 1985), published under the auspices of the Stockholm International Peace Research Institute. It contains papers presented at a conference in Stockholm in September 1983, commenting on the April 1982 report of the Independent Commission on Disarmament and Security Issues, commonly known as the Palme Commission. Many of the papers would support that part of President Reagan's philosophy that depreciates deterrence as a long run concept. Most of those papers part on the issue of whether escape from reliance on deterrence should be through common action or unilateral defense. I tend to believe that neither holds any promise, not unilateral defense nor some international movement that desperately seeks an early alternative to deterrence.

As I mentioned at the outset, I find those forty years of living with nuclear weapons without war to be not only some evidence that war can be avoided but part of the reason why it can be, namely, increasing experience in living with the weapons without precipitating a war, increasing confidence on both sides that neither wishes to risk nuclear war. I go further than that. I think healthy restraint from aggressive violence that is based on an acknowledgment that the world is too small to support a nuclear war without all parties getting horribly damaged is a healthier basis for peace than unilateral efforts to build defenses. I like the notion that East and West have exchanged hostages on a massive scale and that as long as they are unprotected civilization depends on the avoidance of military aggression that could escalate to nuclear war.

I think most of what we call civilization depends on a kind of reciprocal vulnerability. I am defenseless against almost everybody that I know, and while most of them would have no interest in harming me there must be some that would. I feel safer in an environment of deterrence than I would in an environment of defense.

It is often said that terror is a poor basis for civilization, and the balance of terror is not a permanently viable foundation for the avoidance of war. Fear may promote hostility, and fear can lead to faulty thinking, especially in a crisis. I agree, but I do not equate a balance of deterrence with a balance of terror, even though the roots of "deterrence" and "terror" are the same.

I regularly stand at the curb watching trucks, buses, and cars hurtle past at speeds that guarantee injury and threaten death if I so much as attempt to cross against the traffic. I am absolutely deterred. But there is absolutely no fear. I just know better. If fear is some emotion that addles my brain or spoils human relationships, there is none of any such thing as I stand recognizing that almost certain death will attend my venturing into the street before the traffic subsides.

Let me quote a few lines that I wrote twenty years ago and still believe:

> The extent of the "fear" involved in any arrangement—total disarmament, negotiated mutual deterrence, or stable weaponry achieved unilaterally by conscious design—is a function of confidence. If the consequences of transgression are plainly bad—bad for all parties, little dependent on who trangresses first, and not helped by rapid mobilization—we can take the consequences for granted and call it a "balance of prudence".

DISCUSSIONS

Phil Williams

Professor Schelling's analysis of what went wrong with arms control in the 1970s and early 1980s is in most respects very compelling. Arms control is certainly not what it was. It has lost its sense of direction and in recent years arms control negotiations have had more to do with alliance management and with legitimizing new weapons systems than with promoting strategic stability. The American position in the INF talks, for example, was designed primarily to legitimize deployment of cruise and Pershing missiles, while the Soviet stance was intended simply to prevent that deployment. Furthermore, both superpowers have used arms control as a propaganda device, with each trying to blame the impasse on the obduracy of the other. Negotiations seem to have degenerated into the kind of gamesmanship that characterized the disarmament negotiations of the 1950s. This is doubly ironic since it was the futility of these negotiations which prompted Schelling and other analysts such as Hedley Bull into developing imaginative new concepts of arms control based on the assumption that the superpowers, while remaining adversaries, had a common interest in minimizing the likelihood of nuclear war. Professor Schelling's analysis can be understood as a reaffirmation of some of these ideas.

For all its persuasiveness, however, the paper leaves a number of questions unanswered. These can be discussed under three headings: the initial arms control design or architecture, the question of what went wrong, and the future prospects for arms control.

The Arms Control Design

Acceptance of the principle that adversaries could have common interests was a prerequisite for serious arms control negotiations. Yet translating these common interests into mutually acceptable agreements proved more difficult than arms control theory had anticipated. The reason for this lies in the dynamics of the bargaining process itself. Although the very existence of negotiations reflects the fact that both participants see potential advantage in a possible agreement, once the process begins there is a natural, and probably inescapable, tendency for each government to use it to maximize its advantages and to minimize its disadvantages. The result is that arms control negotiations, in contrast to arms control theory, become an extension of arms competition. This has important implications for assessments of the 1972 Anti-Ballistic Missile Treaty which is held up by Schelling as the most important product of the "golden age" of arms control thinking. It is arguable that the ABM Treaty was less the result of common interests and shared strategic assumptions between the superpowers than of a temporary and almost fortuitous coincidence of interests. Far from signifying Soviet acceptance of the logic of Western arms control theory and notions of strategic stability that were developed in the writings of Schelling and others and were taken up by Secretary of Defense McNamara and subsequently by Henry Kissinger, the ABM Treaty was the result of a Soviet desire to avoid a weapons race that it was going to lose. For its part the Nixon Administration was happy to accept restrictions on systems which were not only of doubtful strategic utility but were politically controversial at a time when the US defense budget was coming under enormous pressure from Congress.

In one sense, of course, the reasons why the ABM Treaty was signed matter less than the consequences. And the Treaty, by legitimizing the idea of mutual vulnerability, did contribute significantly to strategic stability. Such stability, however, seems to result as much from technological conditions as from deliberate design. At some points in the paper Professor Schelling emphasizes the importance of technology. He acknowledges, for example, that in the early 1960s technology proved extremely benign. "The vulnerability (of retaliatory systems) problem was temporarily shelved by unilateral actions without any boost from explicit arms control". If there was a happy marriage between the existing technology and the prevalent concepts of arms control in the 1960s, however, the two came apart simultaneously in the 1970s. Schelling emphasizes the retrogression in the doctrine, but greater attention could have been paid to the technology which became both more complex and less benign in its impact. The problems were posed primarily by MIRV technology, yet this was in large part a consequence of the failure to restrict MIRVs in SALT I. While this enabled the United States to accept unequal ceilings and thereby facilitated agreement, it does suggest that the "golden age" of arms control was less successful than the paper implies and that the break between the periods before and after 1972 was not as pronounced as Schelling argues. The failure to deal with MIRV at this stage made the arms control problems throughout the remainder of the 1970s much more intractable.

Another difficulty with the arms control design offered by Professor Schelling is its sheer breadth. The idea of restricting war in Europe to conventional weapons is presented as an element in arms control, and the build-up of conventional forces by both NATO and the Warsaw Pact is consequently treated as something to be applauded. Yet, it could equally well be argued that, insofar as the primary aim of arms control is to stabilize deterrence, such a build-up, by raising the nuclear threshold and thereby lowering the risks inherent in hostilities in Europe, may prove counter-productive. From the perspective of the Europeans—who would after all provide the battleground—deterrence based on the strong probability of escalation and reliance on what Schelling described in earlier works as "threats that leave something to chance" may be preferable to the idea of prolonged conventional hostilities. Certainly this is an issue on which there are difficult trade-offs between the desire to maximize deterrence and the concern with limiting hostilities in the event that deterrence should fail. The situation is further complicated by the fact that the NATO allies have different vulnerabilities and potentially divergent interests. In these circumstances the role of arms control is much more problematical than Schelling suggests. If it is possible to dissent from the Schelling arms control design in some of its incidentals, however, the main thrust of the argument is persuasive. So too is Schelling's assessment of what went wrong in the 1970s. Yet there are some areas of this analysis which can usefully be elaborated.

What Went Wrong with Arms Control?

According to Schelling's account, the arms control negotiations of the 1970s became increasingly purposeless as they lacked a guiding philosophy. Schelling particularly regrets the shift of focus from the character of weapons system—and in particular whether they were stabilizing or destabilizing—to numbers. Yet this shift may well have been inevitable as arms control became the focus of increasing political attention and maneuvering. One of the key events was the Jackson Amendment to SALT I which mandated that any future agreement should contain equal ceilings on Soviet and American forces. The passage of this Amendment marked a shift of emphasis from the Nixon concept of sufficiency (which was elastic in interpretation but fairly relaxed in its approach to the strategic balance) to the Jackson concept of numerical parity, based on the belief that any strategic asymmetries between the superpowers had considerable political significance. This transformation was taken further with the promulgation of the Schlesinger doctrine. With its emphasis on maintaining essential equivalence of both capabilities and options with the Soviet Union, the Schlesinger doctrine can be understood as the operational equivalent of the Jackson Amendment. But if both doctrine and politics contributed to the preoccupation with numbers this may have occurred anyway in a nation which treats numerical assessments with considerable deference. It was also a function of the fact that the Soviet Union had achieved a rough equality of strategic power. In these circumstances numbers seemed to matter more than they did when the United States possessed unequivocal superiority. Furthermore, as the debate over arms control and the strategic balance became more public, there was inevitably a focus on relatively simple quantitative indicators rather than more complex qualitative factors.

The result of all this was that it became increasingly difficult to reconcile the force posture deemed necessary for the 1970s and 1980s with the concepts of arms control that had been developed in the 1960s. Nor have the resulting dilemmas disappeared. The Midgetman missile, for example, appears very attractive in terms of strategic stability but seems likely to be severely criticized for its limited cost-effectiveness by those whose primary concern is with the American capacity for nuclear war-fighting.

If arms control was derailed as a result of domestic political pressures in the United States, this was not entirely surprising.

Whereas arms control theory had treated states as monolithic actors, arms control·negotiations are carried out by governments consisting of competing coalitions of organizations and individuals with differing perspectives, interests, and vulnerabilities. Inevitably, compromises have to be made. Indeed, there were several attempts in the 1970s to reconcile military requirements and arms control considerations. Contrary to the views of the American right, however, these generally took the form of concessions to the military in order to obtain their support for arms control. For example, President Nixon agreed to speed up the Trident program in order to get the support of the Joint Chiefs of Staff for SALT I. If this contributed to a rechanneling of the arms race into areas not subject to constraint, an even more pernicious development was the bargaining chip philosophy. Schelling's paper shows how absurd this approach became when it was used to justify the deployment of the MX missile in a potentially vulnerable basing-mode. Even though bargaining chips are rarely if ever bargained away, however, the idea retains a certain currency.

The bargaining chip theory contributed to the growing strategic arsenals of the superpowers. While Schelling rightly casts doubt on the belief that smaller numbers are invariably better than bigger ones, those critics who became disillusioned with arms control because it appeared to permit continued increases in the number of weapons deployed by the superpowers do have more of a point than is acknowledged in the paper. These critics are at least asking questions about where the arms race is likely to end. They recognize too that continued deployments are not bringing commensurate increases in the security of either side and may in some instances be adding to insecurity. In these circumstances calls for reassessment of arms control are readily understandable. Indeed, it is to the question of where arms control goes from here that attention must now be given.

The Future of Arms Control

Although Professor Schelling's paper concentrates more on what has gone wrong with arms control than with charting a new path, there are indications of possible directions he would like to see arms control take.

For Schelling arms control is first and foremost a conceptual matter. The implication is that it does not depend upon negotiation, so much as on philosophy. Indeed, if both superpowers had procurement philosophies based on mutually accepted arms control criteria then there would be no need for formal negotiations. A step towards this would be to put more emphasis on unilateral and tacit restraint. Yet it is not clear how well this would work: without some form of reciprocity from the adversary it would almost certainly become discredited. Nevertheless, there are some measures that may add to security and stability even if they do not elicit similar action from the adversary. Joseph Nye, for example, has emphasized the importance of "transparency and communication" in reassuring the adversary. Indeed, this may be an essential element in a deterrence posture designed to frighten the adversary into inaction without simultaneously frightening him into irrationality. This is all the more important if it is accepted that the real challenges to deterrence occur not from opportunity but from need. The most dangerous situations may well be those in which the adversary is operating not on a cost-gain calculus but on what might be termed a cost-cost calculus. The less tolerable the perceived costs of inaction the more likely is deterrence to break down.

This in turn suggests that there needs to be a refocussing of the arms control effort in ways which lead back to the early ideas propounded by Schelling about minimizing the incentives for pre-emptive attack, and which focus on the psychological factors that may exacerbate the security dilemma inherent in the superpower relationship. In this connexion, an extremely helpful step would be the creation of crisis management or nuclear risk reduction centers in both Washington and Moscow.

As part of this reorientation of arms control it may be necessary to consider more carefully precisely what is meant by strategic stability. Schelling, for example, is fairly complacent about the extensive deployment of sea-launched cruise missiles on the grounds that these are not first-strike weapons. Yet nuclear and conventional SLCMs may be difficult to distinguish from each other. The same kind of problem could arise in Europe if NATO deploys conventional cruise missiles alongside its nuclear cruise. It seems pertinent to ask, therefore, to what extent strategic stability requires the kind of salient thresholds based on prominent distinctions that Schelling discussed in the 1960s?

Although the gradual blurring of traditional distinctions between categories of weapons may pose a long-term problem for arms control, a more immediate challenge stems from President Reagan's Strategic Defense Initiative (SDI). It is still not clear whether SDI will simply be a means of upholding deterrence through retaliation or a way of transcending this approach and replacing it with what is called deterrence through denial. This latter possibility has considerable attraction for those who dislike the reliance on Soviet restraint that is inescapable in a situation where both Soviet and American societies are vulnerable to nuclear retaliation. Supporters of deterrence through retaliation accept the paradox that Professor Schelling ends with. Yet this is not a particularly comfortable position. This is why the challenge to arms control—and its major achievement the ABM Treaty—from the proponents of SDI is likely to be even more serious than the difficulties encountered in the 1970s. It may well be, therefore, that we have to develop more robust or resilient concepts of arms control which have relevance in unfavorable conditions. It is only to be hoped that Professor Schelling will take the lead in this as he did in developing the initial arms control design of the 1960s.

Raimo Väyrynen

Professor Schelling conveys to us the message that until the early 1970s arms control was an intellectual and political achievement, as it ensured arms-race stability. Arms control was tailored to restrain the destabilizing functions and missions of various nuclear-weapon systems and consequently mutual deterrence between the great powers was strengthened, in particular by the conclusion of the ABM Treaty in 1972. Arms-control agreements produced a stable deterrence which promoted, in turn, a measure of true confidence between the United States and the Soviet Union. In Professor Schelling's opinion, since 1972 arms-control efforts have lost most of their relevance and beneficial effects, largely due to institutionalization and rutinization of arms-control negotiations which have for this reason lost touch with the strategic reality.

To my mind, Professor Schelling makes an important point here by stressing that the tendency of negotiations to deal not only with numbers, but also with fixed categories of weapons alienates them from the true world of the strategic arms race. This world is both technologically and politically so complex that it cannot be reduced to simple categories of weapons. Nowhere does this problem become clearer than in the SALT II Treaty and in its "Agreed Statements and Common Understandings Regarding the Treaty between the United States of America and the Union of Soviet Socialist Republics on the Limitation of Strategic Offensive Arms". This appendix to the Treaty contains about one hundred "agreed statements" and "common understandings" which specify the implications of various military technologies and create a consensus between the parties on these implications.

To take just one example, one may refer to the agreed statement to paragraph 4 of article V of the Treaty: "if a bomber is equipped with MIRVs, all bombers of that type shall be considered to be equipped for ASBMs equipped with MIRVs". I am convinced that it is impossible to continue on this road and try to develop increasingly complicated political agreements to curb the technological arms race. This dilemma is well expressed by Strobe Talbott in his seminal study of the SALT II process, "Endgame", that "part of the maddening dynamic of SALT has been that the resolution of a general problem often confronts the negotiators with a MIRV-like cluster of specific problems of definition and detail". On this score Schelling appears to share Talbott's conclusion. He does not tell us, however, why arms control has really deteriorated since 1972 and has been able to produce only few results.

There seem to be two major approaches to this problem that tend to contend with each other. The view stressing the *primacy of politics* argues that power politics, ideological incompatibilities, and economic differences create an atmosphere of political distrust fostering the arms competition. Another view, emphasizing the *primacy of arms race*, contends that the dynamics of arms race itself is the main force behind the continuation of the military build-up. The latter perspective is advocated by, among others, George Quester and Robert Jervis, who regard qualitative characteristics of weapons systems and their politico-military missions as central in the analysis of the *security dilemma*. This dilemma should, in fact, be the most crucial dependent variable in the study of security issues. The distinction between offense and defense, albeit occasionally difficult to make, is more central in the analysis of security dilemma than the mere number of weapons.

According to Jervis, the security dilemma is at its deepest when *defense* has preponderance over *offense* and when they are indistinguishable one from the other. At the present moment the nuclear relationship between the United States and the Soviet Union is moving in the direction in which defense is becoming progressively more important (so-called defensive transition). Simultaneous development of offensive and defensive weapons (SDI and the MX missile in the United States) tends to eliminate the differences in their military missions. The defensive transition coupled with the accumulation of offensive nuclear weapons is *destabilizing* and should be transformed to a more stable solution by arms-control agreements.

Though this philosophy is not fully spelled out in Professor Schelling's paper he appears to depart from its premises. In so doing he criticizes arms-control proposals on strategic offensive weapons as "mostly mindless, without a guiding philosophy". That is why the decision was made to procure MX missiles instead of the sea-based Trident solution. The MX solution was further motivated by the bargaining chip theory which seldom if ever has really worked. The Trident solution can be justified by its tendency to enhance invulnerable retaliatory capacity which so far at least has had very limited counterforce capability. In that way deterrence in the sense of assured capability for mutual destruction, would have been strengthened. The primacy of *stable deterrence* appears to be the central objective in Professor Schelling's thinking. It also provides ammunition with which to criticize the Strategic Defense Initiative which for him is a destabilizing and unilateral measure devoid of sound strategic theory. In general, Professor Schelling feels himself "safer in an environment of deterrence than in an environment of defense".

Professor Schelling believes in neither unilateral defense nor in any early alternative to deterrence. Are there, however, any concrete steps that could be taken in the arms-control nego- tiations that would stabilize deterrence and provide in that way preconditions for the subsequent reductions in nuclear arsenals? Professor Schelling, perhaps due to his lack of belief in arms control, is short on this point. If strategic stability is an inter- mediate objective, focus should be on the functional character- istics of the weapons rather than on their mere number. Follow- ing Jervis's advice, particular attention should be paid to the distinction between offensive and defensive weapons. Arms- control efforts should be directed at the control of defensive weapons that can be used to strengthen the offensive capability and its usability. This means in concrete terms the necessity to uphold the ABM Treaty, to limit and ultimately ban the ASAT technologies and to place limitations on the continued sophisti- cation of ASW technologies. Ballistic missile defenses, including the SDI, the ability to destroy satellites and to threaten missile- carrying strategic submarines all undermine the credible retali- atory capacity on which the stability of deterrence rests.

On this score I am somewhat skeptical as to whether a distinc- tion between "good" and "bad" ABM can be made in the Professor Schelling manner. The logic of his argument seems to be that a "good" ABM aims at defending the retaliatory wea- pons. It neglects, however, the fact that invulnerable retaliatory weapons, in which category Schelling includes the MX missile, can be used also for first-strike purposes. That is why I tend to be cautious in advocating any limited ballistic missile-defense systems. Focus would be better on the limitation of yet another category of destabilizing weapons, viz. accurate, multiple-war- head strategic missiles. It is often stressed that the multiplication of effective nuclear warheads in the strategic arsenals of great powers poses an increasing threat to the retaliatory capacity of the opponent. That is why deep cuts not only in the number of launchers, but even more importantly in the number of war- heads would be a stabilizing decision. That is why to my mind the strategic build-down program, proposed by the Reagan Administration in 1983, deserves attention. It is in fact one of the few initiatives by this administration which deserves such attention.

The above guidelines demand more action from the United States and the Soviet Union than these nations have been prepared to take during the last few years. Their application in the Geneva negotiations, however, might restore the strategic logic which in Professor Schelling's opinion was lost in 1972. Arms-control talks, in order to progress and to lead to concrete results, have to have an underlying political and strategic theory. Such a theory should, in the first instance, provide the basis for stabilizing the arms race and deterrence; thereafter there may be the opportunity to progress further toward quantitative reductions and in particular toward qualitative limitations. I rather doubt whether any more far-reaching measures can be implemented without a prior state of stability in the strategic relationship between the great powers.

One problem is making the *interest structures* of the great powers compatible to the extent that agreements on arms control might again be possible. In the present situation no such coincidence of interests and doctrines seems to prevail between the United States and the Soviet Union. That is why formal agreements codifying the strategic stability between the great powers will probably be difficult to negotiate. This being the case, a more indirect approach could perhaps be attempted, i.e. the route of informal agreements which could be gradually codified and institutionalized. In an article published in 1975, Thomas Schelling spoke in favor of "unwritten agreements". His argument was that the sufficient coincidence of interest structures of negotiating parties would "lead to fairly self-enforcing understandings without treaties if there can be a sufficient exploration of where the common interest lies". In that way one might "get a lot less arms control as posturing if what one has is private understandings, non-committal understandings arrived at between two sides, non-binding understanding with merely better appreciation on each side of what the other's behaviour would be". It is relatively easy to ridicule the case for informal agreements, but is there anyone who can deny in his right mind that they are imperative for the conclusion of any formal treaties? That is why they should be deliberately promoted and in this way bring the interest structures of the great powers closer to each other.

General discussion

The discussion to some extent represents a continuation of the discussions following Professor Freedman's paper. It revolves mainly around fairly technical questions concerning the mechanics of arms control, and around the problem of why arms control negotiations failed during the 1970s.

A number of discussants raise the problem of sufficiency and bargaining processes between the superpowers, linking the present debate to the theoretical work performed by Schelling and others in the early 1960s. This leads into a discussion of the fascination with numbers in the arms debate, and the question of matching weapons systems category by category.

There is considerable support for emphasizing that within this field we are dealing with immeasurables. Furthermore, within the field of arms control the superpowers are constantly facing problems of both technical innovation and basic scientific development being conducted on a continuous basis. It is fairly reasonable to assume that the results will feed into weapons systems, and certainly reasonable to conclude that the superpowers work on the assumption that the other side is "doing it", so it is not possible for them to abstain.

Several discussants are therefore of the opinion that formal arms control agreements are not necessarily the best basis for security. Good arms technology is preferable when combined with open lines of communication and reciprocal restraint. On the other hand, such an approach is hardly politically feasible. Arms control is important to a public in the West that may not be willing to spend what is necessary for effective deterrence. Discussants emphasize that fallout would be significant if the negotiations in Geneva were to fail as a consequence of American policies.

The problems of crisis avoidance or crisis management are recurrent themes in the technical discussions, just as they were in the discussion on the decline of arms control during the 1970s and the drift towards unilateralism. The question is how to regulate the relationship between the superpowers.

A major cause for the decline is the American assumption that superpower cooperation would not extend merely to arms control, but would involve more general cooperation in securing an international order. The Soviet Union does not share this assumption. Several discussants support the interpretation that the United States would not accept what could be considered the consequential Soviet assumption of equality in the international order.

The influence of public opinion is considered crucial by most discussants. In 1972, arms control became for the first time an important domestic political issue. As a consequence a number of irrelevant and/or irrational considerations were drawn into the negotiation process. The simplifications of the public debate forced the treaty discussion off its tracks. It is maintained that the whole negotiating process was derailed by the intrusion of outsiders into a set of agreements reached by insiders.

The discussion concerning the failure of arms agreements in the 1970s also involves an exchange of opinion of the agreements of the 1960s. The main issue is the possible impact of the Vietnam War on American willingness to negotiate an agreement. Against opposing views, it is quite strongly maintained that domestic problems arising out of the Vietnam War constitute no necessary condition for willingness to negotiate. Henry Kissinger is on record as wanting a treaty even before Nixon was inaugurated.

Part Three
The International System

5

The Post-war International System: Elements of Stability and Instability

JOHN LEWIS GADDIS

I should like to begin this essay with a fable. Once upon a time there was a great war that involved the slaughter of millions upon millions of people. When, after years of fighting, one side finally prevailed over the other and the war ended, everyone said that it must go down in history as the last great war ever fought. To that end, the victorious nations sent all of their wisest men to a great peace conference, where they were given the task of drawing up a settlement that would be so carefully designed, so unquestionably fair to all concerned, that it would eliminate war as a phenomenon of human existence. Unfortunately, that settlement lasted only twenty years.

There followed yet another great war involving the slaughter of millions upon millions of people. When, after years of fighting, one side finally prevailed over the other and the war ended, everyone said that it must go down in history as the last great war ever fought. To everyone's horror, though, the victors in that conflict immediately fell to quarreling among themselves, with the result that no peace conference ever took place. Within a few years each of the major victors had come to regard each other, and not their former enemies, as the principal threat to their survival; each sought to ensure that survival by developing weapons capable, at least in theory, of ending the survival of everyone on earth. Paradoxically, that arrangement lasted twice as long as the first one, and as the fable ended showed no signs of coming apart anytime soon.

It is, of course, just a fable, and as a general rule one ought not to take fables too seriously. There are times, though, when fables can illuminate reality more sharply than conventional forms of explanation are able to do, and this may well be one of them. For it is the case that the post-Second World War system of international relations, which nobody designed or even thought could last for very long, which was based not upon the dictates of morality and justice but rather upon an arbitrary and strikingly artificial division of the world into spheres of influence, and which incorporated within it some of the most bitter and persistent antagonisms short of war in modern history, has now survived twice as long as the far more carefully-designed First World War settlement, has approximately equaled in longevity the great nineteenth century international systems of Metternich and Bismarck, and unlike those earlier systems after four decades of existence shows no perceptible signs of disintegration. It is, or ought to be, enough to make one think.

To be sure, the term "peace" is not the first that comes to mind when one recalls the history of the past forty years. That period, after all, has seen the greatest accumulation of armaments the world has ever known, a whole series of protracted and devastating limited wars, an abundance of revolutionary, ethnic, religious and civil violence, as well as some of the deepest and most intractable ideological rivalries in human experience. Nor have those more ancient scourges—famine, disease, poverty, injustice—by any means disappeared from the face of the earth. Is it not stretching things a bit, one might well ask, to take the moral and spiritual desert in which the nations of the world conduct their affairs, and call it "peace"?

It is, of course, but that is just the point. Given all the conceivable reasons for having had a major war in the past four decades—reasons that in any other age would have provided ample justification for such a war—it seems worthy of comment that there has not in fact been one; that despite the unjust and wholly artificial character of the post-Second World War settlement, it has now persisted for the better part of half a century. That may not be grounds for celebration, but it is at least grounds for investigation: for trying to comprehend how this great power peace has managed to survive for so long in the face of so much provocation, and for thinking about what might be done to perpetuate that situation. For, after all, we could do worse.

I

Anyone attempting to understand why there has been no third world war confronts a problem not unlike that of Sherlock Holmes and the dog that did not bark in the night: how does one account for something that did not happen? How does one explain why the great conflict between the United States and the Soviet Union, which by all past standards of historical experience should have developed by now, has not in fact done so? The question involves certain methodological difficulties, to be sure: it is always easier to account for what did happen than what did not. But there is also a curious bias among students of international relations that reinforces this tendency: "For every thousand pages published on the causes of wars," Geoffrey Blainey has commented, "there is less than one page directly on the causes of peace."[1] Even the discipline of "peace studies" suffers from this disproportion: it has given far more attention to the question of what we must do to avoid the apocalypse than it has to the equally interesting question of why, given all the opportunities, it has not happened so far.

It might be easier to deal with this question if the work that has been done on the causes of war had produced something approximating a consensus on why wars develop: we could then apply that analysis to the post-1945 period and see what it is that has been different about it. But, in fact, these studies are not much help. Historians, political scientists, economists, sociologists, statisticians, even meteorologists, have wrestled for years with the question of what causes wars, and yet the most recent review of that literature concludes that "our understanding of war remains at an elementary level. No widely accepted theory of the causes of war exists and little agreement has emerged on the methodology through which these causes might be discovered."[2]

Nor has the comparative work that has been done on international systems shed much more light on the matter. The difficulty here is that our actual experience is limited to the operations of a single system—the balance of power system—operating either within the "multipolar" configuration that characterized international politics until the Second World War, or the "bipolar" configuration that has characterized them since. Alternative systems remain abstract conceptualizations in the minds of theorists, and are of little use in advancing our knowledge of how wars in the real world do or do not occur.[3]

But "systems theory" itself is something else again: here one can find a useful point of departure for thinking about the nature of international relations since 1945. An "international system" exists, political scientists tell us, when two conditions are met: first, interconnections exist between units within the system, so that changes in some parts of it produce changes in other parts as well; and, second, the collective behavior of the system as a whole differs from the expectations and priorities of the individual units that make it up.[4] Certainly demonstrating the "interconnectedness" of post-Second World War international relations is not difficult: one of its most prominent characteristics is the tendency of major powers to assume that little if anything can happen in the world without in some way enhancing or detracting from their own immediate interests.[5] Nor has the collective behavior of nations corresponded to their individual expectations: the very fact that the interim arrangements of 1945 have remained largely intact for four decades would have astonished—and quite possibly appalled—the statesmen who cobbled them together in the hectic months that followed the surrender of Germany and Japan.[6]

A particularly valuable feature of systems theory is that it provides criteria for differentiating between stable and unstable political configurations: this can help to account for the fact that some international systems outlast others. Karl Deutsch and J. David Singer have defined "stability" as "the probability that the system retains all of its essential characteristics; that no single nation becomes dominant; that most of its members continue to survive; and that large-scale war does not occur". It is characteristic of such a system, Deutsch and Singer add, that it has the capacity for self-regulation: the ability to counteract stimuli that would otherwise threaten its survival, much as the automatic pilot on an airplane or the governor on a steam engine would do. "Self-regulating" systems are very different from what they call "self-aggravating" systems, situations that get out of control, like forest fires, drug addiction, runaway inflation, nuclear fission, and of course, although they themselves do not cite the example, all-out war.[7] Self-regulating mechanisms are most likely to function, in turn, when there exists some fundamental agreement among major states within the system on the objectives they are seeking to uphold by participating in it, when the structure of the system reflects the way in which power is distributed among its respective members, and when agreed-upon procedures exist for resolving differences among them.[8]

Does the post-Second World War international system fit these criteria for "stability"? Certainly its most basic characteristic—bipolarity—remains intact, in that the gap between the world's two greatest military powers and their nearest rivals is not substantially different from what it was forty years ago.[9] At the same time, neither the Soviet Union nor the United States nor anyone else has been able wholly to dominate the system; the nations most active within it in 1945 are for the most part still active today. And of course the most convincing argument for "stability" is that, so far at least, the Third World War has not occurred. On the surface, then, the concept of a "stable" international system makes sense as a way of understanding the experience through which we have lived these past forty years.

But what have been the self-regulating mechanisms? How has an environment been created in which they are able to function? In what way do those mechanisms—and the environment in which they function—resemble or differ from the configuration of other international systems, both stable and unstable, in modern history? What circumstances exist that might impair their operation, transforming self-regulation into self-aggravation? These are questions that have not received the attention they deserve from students of the history and politics of the postwar era. What follows is a series of speculations—it can hardly be more than that, given present knowledge—upon these issues, the importance of which hardly needs to be stressed.

I should like to emphasize, though, that this essay's concentration on the way the world is and has been is not intended to excuse or to justify our current predicament. Nor is it meant to preclude the possibility of moving ultimately toward something better. We can all conceive of international systems that combine stability with greater justice and less risk than the present one does, and we ought to continue to think about these things. But short of war, which no one wants, change in international relations tends to be gradual and evolutionary. It does not happen overnight. That means that alternative systems, if they ever develop, probably will not be total rejections of the existing system, but rather variations proceeding from it. All the more reason, then, to try to understand the system we have, to try to distinguish its stabilizing from its destabilizing characteristics, and to try to reinforce the former as a basis from which we might, in time and with luck, do better.

II

Any such investigation should begin by distinguishing the structure of the inter of the nations that make it up.[10] The reason for this is simple: behavior alone will not ensure stability if the structural prerequisites for it are absent, but structure can under certain circumstances impose stability even when its behaviorial prerequisites are unpromising.[11] One need only compare the settlement of 1945 with its predecessor of 1919 to see the point.

If the intentions of statesmen alone had governed, the Paris Peace Conference of 1919 would have ushered in an era of stability in world politics comparable to that brought about in Europe by the Congress of Vienna almost a century earlier. Certainly the diplomats at Paris had that earlier precedent very much in mind;[12] conscious of what victory had cost, they approached their task wondering whether war had not altogether lost its usefulness as a means of resolving disputes among nations.[13] Few if any peace negotiators have been able to draw upon such an impressive array of technical expertise as was available in 1919.[14] Moreover, the most influential of them, Woodrow Wilson, had determined to go beyond the practices and procedures of the "old diplomacy" to construct a settlement that would integrate power with morality. "Tell me what's right and I'll fight for it," Wilson is said to have demanded of his advisers,[15] and at least as far as the idea of self-determination was concerned, the Versailles Treaty did come about as close as any in modern history to incorporating within itself the principles of justice.[16]

Unfortunately, in so doing, it neglected the realities of power.

It broke up the old Austro-Hungarian Empire, a move that reflected accurately enough the aspirations of the nationalities involved, but that failed to provide the successor states of Poland, Czechoslovakia, Austria, and Hungary with the military or economic means necessary to sustain their new-found sovereignty.[17] Even more shortsightedly, the treaty made no effort to accommodate the interests of two nations whose population and industrial strength were certain to guarantee them a major influence over post-war European developments—Germany and Soviet Russia. It should have been no surprise, therefore, that when the Versailles system finally broke down in 1939, it did so largely as the result of a deal cut at the expense of the East Europeans between these two countries whose power had been ignored, twenty years earlier, in the interests of justice.[18]

Nobody, in contrast, would picture the post-Second World War settlement as a triumph of justice. That settlement arbitrarily divided sovereign nations like Germany, Austria and Korea, not because anyone thought it was right to do so, but because neither the United States nor the Soviet Union could agree on whose occupation forces would withdraw first.[19] It did nothing to prevent the incorporation of several of the countries whose independence the 1919 settlement had recognized—and, in the case of Poland, whose independence Great Britain had gone to war in 1939 to protect—into a Soviet sphere of influence, where they remain to this day.[20] It witnessed, in response to this, the creation of an American sphere of influence in Western Europe, the Mediterranean and the Pacific, which although different from its Soviet counterpart in the important fact that the nations lying within it for the most part voluntarily associated themselves with the United States,[21] nonetheless required, however willingly, some sacrifice of national independence as well.

What resulted was the first true polarization of power in modern history. The world had had limited experience with bipolar systems in ancient times, it is true: certainly Thucydides' account of the rivalry between Athens and Sparta carries an eerie resonance for us today; nor could statesmen of the Cold War era forget what they had once learned, as schoolboys, of the antagonism between Rome and Carthage.[22] But these had been regional, not global conflicts: not until 1945 could one plausibly speak of a *world* divided into two competing spheres of influence, or of the *superpowers* that controlled them. The international situation had been reduced, Hans Morgenthau wrote in 1948, "to the primitive spectacle of two giants eyeing each other with watchful suspicion ... Thus contain or be contained, conquer or be conquered, destroy or be destroyed, become the watchwords of the new deplomacy".[23]

Now, bipolarity may seem to many today—as it did forty years ago—an awkward and dangerous way to organize world politics.[24] Simple geometric logic would suggest that a system resting upon three or more points of support would be more stable than one resting upon two. But politics is not geometry: the passage of time and the accumulation of experience has made clear certain structural elements of stability in the bipolar system of international relations that were not present in the "multipolar" systems that preceded it:

(1) The post-war bipolar system realistically reflected the facts of where military power resided at the end of the Second World War[25]—and where it still does today, for that matter. In this sense, it differed markedly from the settlement of 1919, which made so little effort to accommodate the interests of Germany and Soviet Russia. It is true that in other categories of power—notably the economic—states have since arisen capable of challenging or even surpassing the Soviet Union and the United States in the production of certain specific commodities. But as the *political* position of nations like West Germany, Brazil, Japan, South Korea, Taiwan and Hong Kong suggests, the ability to make video recorders, motorcycles, even automobiles and steel efficiently has yet to translate into anything approaching the capacity of Washington or Moscow to shape events in the world as a whole.

(2) The post-1945 bipolar structure was a simple one that did not require sophisticated leadership to maintain it. The great multipolar systems of the nineteenth century collapsed in large part because of their intricacy: they required a Metternich or a Bismarck to hold them together, and when statesmen of that calibre were no longer available, they tended to come apart.[26] Neither the Soviet nor the American political systems have been geared to identifying statesmen of comparable prow-

ess and entrusting them with responsibility; demonstrated skill in the conduct of foreign policy has hardly been a major prerequisite for leadership in either country. And yet, a bipolar structure of international relations—because of the inescapably high stakes involved for its two major actors—tends, regardless of the personalities involved, to induce in them a sense of caution and restraint, and to discourage irresponsibility. "It is not," Kenneth Waltz notes, "that one entertains the utopian hope that all future American and Russian rulers will combine in their persons ... nearly perfect virtues, but rather that the pressures of a bipolar world strongly encourage them to act internationally in ways better than their characters may lead one to expect."[27]

(3) Because of its relatively simple structure, alliances in this bipolar system have tended to be more stable than they had been in the nineteenth century and in the 1919-1939 period. It is striking to consider that the North Atlantic Treaty Organization has now equaled in longevity the most durable of the pre-First World War alliances, that between Germany and Austria-Hungary; it has lasted almost twice as long as the Franco-Russian alliance, and certainly much longer than any of the tenuous alignments of the inter-war period. Its principal rival, the Warsaw Treaty Organization, has been in existence for almost as long. The reason for this is simple: alliances, in the end, are the product of insecurity;[28] so long as the Soviet Union and the United States each remain for the other and for their respective clients the major source of insecurity in the world, neither superpower encounters very much difficulty in maintaining its alliances. In a multipolar system, sources of insecurity can vary in much more complicated ways; hence it is not surprising to find alliances shifting to accommodate these variations.[29]

(4) At the same time, though, and probably because of the overall stability of the basic alliance systems, defections from both the American and Soviet coalitions—China, Cuba, Vietnam, Iran, and Nicaragua, in the case of the Americans; Yugoslavia, Albania, Egypt, Somalia, and China again in the case of the Russians—have been tolerated without the major disruptions that might have attended such changes in a more delicately balanced multipolar system. The fact that a state the size of China was able to reverse its alignment twice during the Cold

War without any more dramatic effect upon the position of the superpowers says something about the stability bipolarity brings; compare this record with the impact, prior to 1914, of such apparently minor episodes as Austria's annexation of Bosnia and Herzegovina, or the question of who was to control Morocco. It is a curious consequence of bipolarity that although alliances are more durable than in a multipolar system, defections are at the same time more tolerable.[30]

In short, without anyone's having designed it, and without any attempt whatever to consider the requirements of justice, the nations of the post-war era lucked into a system of international relations that, because it has been based upon realities of power, has served the cause of order—if not justice—better than one might have expected.

III

But if the structure of bipolarity in itself encouraged stability, so too did certain inherent characteristics of the bilateral Soviet-American relationship. It used to be fashionable to point out, in the days before the Cold War began, that despite periodic outbreaks of tension between them Russians and Americans had never actually gone to war with one another; the same claim could not be made for the history of either country's relations with Great Britain, Germany, Italy, Austria-Hungary, Japan, or (if the Americans' undeclared naval war of 1798-1800 is counted), France. This record was thought to be all the more remarkable in view of the fact that, in ideological terms, Russian and American systems of government could hardly have been more different. Soviet–American friendship would not evolve easily, historian Foster Rhea Dulles noted in the wake of the first meeting between Roosevelt and Stalin in 1943, but the fact that "its roots were so deep in the past, and that it had developed through the years out of common interests transcending all other points of difference, marked the effort toward a new rapprochement as conforming not only to the immediate but also to the long-term interests of the two nations".[31]

The onset of the Cold War made this argument seem less than convincing. To assert that relations between Russia had once been good, students of the subject now suggested, was to confuse harmony with inactivity: given the infrequency of contacts between Russia and the United States in the nineteenth century, their tradition of "friendship" had been decidedly unremarkable. Once contacts became more frequent, as they had by the beginning of the twentieth century, conflicts quickly followed, even before Western statesmen had begun to worry about the impact of the Bolshevism, or the imminence of the international proletarian revolution.[32] But even after this breakdown in cordiality—and regardless of whether that cordiality had been real or imagined—Dulles's point remained valid: there still had been no Russian-American war, despite the fact that Russians and Americans had at one time or another fought virtually every other major power. This raises the question of whether there are not structural elements in the Russian-American relationship itself that contribute to stability, quite apart from the policies actually followed by Russian and American governments.

It has long been an assumption of classical liberalism that the more extensive the contacts that take place between nations, the greater are the chances for peace. Economic interdependence, it has been argued, makes war unlikely because nations who have come to rely upon one another for vital commodities cannot afford it. Cultural exchange, it has been suggested, causes peoples to become more sensitive to each other's concerns, and hence reduces the likelihood of misunderstandings. "People to people" contacts, it has been assumed, make it possible for nations to "know" one another better; the danger of war between them is, as a result, correspondingly reduced.[33]

These are pleasant things to believe, but there is remarkably little historical evidence to validate them. As Kenneth Waltz has pointed out, "the fiercest civil wars and the bloodiest international ones are fought within arenas populated by highly similar people whose affairs are closely knit".[34] Consider, as examples, the costliest military conflicts of the past century and a half, using the statistics conveniently available now through the University of Michigan "Correlates of War" project: of the ten bloodiest inter-state wars, every one of them grew out of conflicts between countries that either directly adjoined one another, or were involved actively in trade with one another.[35]

Certainly economic interdependence did little to prevent Germany, France, Britain, Russia, and Austria-Hungary from going to war in 1914; nor did the fact that the United States was Japan's largest trading partner deter that country from attacking Pearl Harbor in 1941. Since 1945, there have been more civil wars than inter-state wars;[36] that fact alone should be sufficient to call into question the proposition that interdependence necessarily breeds peace.

The Russian-American relationship, to a remarkable degree for two nations so extensively involved with the rest of the world, has been one of mutual *in*dependence. The simple fact that they occupy opposite sides of the earth has had something to do with this: geographical remoteness from one another has provided little opportunity for the emergence of irredentist grievances comparable in importance to historic disputes over, say, Alsace-Lorraine, or the Polish Corridor, or the West Bank, the Gaza Strip, and Jerusalem. In the few areas where Soviet and American forces—or their proxies—have come into direct contact, they have erected artificial barriers like the Korean demilitarized zone, or the Berlin Wall, perhaps in unconscious recognition of an American poet's rather chilly precept that "good fences make good neighbors".

Nor have the two nations been economically dependent upon one another in any critical way. Certainly the United States requires nothing in the form of imports from the Soviet Union that it cannot obtain elsewhere. The situation is different for the Russians, to be sure, but even though the Soviet Union imports large quantities of food from the United States—and would like to import advanced technology as well—it is far from being wholly dependent upon these items, as the failure of recent attempts to change Soviet behavior by denying them has shown. The relative invulnerability of Russians and Americans to one another in the economic sphere may be frustrating to their respective policy-makers, but it is probably fortunate, from the standpoint of international stability, that the two most powerful nations in the world are also its two most self-sufficient.[37]

But what about the argument that expanded international communication promotes peace? Is not the failure of Russians and Americans to understand one another better a potential source of instability in their relationship? Obviously it can be if misunderstandings occur at the level of national leadership: the most serious Soviet-American confrontation of the post-war era, the Cuban missile crisis, is generally regarded as having arisen from what appear in retrospect to have been quite remarkable misperceptions of each side's intentions by the other.[38] But "people to people" contacts are another matter. The history of international relations is replete with examples of familiarity breeding contempt as well as friendship: there are too many nations whose people have known each other all too well and have, as a result, taken an intense dislike to one another— French and Germans, Russians and Poles, Japanese and Chinese, Greeks and Turks, Arabs and Israelis—to lend very much credence to the invariably pacifying effects of "people to people" contacts.[39] Moreover, foreign policy in the United States depends only to a limited extent upon mass perceptions; in the Soviet Union, it depends upon them not at all.[40] There is little reason to think that opportunities for travel, academic and cultural exchanges, and even "sister city" contacts have any consistently destabilizing effect on relations between the United States and the Soviet Union; but there is little evidence of their consistently stabilizing effect either.

It may well be, then, that the extent to which the Soviet Union and the United States have been independent of one another rather than interdependent—the fact that there have been so few points of economic leverage available to each, the fact that two such dissimilar people have had so few opportunities for interaction—has in itself constituted a structural support for stability in relations between the two countries, whatever their respective governments have actually done.

IV

Structure can affect diplomacy from another angle, though: that has to do with the domestic roots of foreign policy. It was Karl Marx who first called attention to the effect of social and economic forces upon political behavior; John A. Hobson and

V. I. Lenin subsequently derived from this the proposition that capitalism causes both imperialism and war. Meanwhile, Joseph Schumpeter was working out an alternative theory that placed the origins of international conflict in the "atavistic" insecurities of aristocracies, bureaucracies, and individual leaders.[41] Historians of both Marxist and non-Marxist persuasions have stressed the importance of domestic structural influences in bringing about the First World War;[42] and there has been increasing scholarly interest as well in the role of such factors in inter-war diplomacy.[43] But to what extent can one argue that domestic structures have shaped the behavior of the Soviet Union and the United States toward each other since 1945? What has been the effect of such influences upon the stability of the post-Second World War international system?

The literature on the relationship betweecertainly there is no clear consensus on how internal influences determine behavior toward the world at large.[44] There has been, though, a persistent effort to link the structure of the American economy to foreign policy, most conspicuously through the assertion that capitalism requires an aggressive search for raw materials, markets, and investment opportunities overseas in order to survive. The theory itself pre-dates the Cold War, having been suggested by Charles A. Beard during the 1920s and 1930s, but it was left to William Appleman Williams to work out the most influential characterization of what he called "open door" expansionism in his classic work, *The Tragedy of American Diplomacy*, first published in 1959.[45] More recently—and in a much more sophisticated way—the linkage between domestic economic structure and foreign policy has taken the form of studies demonstrating the effects of "corporatism": the *cooperation* of business, labor, and government to shape a congenial external environment.[46]

Both the "open door" and "corporatist" models have been criticized, with some justification, for their tendency toward reductionism: the explanation of complex phenomena in terms of single causes.[47] But for the purposes of this analysis, these criticisms are beside the point. What is important here is that these most frequently-advanced arguments linking the structure of American capitalism with American foreign policy do not assume, from that linkage, the inevitability of war. One of the great advantages of the "open door", Williams has pointed out, was precisely the fact that it *avoided* military confrontations: it was a way to "extend the American system throughout the world without the embarrassment and inefficiency of traditional colonialism"; "*it was conceived and designed to win the victories without the wars.*"[48] Similarly, "corporatist" historiography stresses the stabilizing rather than the de-stabilizing effects of American intervention in Europe after the First and Second World Wars; here, if anything, attempts to replicate domestic structure overseas are seen as reinforcing rather than undermining existing international systems.[49] Neither the "open door" nor the "corporatist" paradigms, therefore, offer evidence sufficient to confirm the old Leninist assertion that a society committed to capitalism is necessarily precluded from participation in a stable world order.

There have been, of course, Schumpeterian as well as Leninist explanations of how domestic influences affect American foreign policy. C. Wright Mills some three decades ago stressed the interlocking relationship of businessmen, politicians, and military officers whose "power elite" had imposed a form of "naked and arbitrary power" upon the world;[50] subsequent analysts, no doubt encouraged by Dwight D. Eisenhower's perhaps inadvertent endorsement of the term,[51] transformed Mills's argument into a full-blown theory of a "military-industrial complex" whose interests necessarily precluded any significant relaxation of world tensions.[52] There were, to be sure, certain difficulties with this model: it did not plausibly explain the Truman administration's low military budgets of the 1945-50 period, nor did it deal easily with the dramatic shift from defense to welfare expenditures presided over by Richard Nixon during the early 1970s.[53] It neglected evidence that a "military-industrial complex" existed inside the Soviet Union as well.[54] But even if one overlooked these problems, it was not clear how the existence of such a "military-industrial complex" necessarily made war anymore likely, given the opportunities deterrence offered to develop and deploy a profusion of military hardware without the risks war would pose to one's ability to continue doing precisely this.

More recently, attention has been given to the problems created by the structure of American domestic politics in attempting to formulate coherent policies for dealing with the

Soviet Union. There is, of course, nothing new about this: the constitutionally-mandated division of authority over foreign affairs has always made policy formulation in the United States a less than orderly process. But there is reason to think the problem is getting worse, partly because of the increasing number of government departments, Congressional committees, and interest groups who have a stake in foreign policy decisions, partly because of an increasingly protracted presidential selection process that has eroded an already imperfect tradition of keeping electoral politics apart from world politics.[55] Even here, though, the effect of such disarray on the long-term Soviet-American relationship has not been as great as might have been expected: what is impressive, when one considers all of the domestically-motivated mutations American foreign policy has gone through during the past four decades, is how consistent its fundamental objectives in dealing with the Soviet Union have nonetheless remained.[56]

But what about domestic structural constraints inside the Soviet Union? Here, of course, there is much less hard information with which to work; generalizations, as a result, are not as firmly grounded or as richly developed as they are with regard to the United States. One point seems clear enough, though: in attempting to understand the effect of internal influences on Soviet foreign policy, American analysts have found Schumpeter a more reliable guide than Lenin; they have stressed the extent to which the structural requirements of legitimizing internal political authority have affected behavior toward the outside world. It was George F. Kennan who most convincingly suggested this approach with his portrayal, in the famous "long telegram" of February, 1946, of a Soviet leadership at once so insecure and so unimaginative that it felt obliged to cultivate external enemies in order to maintain itself in power. Without at least the image of outside adversaries, he argued, "there would be no justification for that tremendous crushing bureaucracy of party, police and army, which now lives off the labor and idealism of [the] Russian people".[57] Whatever the validity of this theory—and however limited Kennan himself considered its application to be[58]—this characterization of a Kremlin leadership condemned by its own nervous ineptitude to perpetual distrust nonetheless remains the most influential explanation in the West of how domestic structure influences Soviet foreign policy.[59]

But this theory, too, did not assume the inevitability of war. Institutionalized suspicion in the USSR resulted from weakness, not strength, Kennan argued; as a consequence, the Kremlin was most unlikely actually to initiate military action.[60] With rare exceptions,[61] American officials ever since have accepted this distinction between the likelihood of hostility and the probability of war: indeed, the whole theory of deterrence has been based upon the assumption that paranoia and prudence can co-exist.[62] By this logic, then, the domestic structures of the Soviet state, however geared they may have been to picturing the rest of the world in the worst possible light, have not been seen as likely in and of themselves to produce a war.

One should not make too much of these attempts to attribute to domestic constraints the foreign policy of either the United States or the Soviet Union. International relations, like life itself, are a good deal more complicated than these various models would tend to suggest. But it is significant that these efforts to link internal structure to external behavior reveal no obvious proclivity on either side to risk war; that despite their striking differences, Soviet and American domestic structures appear to have posed no greater impediment to the maintenance of a stable international system than has bipolarity itself or the bilateral characteristics of the Soviet-American relationship.

V

Stability in international systems is only partly a function of structure, though; it depends as well upon the conscious behavior of the nations that make them up. Even if the Second World War settlement had corresponded to the distribution of power in the world, even if the Russian-American relationship had been one of minimal interdependence, even if domestic constraints had not created difficulties, stability in the post-war era still might not have resulted if there had been, among either of the dominant powers in the system, the same willingness to risk war that has existed at other times in the past.

Students of the causes of war have pointed out that war is rarely something that develops from the workings of impersonal social or economic forces, or from the direct effects of arms races, or even by accident. It requires deliberate decisions on the part of national leaders; more than that, it requires calculations that the gains to be derived from war will outweigh the possible costs. "Recurring optimism," Geoffrey Blainey has written, "is a vital prelude to war. Anything which increases that optimism is a cause of war. Anything which dampens that optimism is a cause of peace."[63] Admittedly, those calculations are often in error: as Kennan, in his capacity as a historian, has pointed out, whatever conceivable gains the statesmen of 1914 might have had in mind in risking war, they could not have come anywhere close to approximating the costs the ensuing four-year struggle would actually entail.[64] But it seems hard to deny that it is from such calculations, whether accurately carried out, as Bismarck seemed able to do in his wars against Denmark, Austria and France in the mid-nineteenth century, or inaccurately carried out, as was the case in 1914, that wars tend to develop. They are not something that just happens, like earthquakes, locust plagues, or (some might argue) the selection of presidential candidates in the United States.

For whatever reason, it has to be acknowledged that the statesmen of the post-1945 superpowers have, compared to their predecessors, been exceedingly cautious in risking war with one another.[65] In order to see this point, one need only run down the list of crises in Soviet-American relations since the end of the Second World War: Iran, 1946; Greece, 1947; Berlin and Czechoslovakia, 1948; Korea, 1950; the East Berlin riots, 1953; the Hungarian uprising, 1956; Berlin again in 1958-59; the U-2 incident, 1960; Berlin again, 1961; the Cuban missile crisis, 1962; Czechoslovakia again, 1968; the Yom Kippur war, 1973; Afghanistan, 1979; Poland, 1981; the Korean airliner incident, 1983—one need only run down this list to see how many occasions there have been in relations between Washington and Moscow that in almost any other age, and among almost any other antagonists, would sooner or later have produced war.

That they have not cannot be chalked up to the invariably pacific temperament of the nations involved: the United States participated in eight international wars involving a thousand or more battlefield deaths between 1815 and 1980; Russia participated in nineteen.[66] Nor can this restraint be attributed to any unusual qualities of leadership on either side: the vision and competency of post-war Soviet and American statesmen does not appear to have differed greatly from that of their predecessors. Nor does weariness growing out of participation in two world wars fully explain this unwillingness to resort to arms in their dealings with one another: during the post-war era both nations have employed force against third parties—in the case of the United States in Korea and Vietnam; in the case of the Soviet Union in Afghanistan—for protracted periods of time, and at great cost.

It seems inescapable that what has really made the difference in inducing this unaccustomed caution has been the workings of the nuclear deterrent.[67] Consider, for a moment, what the effect of this mechanism would be on a statesman from either superpower who might be contemplating risking war. In the past, the horrors and the costs of wars could be forgotten with the passage of time. Generations like the one of 1914 had little sense of what the Napoleonic Wars—or even the American Civil War—had revealed about the brutality, expense, and duration of military conflict. But the existence of nuclear weapons —and, more to the point, the fact that we have direct evidence of what they can do when used against human beings[68]—has given this generation a painfully vivid awareness of the realities of war that no previous generation has had. It is difficult, given this awareness, to generate the optimism that historical experience tells us prepares the way for war; pessimism, it appears, is a permanent accompaniment to our thinking about war, and that, as Blainey reminds us, is a cause of peace.

That same pessimism has provided the superpowers with powerful inducements to control crises resulting from the risk-taking of third parties. It is worth recalling that the first World War grew out of the unsuccessful management of a situation neither created nor desired by any of the major actors in the international system. There were simply no mechanisms to put a lid on escalation: to force each nation to balance the short-term temptation to exploit opportunities against the long-term danger that things might get out of hand.[69] The nuclear deterrent provides that mechanism today, and as a result the United States and the Soviet Union have successfully managed a whole series of crises—most notably in the Middle East—that grew out of the actions of neither but that could have involved them both.

None of this is to say, of course, that war cannot occur: if the study of history reveals anything at all it is that one ought to expect, sooner or later, the unexpected. Nor is it to say that the nuclear deterrent could not function equally well with half, or a fourth, or even an eighth of the nuclear weapons now in the arsenals of the superpowers. Nor is it intended to deprecate the importance of refraining from steps that might destabilize the existing stalemate, whether through the search for techno- logical breakthroughs that might provide a decisive edge over the other side, or through so mechanical a duplication of what the other side has that one fails to take into account one's own probably quite different security requirements, or through strategies that rely upon the first use of nuclear weapons in the interest of achieving economy, forgetting the far more funda- mental systemic interest in maintaining the tradition, dating back four decades now, of never actually employing these wea- pons for military purposes.

I am suggesting, though, that the development of nuclear weapons has had, on balance, a stabilizing effect on the post- war international system. They have served to discourage the process of escalation that has, in other eras, too casually led to war. They have had a sobering effect upon a whole range of statesmen of varying degrees of responsibility and capability. They have forced national leaders, every day, to confront the reality of what war is really like, indeed to confront the prospect of their own mortality, and that, for those who seek ways to avoid war, is no bad thing.

VI

But although nuclear deterrence is the most important behav- ioral mechanism that has sustained the post-Second World War international system, it is by no means the only one. Indeed, the very technology that has made it possible to deliver nuclear weapons anywhere on the face of the earth has functioned also to lower greatly the danger of surprise attack, thereby supplementing the self-regulating features of deterrence with the assurance that comes from knowing a great deal more than in the past about adversary capabilities. I refer here to what might be called the "reconnaissance revolution", a development that may well rival in importance the "nuclear revolution" that preceded it, but one that rarely gets the attention it deserves.

The point was made earlier that nations tend to start wars on the basis of calculated assessments that they have the power to prevail. But it was suggested as well that they have often been wrong about this: they either have failed to anticipate the nature and the costs of war itself, or they have misjudged the intentions and the capabilities of the adversary they have chosen to confront.[70] Certainly the latter is what happened to Napoleon III in choosing to risk war with Prussia in 1870, to the Russians in provoking the Japanese in 1904, to the Germans in the First World War when they brought about American entry by resuming unrestricted submarine warfare, to the Japanese in the Second World War by attacking Pearl Harbor and to Adolf Hitler in that same conflict when he managed within six months to declare war on *both* the Soviet Union and the United States, and most recently, to General Galtieri and the Argentine junta in deciding to take on Mrs. Thatcher.

Now, it would be foolish to argue that Americans and Russians have become anymore skillful than they ever were at discerning the other's *intentions*: clearly the United States invasion of Grenada surprised Moscow as much as the Soviet invasion of Afghanistan surprised Washington. The capacity of each nation to behave in ways that seem perfectly logical to it but quite unfathomable to the other remains about what it has been throughout the entire Cold War. But both sides are able—and indeed have been able for at least two decades—to evaluate each other's *capabilities* to a degree that is totally unprecedented in the history of relations between great powers.

What has made this possible, of course, has been the development of the reconnaissance satellite, a device that if rumors are correct allows the reading of automobile license plates or newspaper headlines from a hundred or more miles out in space, together with the equally important custom that has evolved among the superpowers of allowing these objects to pass unhindered over their territories.[71] The effect has been to give each side a far more accurate view of the other's military capabilities —and, to some degree, economic capabilities as well—than could have been provided by an entire phalanx of the best spies in the long history of espionage. The resulting intelligence does not rule out altogether the possibility of surprise attack, but it does render it far less likely, at least as far as the superpowers are concerned. And that is no small matter, if one considers the number of wars in history—from the Trojan War down through Pearl Harbor—in the origins of which deception played a major role.[72]

The "reconnaissance revolution" also corrects, at least to an extent, the asymmetry imposed upon Soviet-American relations by the two countries' sharply-different forms of political and social organization. Throughout most of the early Cold War years the Soviet Union enjoyed all the advantages of a closed society in concealing its capabilities from the West; the United States and its allies, in turn, found it difficult to keep anything secret for very long.[73] That problem still exists, but the ability now to see both visually and electronically into almost every part of the Soviet Union helps to compensate for it. And, of course, virtually none of the limited progress the two countries have made in the field of arms control would have been possible had Americans and Russians not tacitly agreed to the use of reconnaissance satellites and other surveillance techniques to monitor compliance;[74] clearly any future progress in that field will depend heavily upon these devices as well.

There is no little irony in the fact that these instruments, which have contributed so significantly toward stabilizing the post-war international system, grew directly out of research on the intercontinental ballistic missile and the U-2 spy plane.[75] Technological innovation, therefore, is not always a destabilizing force in the Soviet-American relationship. There have been —as in this case—and there could be again instances in which the advance of technology, far from increasing the danger of war, could actually lessen it. It all depends upon the uses to which the technology is put, and that, admittedly, is not an easy thing to foresee.

VII

If technology has had the potential either to stabilize or destabilize the international system, the same cannot as easily be said of ideology. One cannot help but be impressed, when one looks at the long history of national liberation movements, or revolutions against established social orders, or racial and religious conflict, by the continuing capacity of ideas to move nations, or groups within nations, to fight one another.[76] It is only by reference to a violent and ultimately self-destructive ideological impulse that one can account for the remarkable career of Adolf Hitler, with all of its chaotic consequences for the post-First War international system.[77] Since 1945, the ideology of self-determination has not only induced colonies to embroil colonial masters in protracted and costly warfare; it has even led factions within newly-independent states forcibly to seek their own separate political existence.[78] Ideologically-motivated social revolution, too, has been a prominent feature of the post-war international scene, what with major upheavals in nations as diverse as China, Cuba, Vietnam, Cambodia, and Nicaragua. But the most surprising evidence of the continuing influence of ideology has come in the area of religion, where conflicts between Hindus and Moslems, Arabs and Israelis, Iranians and Iraqis, and even Catholics and Protestants in Northern Ireland provide little reason to think that ideas– even ideas once considered to have little relevance other than for historians—will not continue to have a major disruptive potential for international order.[79]

The relationship between the Soviet Union and the United States has not been free from ideological rivalries; it could be argued, in fact, that these are among the two most ideological nations on the face of the earth.[80] Certainly their respective ideologies could hardly have been more antithetical, given the self-proclaimed intention of one to overthrow the other.[81] And yet, since their emergence as superpowers, both nations have demonstrated an impressive capacity to subordinate antagonistic ideological interests to a common goal of preserving international order. The reasons for this are worth examining.

If there were ever a moment at which the priorities of order overcame those of ideology, it would appear to be the point at which Soviet leaders decided that war would no longer advance the cause of revolution. That clearly had not been Lenin's position: international conflict, for him, was good or evil according to whether it accelerated or retarded the demise of capitalism.[82] Stalin's attitude on this issue was more ambivalent:

he encouraged talk of an "inevitable conflict" between the "two camps" of communism and capitalism in the years immediately following the Second World War, but he also appears shortly before his death to have anticipated the concept of "peaceful coexistence".[83] It was left to Georgii Malenkov to admit publicly, shortly after Stalin's death, that a nuclear war would mean "the destruction of world civilization"; Nikita Khrushchev subsequently refined this idea (which he had initially condemned) into the proposition that the interests of world revolution, as well as those of the Soviet state, would be better served by working within the existing international order than by trying to overthrow it.[84]

The reasons for this shift of position are not difficult to surmise. First, bipolarity—the defining characteristic of the post-war international system—implied unquestioned recognition of the Soviet Union as a great power. It was "no small thing", Khrushchev later acknowledged in his memoirs, "that we have lived to see the day when the Soviet Union is considered, in terms of its economic and military might, one of the two most powerful countries in the world".[85] Second, the international situation in the 1950s and early 1960s seemed favorable, especially because of the decline of colonialism and the rise of newly-independent nations likely to be suspicious of the West, to the expansion of Soviet influence in the world.[86] But third, and most important, the proliferation of nuclear capabilities on both sides had confirmed Malenkov's conclusion that in any future war between the great powers, there would be no victors at all, whether capitalist or communist. "[T]he atomic bomb," Soviet leaders reminded their more militant Chinese comrades in 1963, "does not observe the class principle."[87]

The effect was to transform a state which, if ideology alone had governed, should have sought a complete restructuring of the existing international system, into one for whom that system now seemed to have definite benefits, within which it now sought to function, and for whom the goal of overthrowing capitalism had been postponed to some vague and indefinite point in the future.[88] Without this moderation of ideological objectives, it is difficult to see how the stability that has characterized great power relations since the end of the Second World War could have been possible.

Ideological considerations have traditionally played a less prominent role in shaping American foreign policy, but they have had their influence nonetheless. Certainly the Wilsonian commitment to self-determination, revived and ardently embraced during the Second World War, did a great deal to alienate Americans from their Soviet allies at the end of that conflict. Nor had their military exertions moderated Americans' long-standing aversion to collectivism—of which the Soviet variety of communism appeared to be the most extreme example.[89] But there had also developed, during the war, an emphatic hostility toward "totalitarianism" in general: governments that relied upon force to sustain themselves in power, it was thought, could hardly be counted on to refrain from the use of force in the world at large. Demands for the "unconditional surrender" of Germany and Japan reflected this ideological positon: there could be no compromise with regimes for whom arbitrary rule was a way of life.[90]

What is interesting is that although the "totalitarian" model came as easily to be applied to the Soviet Union as it had been to Germany and Japan,[91] the absolutist call for "unconditional surrender" was not. To be sure, the United States and the USSR were not at war. But levels of tension were about as high as they can get short of war during the late 1940s, and we now know that planning for the *contingency* of war was well underway in Washington—as it presumably was in Moscow as well.[92] Nevertheless, the first of these plans to be approved by President Truman, late in 1948, bluntly stated that, if war came, there would be no "predetermined requirement for unconditional surrender".[93] NSC-68, a comprehensive review of national security policy undertaken two years later, elaborated on the point: "[O]ur over-all objectives ... do not include unconditional surrender, the subjugation of the Russian peoples or a Russia shorn of its economic potential." The ultimate goal, rather, was to convince the Soviet government of the impossibility of achieving its self-proclaimed ideological objectives; the immediate goal was to "induce the Soviet Union to accommodate itself, with or without the conscious abandonment of its [ideological] design, to coexistence on tolerable terms with the non-Soviet world."[94]

It is no easy matter to explain why Americans did not commit themselves to the eradication of Soviet "totalitarianism" with the same single-minded determination they had earlier applied to German and Japanese "totalitarianism". One reason, of course, would have been the daunting prospect of attempting to occupy a country the size of the Soviet Union, when compared to the more manageable adversaries of the Second World War.[95] Another was the fact that, despite the hostility that had developed since 1945, American officials did not regard their Russian counterparts as irredeemable: the very purpose of "containment" had been to change the *psychology* of the Soviet leadership; but not, as had been the case with Germany and Japan, the leadership itself.[96]

But Washington's aversion to an "unconditional surrender" doctrine for the Soviet Union stemmed from yet another less obvious consideration; it had quickly become clear to American policy-makers, after the Second World War, that insistence on the total defeat of Germany and Japan had profoundly destabilized the post-war balance of power. Only by assuming responsibility for the rehabilitation of these former enemies as well as the countries they had ravaged had the United States been able to restore equilibrium, and even then it was clear that the American role in this regard would have to be a continuing one. It was no accident that the doctrine of "unconditional surrender" came under severe criticism, after 1945, from a new school of "realist" geopoliticians given to viewing international stability in terms of the wary toleration of adversaries rather than, as a point of principle, their annihilation.[97]

Largely as a result of such reasoning, American officials at no point during the history of the Cold War seriously contemplated, as a deliberate political objective, the elimination of the Soviet Union as a major force in world affairs. By the mid-1950s, it is true, war plans had been devised that, if executed, would have quite indiscriminately annihilated not only the Soviet Union but several of its communist and non-communist neighbors as well.[98] What is significant about those plans, though, is that they reflected the organizational convenience of the military services charged with implementing them, not any conscious policy decisions at the top. Both Eisenhower and Kennedy were appalled on learning of them; both considered them ecologically as well as strategically impossible; and during the Kennedy administration steps were initiated to devise strategies that would leave open the possibility of a surviving political entity in Russia even in the extremity of nuclear war.[99]

All of this would appear to confirm, then, the proposition that systemic interests tend to take precedence over ideological interests.[100] Both the Soviet ideological aversion to capitalism and the American ideological aversion to totalitarianism could have produced policies—and indeed had produced policies in the past—aimed at the complete overthrow of their respective adversaries. That such ideological impulses could be muted to the extent they have been during the past four decades testifies to the stake both Washington and Moscow have developed in preserving the existing international system: the moderation of ideologies must be considered, then, along with nuclear deterrence and reconnaissance, as a major self-regulating mechanism of post-war politics.

VIII

The question still arises, though: how can order emerge from a system that functions without any superior authority? Even self-regulating mechanisms like automatic pilots or engine governors cannot operate without someone to set them in motion; the prevention of anarchy, it has generally been assumed, requires hierarchy, both at the level of interpersonal and international relations. Certainly the statesmen of the Second World War expected that some supra-national structure would be necessary to sustain a future peace, whether in the form of a new collective security organization to replace the ineffectual League of Nations, or through perpetuation of the great-power consensus that Churchill, Roosevelt, and Stalin sought to forge.[101] All of them would have been surprised by the extent to which order has been maintained since 1945 in the absence of any effective supra-national authority of any kind.[102]

This experience has forced students of international politics to recognize that their subject bears less resemblance to local, state or national politics, where order does in fact depend upon legally-constituted authority, than it does to the conduct of games, where order evolves from mutual agreement on a set of "rules" defining the range of behavior each side anticipates from the other. The assumption is that the particular "game" being played promises sufficient advantages to each of its "players" to outweigh whatever might be obtained by trying to upset it; in this way, rivalries can be pursued within an orderly framework, even in the absence of a referee. Game theory therefore helps to account for the paradox of order in the absence of hierarchy that characterizes the post-war superpower relationship: through it one can get a sense of how "rules" establish limits of acceptable behavior on the part of nations who acknowledge only themselves as the arbiters of behavior.[103]

These "rules" are, of course, implicit rather than explicit: they grow out of a mixture of custom, precedent, and mutual interest that takes shape quite apart from the realm of public rhetoric, diplomacy, or international law. They require the passage of time to become effective; they depend, for that effectiveness, upon the extent to which successive generations of national leadership on each side find them useful. They certainly do not reflect any agreed-upon standard of international morality: indeed they often violate principles of "justice" adhered to by one side or the other. But these "rules" have played an important role in maintaining the international system that has been in place these past four decades: without them the correlation one would normally anticipate between hostility and instability would have become more exact than it has in fact been since 1945.

No two observers of superpower behavior would express these "rules" in precisely the same way; indeed it may well be that their very vagueness has made them more acceptable than they otherwise might have been to the nations that have followed them. What follows is nothing more than my own list, derived from an attempt to identify *regularities* in the post-war Soviet-American relationship whose pattern neither side could now easily disrupt.

(1) *Respect spheres of influence.* Neither Russians nor Americans officially admit to having such "spheres", but in fact much of the history of the Cold War can be written in terms of the efforts both have made to consolidate and extend them. One should not, in acknowledging this, fall into so mechanical a comparison of the two spheres as to ignore their obvi-

ous differences: the American sphere has been wider in geo-graphical scope than its Soviet counterpart, but it has also been a much looser alignment, participation in which has more often than not been a matter of choice rather than coercion.[104] But what is important from the standpoint of superpower "rules" is the fact that, although neither side has ever publicly endorsed the other's right to a sphere of influence, neither has ever directly challenged it either.[105]

Thus, despite publicly condemning it, the United States never attempted seriously to undo Soviet control in Eastern Europe; Moscow reciprocated by tolerating, though never openly ap-proving of, Washington's influence in Western Europe, the Mediterranean, the Near East, and Latin America. A similar pattern held up in East Asia, where the Soviet Union took no more action to oppose United States control over occupied Japan than the Truman administration did to repudiate the Yalta agreement, which left the Soviet Union dominant, at least for the moment, on the Northeast Asian mainland.[106]

Where the relation of particular areas to spheres of influence had been left unclear—as had been the case with the Western-occupied zones of Berlin prior to 1948, or with South Korea prior to 1950—or where the resolve of one side to maintain its sphere appeared to have weakened—as in the case of Cuba following the failure of the Bay of Pigs invasion in 1961—at-tempts by the other to exploit the situation could not be ruled out: the Berlin Blockade, the invasion of South Korea, and the decision to place Soviet missiles in Cuba can all be understood in this way.[107] But it appears also to have been understood, in each case, that the resulting probes would be conducted cau-tiously, and that they would not be pursued to the point of risking war if resistance was encountered.[108]

Defections from one sphere would be exploited by the other only when it was clear that the first either could not or would not reassert control. Hence, the United States took advantage of departures from the Soviet bloc of Yugoslavia and—ulti-mately—the Peoples' Republic of China; it did not seek to do so in the case of Hungary in 1956, Czechoslovakia in 1968, or (in what was admittedly a more ambiguous situation) Poland in 1981. Similarly, the Soviet Union exploited the defection of Cuba after 1959, but made no attempt to contest the reassertion of American influence in Iran in 1953, Guatemala in 1954, the Dominican Republic in 1965, or Grenada in 1983.[109]

(2) *Avoid direct military confrontation.* It is remarkable, in retrospect, that at no point during the long history of the Cold War have Soviet and American military forces engaged each other directly in sustained hostilities. The superpowers have fought three major limited wars since 1945, but in no case with each other: the possibility of direct Soviet–American military involvement was greatest—although it never happened—during the Korean War; it was much more remote in Vietnam and has remained so in Afghanistan as well. In those few situations where Soviet and American military units have confronted one another directly—the 1948 Berlin blockade, the construction of the Berlin Wall in 1961, and the Cuban missile crisis the following year—great care was taken on both sides to avoid incidents that might have triggered hostilities.[110]

Where the superpowers have sought to expand or to retain areas of control, they have tended to resort to the use of proxies or other indirect means to accomplish this: examples would include the Soviet Union's decision to sanction a North Korean invasion of South Korea,[111] and its more recent reliance on Cuban troops to promote its interests in sub-Saharan Africa; on the American side covert intervention has been a convenient (if not invariably successful) means of defending spheres of influence.[112] In a curious way, clients and proxies have come to serve as buffers, allowing Russians and Americans to pursue their competition behind a facade of "deniability" that minimizes the risks of open—and presumably less manageable—confrontation.

The two superpowers have also been careful not to allow the disputes of third parties to embroil them directly: this pattern has been most evident in the Middle East, which has witnessed no fewer than five wars between Israel and its Arab neighbors since 1948; but it holds as well for the India-Pakistan conflicts of 1965 and 1971, and for the more recent—and much more protracted—struggle between Iran and Iraq. The contrast between this long tradition of restraint and the casualness with which great powers in the past have allowed the quarrels of others to become their own could hardly be more obvious.[113]

(3) *Use nuclear weapons only as an ultimate resort.* One of

the most significant—though least often commented upon—of the superpower "rules" has been the tradition that has evolved, since 1945, of maintaining a sharp distinction between conventional and nuclear weapons, and of reserving the military use of the latter only for the extremity of total war. In retrospect, there was nothing at all inevitable about this: the Eisenhower administration announced quite publicly its willingness to use nuclear weapons in limited war situations;[114] Henry Kissinger's *Nuclear Weapons and Foreign Policy* strongly endorsed such use in 1957 as a way to keep alliance commitments credible;[115] and Soviet strategists have traditionally insisted as well that in war both nuclear and conventional means would be employed.[116] It is remarkable, given this history, that the world has not seen a single nuclear weapon used in anger since the destruction of Nagasaki forty years ago. Rarely has *practice* of nations so conspicuously departed from proclaimed *doctrine*; rarely, as well, has so great a disparity attracted so little public notice.

This pattern of caution in the use of nuclear weapons did not develop solely, as one might have expected, from the prospect of retaliation. As early as 1950, at a time when the Soviet Union had only just tested an atomic bomb and had only the most problematic methods of delivering it, the United States nonetheless effectively ruled out the use of its own atomic weapons in Korea because of the opposition of its allies and the fear of an adverse reaction in the world at large. As one State Department official put it: "[W]e must consider that, regardless of the fact that the military results achieved by atomic bombardment may be identical to those attained by conventional weapons, the effect on world opinion will be vastly different."[117] Despite his public position that there was "no reason why [nuclear weapons] shouldn't be used just exactly as you would use a bullet or anything else," President Eisenhower repeatedly rejected recommendations for their use in limited war situations: "You boys must be crazy," he told his advisers at the time of the collapse of Dien Bien Phu in 1954. "We can use those awful things against Asians for the second time in less than ten years. My God."[118]

It was precisely this sense that nuclear weapons were qualitatively different from other weapons[119] that most effectively deterred their employment by the United States during the first decade of the Cold War, a period in which the tradition of "non-use" had not yet taken hold, within which ample opportunities for their use existed, and during which the possibility of Soviet retaliation could not have been great. The idea of a discrete "threshold" between nuclear and conventional weapons, therefore, may owe more to the moral—and public relations—sensibilities of Washington officials than to any actual fear of escalation. By the time a credible Soviet retaliatory capability was in place, at the end of the 1950s, the "threshold" concept was equally firmly fixed: one simply did not cross it short of all-out war.[120] Subsequent limited war situations—notably Vietnam for the Americans, and more recently Afghanistan for the Russians—have confirmed the continued effectiveness of this unstated but important "rule" of superpower behavior, as have the quiet but persistent efforts both Washington and Moscow have made to keep nuclear weapons from falling into the hands of others who might not abide by it.[121]

(4) *Prefer predictable anomaly over unpredictable rationality*. One of the most curious features of the Cold War has been the extent to which the superpowers—and their respective clients, who have had little choice in the matter—have tolerated a whole series of awkward, artificial, and, on the surface at least, unstable regional arrangements: the division of Germany is, of course, the most obvious example; others would include the Berlin Wall, the position of West Berlin itself within East Germany, the arbitrary and ritualized partition of the Korean peninsula, the existence of an avowed Soviet satellite some ninety miles off the coast of Florida, and, not least, the continued function of an important American naval base within it. There is to all of these arrangements an appearance of wildly illogical improvisation: none of them could conceivably have resulted, it seems, from any rational and premeditated design.

And yet, at another level, they have had a kind of logic after all: the fact that these jerry-built but rigidly-maintained arrangements have lasted for so long suggests an unwillingness on the part of the superpowers to trade familiarity for unpredictability. To try to rationalize the German, Korean, or Cuban anomalies would, it has long been acknowledged, create the unnerving possibility of an uncertain result; far better, Soviet and American leaders have consistently agreed, to perpetuate the anomalies rather than to risk the possibilities for destabilization inherent in trying to resolve them. For however unnatural and unjust these situations may be for the people whose lives they directly affect, it seems nonetheless incontestable that the superpowers' preference for predictability over rationality has, on the whole, enhanced more than it has reduced prospects for a stable relationship.

(5) *Do not seek to undermine the other side's leadership.* The death of Stalin, in March, 1953, set off a flurry of proposals within the United States government for exploiting the vulnerability that was thought certain to result: it was a major American objective, Secretary of State Dulles informed embassies overseas, "to sow doubt, confusion, uncertainty about the new regime".[122] And yet, by the following month President Eisenhower was encouraging precisely that successor regime to join in a major new effort to control the arms race and reduce the danger of war.[123] The dilemma here was one that was to recur throughout the Cold War: if what one wanted was stability at the international level, did it make sense to try to destabilize the other side's leadership at the national level?

The answer, it appears, has been no. There have been repeated leadership crisis in both the United States and the Soviet Union since Stalin's death: one thinks especially of the decline and ultimate deposition of Khrushchev following the Cuban Missile Crisis, of the Johnson administration's all-consuming fixation with Vietnam, of the collapse of Nixon's authority as a result of Watergate, and of the recent paralysis in the Kremlin brought about by the illness and death of three Soviet leaders within less than three years. And yet, in none of these instances can one discern a concerted effort by the unaffected side to exploit the other's vulnerability; indeed there appears to have existed in several of these situations a sense of frustration, even regret, over the difficulties its rival was undergoing.[124] From the standpoint of game theory, a "rule" that acknowledges legitimacy of leadership on both sides is hardly surprising: there have to be players in order for the game to proceed. But when compared to other historical—and indeed other current—situations in which that reciprocal tolerance has not existed,[125] its importance as a stabilizing mechanism becomes clear.

Stability, in great power relationships, is not the same thing as politeness. It is worth noting that despite levels of hostile rhetoric unmatched on both sides since the earliest days of the Cold War, the Soviet Union and the United States have managed to get through the early 1980s without a single significant military confrontation of any kind. Contrast this with the record of Soviet-American relations in the 1970s: an era of far greater politeness in terms of what the two nations *said* about one another, but one marred by potentially dangerous crises over Soviet submarine bases and combat brigades in Cuba, American bombing and mining activities in Vietnam, and a pattern of Soviet interventionism in Angola, Somalia, Ethiopia, South Yemen, and Afghanistan. There was even a major American nuclear alert during the Yom Kippur War in 1973—the only one since the Cuban missile crisis—ironically enough, this occurred at the height of what is now wistfully remembered as the era of "detente".[126]

What stability does require is a sense of caution, maturity, and responsibility on both sides. It requires the ability to distinguish posturing—something in which all political leaders indulge—from provocation, which is something else again. It requires recognition of the fact that competition is a normal rather than an abnormal state of affairs in relations between nations, much as it is in relations between major corporations, but that this need not preclude the identification of certain common—or corporate, or universal—interests as well. It requires, above all, a sense of the relative rather than the absolute nature of security: that one's own security depends not only upon the measures one takes in one's own defense, but also upon the extent to which these create a sense of insecurity in the mind of one's adversary.

It would be foolish to suggest that the Soviet-American relationship today meets all of these prerequisites: the last one especially deserves a good deal more attention than it has heretofore received, on both sides. But to the extent that the relationship has taken on a new maturity—and to see that it has one need only compare the current mood of wary optimism with the almost total lack of communication that existed at the time of the Korean War, or the extreme swings between alarm and amiability that characterized relations in the late 1950s and early 1960s, or the inflated expectations and resulting disillusionments of the 1970s—that maturity would appear to reflect an increasing commitment on the part of both great nations involved to a "game" played "by the rules".

IX

History, as anyone who has spent any time at all studying it would surely know, has a habit of making bad prophets out of both those who make and those who chronicle it. It tends to take expectations and turn them upside down; it is not at all tolerant of those who would seek too self-confidently to anticipate its future course. One should be exceedingly wary, therefore, of predicting how long the current era of Soviet-American stability will last. Certainly it is easy to conceive of things that might in one way or another undermine it: domestic developments in either country could affect foreign policy in unpredictable ways; the actions of third parties could embroil the superpowers in conflict with each other against their will; opportunities for miscalculation and accident are always present; incompetent leadership is always a risk. All that one can—or should—say is that the relationship has survived these kinds of disruptions in the past: if history made bad prophets out of the warmakers of 1914 and 1939-41, or the peacemakers of 1919, all of whom approached their tasks with a degree of optimism that seems to us foolish in retrospect, then so too has it made bad prophets out of the peacemakers of 1945, who had so little optimism about the future.

Whether the Soviet-American relationship could survive something more serious is another matter entirely. We know the answer when it comes to nuclear war; recent scientific findings have only confirmed visions of catastrophe we have lived with for decades.[127] But what about a substantial decline in the overall influence of either great power that did not immediately result in war? Here, it seems to me, is a more probable—if less often discussed—danger. For if history demonstrates anything at all, it is that the condition of being a great power is a transitory one: sooner or later, the effects of exhaustion, overextension and lack of imagination take their toll among nations, just as surely as does old age itself among individuals. Nor is it often that history arranges for great powers to decline simultaneously and symmetrically. Past experience also suggests that the point at which a great power perceives its decline to be beginning is a perilous one: behavior can become erratic, even desperate, well before physical strength itself has dissipated.[128]

The Soviet-American relationship has yet to face this test, although there is no reason to think it will escape it indefinitely. When that time comes, the preservation of stability may require something new in international relations: the realization that great nations can have a stake, not just in the survival, but also the success and prosperity of their rivals. International systems, like tangoes, require at least two reasonably active and healthy participants; it is always wise, before allowing the dance to end, to consider with what, or with whom, one will replace it.

The Cold War, with all of its rivalries, anxieties, and unquestionable dangers, has produced the longest period of stability in relations among the great powers that the world has known in this century; it now compares favorably as well with some of the longest periods of great power stability in all of modern history. We may argue among ourselves as to whether or not we can legitimately call this "peace": it is not, I dare say, what most of us have in mind when we use that term. But I am not at all certain that the contemporaries of Metternich or Bismarck would have regarded their eras as "peaceful" either, even though historians looking back on those eras today clearly do.

Who is to say, therefore, how the historians of the year 2086—if there are any left by then—will look back on us? Is it not at least plausible that they will see our era, not as "the Cold War" at all, but rather, like those ages of Metternich and Bismarck, as a rare and fondly-remembered "Long Peace"? Wishful thinking? Speculation through a rose-tinted word processor? Perhaps. But would it not behoove us to give at least as much attention to the question of how this might happen—to the elements in the contemporary international system that might make it happen—as we do to the fear that it may not?

DISCUSSIONS

Pierre Hassner

My comment on this excellent paper can be summarized by two formulas: "So far so good" and "yes but ..." I think it is absolutely right and illuminating as far as it goes. But the mood of optimism it expresses may be less justified if it is extrapolated—as Gaddis tends to do however carefully and discreetly—in time and space.

In other words, the only real criticism deserved by the paper lies in its title. Gaddis does not really talk about *the* international system (to the debatable extent that it exists), but about two international subsystems: the Soviet-American nuclear relationship and the intra-Western democratic or capitalistic "security community" or "pacific union".

It is perfectly true that the Soviet-American confrontation has respected a certain number of rules which have prevented it from leading to war, and that war became inconceivable among Western democracies. These two realities are fundamentally novel and deserve to be submitted to the kind of admiring but searching scrutiny which Gaddis practices so well. But it is no less true that from every point of view (functional, historical, geographic) they represent only one dimension, one period, one area of international reality, with no guarantee that this dimension, this period, this area, will prove contagious and decisive for the global system.

Functionally, while the strategic, particularly nuclear, US-Soviet relationship has proved remarkably stable, the social, economic, political one has been particularly agitated. More generally, in East-West relations, particularly in Europe, there is a striking contrast between the stability, even the rigidity of the geo-strategic system, based on division and balance, and the dynamics of social and economic evolution and revolutions.

Historically, the geo-strategic situation itself, which has been partly stabilized by nuclear technology may be in turn destabilized by new technological evolutions.

Finally, and most importantly, the direct, intercontinental Soviet-American balance, and the European continent which is, so far, directly linked to it by the physical presence of Soviet

and American troops and nuclear weapons, cover only a com-
paratively modest part of the globe. Everywhere else, wars and
violent revolutions go on as ever. Their intensity and their
potential for escalation may be worsened both by nuclear proliferation and by the globalization of Soviet-American rivalry.

Let me illustrate each of these points very briefly.

On the US-Soviet Nuclear Relationship

First, the new evolutions in technology can be argued to increase
the danger of war both *directly*, by increasing the vulnerability
of land-based missiles today, perhaps of sea-based ones tomor-
row, and hence the temptation to launch a first-strike, and
indirectly by making control more difficult. Anti-missile defense
may introduce a new round in the arms race. While the opposite
case may also be argued, it seems plausible to say that while
deterrence remains stable, crisis instability and arms race instability are increasing.

Second, even if one assumes mutual deterrence between the
two superpowers to be stable, there is a tension between finite
bilateral deterrence and extended deterrence, or between the
doctrine or situation of mutual assured destruction and the
protection of Europe. Many of those who claim that deterrence
is stable also argue for a conventional defense in Europe. This
would then create two separate systems, a superpower and a
theater one. Hence the dilemmas of decoupling or of deterrence
through the threat of escalation are increasing.

Thirdly, Gaddis speaks of the "reconnaissance revolution".
Here again while he describes the past and, perhaps the present,
very acutely, his analysis may not be valid for the future, given
the progress of anti-satellite warfare and the increasing problems of verification. On the other hand, it can be argued that
uncertainty increases deterrence. If the threat of retaliation is
credible, it is best that it should be communicated in the clearest
and most convincing terms possible; but if it loses credibility or
is based on "the rationality of irrationality", then the residual
uncertainty is better for deterrence than the certainty of a non-
response. Here again, there may be a gap between what is
desirable for mutual finite deterrence and what is desirable for

extended deterrence, which may have nothing better to rely on than the unpredictability of the escalation process.

On the Politics of the US-Soviet Relationship and of the European Situation

Here again the key element which might qualify Gaddis's optimism has to do with unpredictability. Gaddis himself stresses the vagaries of the American political system and public opinion; he also mentions the communist and Russian penchant for secrecy and for distrust of the outside world which seems to be intimately tied to the Soviet system. This makes the situation less symmetrical than he would seem to imply, although one may argue that the superpowers are symmetrically unpredictable for asymmetrical reasons.

The same, to some extent, goes for their respective alliance systems. The West is, on balance, remarkably stable socially but political-military centrifugal trends (towards American disengagement or West German search for accommodation, with the Soviet Union for the sake of relations with the GDR, may still create enough political decoupling to throw doubts upon the military coupling on which extended deterrence rests. Conversely, the Soviet Union has not the slightest temptation to disengage from Eastern Europe and the East Europeans have not the slightest chance to escape its embrace; yet, the very inevitability of the marriage may provoke reactions of frustration and repression which in turn may create the dangers for peace which the Sonnenfelt doctrine tried to forestall.

On the Politics of Frustration and Conflict in the Third World

It must be recognized, however, that all these social and political frustrations have not led in Europe either to war or to violent revolutions; herein lies the strength of Gaddis's argument. But herein also lie its limits, since neither war nor revolution have been in short supply, during the same period, in the rest of the world. One need not agree with those Third-World critics who think the tranquillity of the developed world is based, precisely, on the turmoil of the underdeveloped one. But one must fear that the two worlds may not remain isolated for ever and that, through a kind of political Gresham's law, the instability of the Third World is more likely to spread to the developed one than the other way round. The 1973 oil shock provided one example of how this might happen. Nuclear proliferation may provide another. Again, the consequences of the former were more limited than was thought at the time, and nuclear proliferation looks less threatening today than thirty years ago. But while everybody shares an interest in avoiding nuclear war and almost everybody in avoiding a world economic crisis, only the West and more specifically, only the United States has a real interest in keeping the political status quo. Almost everyone else has his own reasons—whether political, social, psychological or economic—for aspiring to change. In the last analysis, however stable nuclear bipolarity may be, the only stability conceivable for the international system as such is one that makes room for change.

Kjell Goldmann

Professor Gaddis's object is to account for the great power peace which has obtained since 1945 (with the exception of the US-Chinese war in Korea and fighting on the Soviet-Chinese border). He argues that the international system has been re-markably stable, in Karl Deutsch's and David Singer's sense, for forty years and explains this stability in the way outlined in Figure 1. In this model, which I hope is a fair representation of the analysis, systemic stability is brought about by the fact that the leaders on both sides have adopted a "realist" view of foreign policy and by the development of rules of the game between them. These stabilizing features have in turn resulted from the combined impact of bipolarity and military tech-nology. Contrary to common belief, moreover, the fact that the two superpowers have been uniquely independent of one an-other has further reduced the probability of war. Also contrary to common belief, the domestic features of the superpowers have not provided any special incentives for conflict.

In the paper, the uncertainty of the argument is emphasized

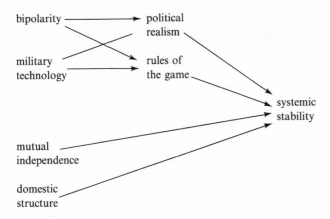

Fig. 1. An outline of Professor Gaddis's account of post-1945 stability.

in two ways. It is pointed out that the analysis is a series of speculations and cannot be more than that, given present knowledge. It is added that one should be exceedingly wary of predicting whether or not the system will remain stable, and it is left an open question whether any historians will exist in the year 2086 (p. 160).

The purpose of these remarks is to consider why this is so —why Professor Gaddis's analysis of "how this great power peace has managed to survive for so long in the face of so much provocation" may be an insufficient basis for "thinking about what might be done to perpetuate that situation" (p. 126). This is not a matter of finding faults with Professor Gaddis's stimulating argument but of indicating some of the unresolved problems in the analysis of war and peace.

Political Realism

It does seem obvious that both the United States and the Soviet Union have demonstrated "an impressive capacity to subordinate antagonistic ideological interests to a common goal of preserving international order" (p. 147), that "systemic interests" have tended "to take precedence over ideological interests", and that this has been "a major self-regulating mechanism of post-war politics" (p. 151). It may not be entirely clear how deep the preference for "realism" goes, however. The *realpolitik* of the Nixon Administration was followed by Jimmy Carter's concern over human rights and then by Ronald Reagan's thoughts about the "evil empire". It is easy to get the impression that an assertive anticommunism has become somewhat less uncommon in the West since the early 1970s. In the Soviet foreign policy doctrine, peaceful coexistence is "a form of class struggle", and the so-called ideological struggle was given especial prominence under détente; much attention was devoted in Soviet pronouncements to clarifying that the international class struggle—including intervention in the Third World—and détente went hand in hand.[1]

This is no more than a question mark in the margin. It remains wildly implausible that either of the superpowers would attack the other for the purpose of ending an evil empire. Still, ideological considerations might provide incentives for action at lower levels. Whether this possibility is stabilizing or destabilizing hinges on the deterrence paradox; see below.

Rules of the Game

It is, of course, a common thought that stabilizing rules of the game have developed in the US-Soviet relationship.[2] No two observers would express them in precisely the same way, as Professor Gaddis points out. However, the main uncertainty with the rules-of-the-game argument is whether we are in fact dealing with rules or merely with behavior patterns. If a behavior pattern does reflect a common norm—an informal political institution—it is provided with extra protection. Professor Gaddis appears to believe that the rules of the game are in fact rules and not just patterns of behavior. He is probably right, but I would have wanted the evidence to be stronger, especially on the Soviet side.

One of the rules, according to Professor Gaddis, is: "Avoid direct military confrontation." It appears to me that this rule is marred by a critical ambiguity even as a mere description of past behavior. It is true, of course, that the United States and the Soviet Union have fought no war against one another. Is it also true that they have consistently taken great care "to avoid incidents that might have triggered hostilities" (p. 154)? Is there systematic evidence of a dramatic decrease in provocative actions since 1945? Isn't it equally plausible to characterize at least some incidents—such as the Cuban Missile Crisis and the Yom Kippur War—as playing with fire? The fact that no fire has occurred may not suffice to prove that care has consistently been taken to avoid it.[3]

It may be argued—although Professor Gaddis doesn't—that if there were no playing with fire, deterrence would not work and the system would be less rather than more stable. This is another aspect of the deterrence paradox, which will be considered shortly.

Independence

Even though interdependence and contact do not "necessarily breed peace" (p. 136), they may not always breed war either. Rather, exchanges seem sometimes to be stabilizing, sometimes to be destabilizing, and sometimes to have no effect at all; this, presumably, depends on a number of third variables. One possibility is that, so far as the leading powers of a bipolar system are concerned, the relationship between cooperation and conflict is non-linear, so that moderate exchanges are more stabilizing than either very limited or very extensive ones. The link between cooperation and conflict remains underresearched, however.

Domestic Structures

Professor Gaddis is right in questioning some common hypotheses to the effect that the United States or the Soviet Union are especially prone to war for reasons of their domestic structure. I should like to add, however, that both countries may be prone to instability in foreign policy.

Foreign policies may be protected by a variety of mechanisms,[4] but some of them may be less unlikely to operate in Washington or Moscow than elsewhere. The matter cannot be elaborated on here. Suffice it to point out that there is in Washington a degree of institutionalized foreign policy pluralism which is hardly rivaled elsewhere; it is common to argue that the instability in US foreign policy during recent decades can be traced back to this feature of the American foreign policy system. As regards the Soviet Union, it may be hypothesized that authoritarian regimes, even when bureaucratic, have more freedom of movement than non-authoritarian ones. The European democracies may represent an intermediate position between pluralism and non-pluralism where foreign policies are more likely to develop into unshakeable institutions than in either superpower.

Military Technology

The "reconnaissance revolution" may not be unambiguously stabilizing. True, there is less reason to fear surprise attack and hence less reason for pre-emption. On the other hand, the better the intelligence, the greater the opportunity for successful attack. Whether the effect is stabilizing or destabilizing would seem to depend on what is the more powerful consideration: to avert threats or to exploit opportunities.

This question, in turn, goes to the heart of the hypothesis that nuclear weapons are a key cause of the post-1945 great power peace. Pessimism, Professor Gaddis argues, is a cause of peace, and therefore the nuclear deterrent has served to induce caution into great power politics. It may be useful to point out why this argument, even though plausible, may not be entirely self-evident.

The issue, first of all, cannot be decided at the theoretical level. If it is rational to avoid risking nuclear war, it is also rational to escalate a conflict in the hope that the adversary will be deterred by his fear of nuclear war from responding. As Morgan suggests, in order for deterrence to work the contenders must be "sensible" and not merely rational.[5] Whether the great powers are sensible is an empirical question.

If in fact the United States and the Soviet Union have "been exceedingly cautious in risking war with one another", it is a very plausible thought that nuclear deterrence has helped to induce this caution. This may be considered an insufficient observation, however. If a war were to start between nuclear powers, escalation to the nuclear level must be considered a serious possibility, and it would probably be difficult to limit a nuclear war. Hence, any great power confrontation carries the possibility of developing into the ultimate catastrophe. From this point of view, even single instances of non-restraint are significant. In this perspective, the main point is that serious crises have in fact occurred.

In effect I am contesting here the very concept of international stability adopted by Professor Gaddis. He, and Deutsch and Singer before him, define stability in terms of the probability rather than the magnitude of war. It could be defined as a function of both. The post-war international system would then appear less stable than in Professor Gaddis's analysis.

Now, as argued by Kaplan in *System and Process in International Politics*, a system is stable as long as it "remains within specified limits for arbitrarily defined variables". The limits and the variables are chosen by the analyst and are not implied in the concept of stability; "the choice of variables is, in effect, a choice of subject matter."[6] Hence, it is neither correct nor incorrect to define stability in one way or the other. What is important is to avoid losing sight of the fact that if there is a trade-off between the probability and the magnitude of war—if a balance of terror tends to induce caution—there may still be a disproportion between an increase in magnitude and a consequent decrease in probability.

This, however, leads to the further question whether crises really represent a higher likelihood of war than non-crisis. Here we encounter the deterrence paradox: the greater the risk of war, the smaller the probability of war. The problem with this assumption is that any evidence can be taken to show that deterrence works. If the contenders do not escalate, this shows that they are deterred. If they do escalate, this is a self-regulating mechanism serving to reduce rather than to increase the probability of war.

The alternative assumption—that escalation is self-aggravating rather than self-regulating—is based on reasoning about conflict dynamics and action-reaction rather than rational calculations. We know for example that both individuals and organizations may malfunction under stress. On this assumption it remains a questionable idea to settle down close to a powder-keg, since people cannot be trusted to consistently abstain from playing with fire.

Whether escalation is self-regulating or self-aggravating is of great importance for assessing proposals for détente, arms control, and crisis management. Empirical research would be useful, in which our interpretation of the evidence were less determined by our preconceptions.

Bipolarity

It is not necessary to recapitulate the debate among international relationists about whether bipolarity is likely to be more or less stabilizing than multipolarity. Reasonable arguments can be given for either hypothesis. Professor Gaddis evidently considers post-1945 experience to show that bipolarity is stabilizing.

It can be argued, however, that this evidence is inconclusive because we cannot control for other variables. There are many differences between pre-1939 and post-1945 world politics, and not just a decrease in the number of "poles"—the reconnaissance and nuclear revolutions, for example.

Professor Gaddis sets out to account for the great power peace since 1945 and is not much concerned with the various ups and downs in superpower relations during this period.[7] It may be argued that these fluctuations are unimportant since there has been a basic stability throughout. It may even be argued that because of the deterrence paradox, the system has been less rather than more stable during détente. Professor Gaddis takes neither position, however. He maintains that in the late 1940s levels of tension were "about as high as they can get short of war", and he refers to the Cold War as a period of "unquestionable dangers".

Détente may be thought of as a safety margin: the better the relationship between two parties, the more is required to trigger a war between them. "Without détente," Nixon stated in October 1973, "we might have had a major conflict in the Middle East. With détente we avoided it."[8] This argument assumes that escalation is not self-regulating. It leads to a concern not just with accounting for the absence of war but with explaining the variations in tension which have occurred between the great powers, in the hope of learning from this experience how to bring about a more stable détente.

From the point of view of the deterrence paradox this is the wrong thing to do. I am not quite sure whether Professor Gaddis is led by his analysis to one conclusion or the other.

General discussion

Gaddis's model may be used as a basis both for explaining why there has so far been no war between the US and the USSR—a fact that may be referred to as "stability"—and for exploring the conditions of peace in the future. The first question, then is, whether the model is a good explanation of the benign outcome so far. It is argued that the model puts too much stress on *bipolarity* as a source of stability, and fails to take into account the vast medium in which the bipolar superpower relationship is, as it were, suspended. This medium is, in large part, the developing world, and it is conjectured that the superpowers have avoided direct war largely because they have been able to fight proxy wars in Africa and Asia. The stability in Europe would therefore have to be seen in relation to this compensatory turbulence; the outcome might have been less benign had the Third World not been there providing the opportunity for superpower tension to be played out.

Conversely, developments in the Third World may be considered a notable source of tension in the superpower relationship. An important aspect of this is the occurrence of *defections*: states moving from one sphere of influence to another. Such moves appear to engender greater tension when there is a direct shift between spheres—as in the cases of Cuba and Vietnam—than when the defecting states adopt an intermediary position, like Iran and Egypt have done. This indicates that changes in Africa and Asia put less stress on the bipolar superpower relationship the less they themselves follow a bipolar logic.

The significance of developments in the developing world is emphasized also with respect to the *predictive* value of the model. It is suggested that the superpower system will come under increasing strain from new sources of disorder in the Third World. One source is the profound changes in attitudes and values which find expression in religious fundamentalism; another is the diffusion of power which, combined with the easy availability of arms, threatens the ability of the superpowers to control local conflicts.

It is suggested that the model might be more useful in thinking about the future if some *historical dynamics* were incorporated in it. In the case of, e.g., spheres of interest, it would be interesting to know when and how these spheres became identifiable and acknowledged as spheres not to be meddled with. Similarly, one could trace the *development* of the acknowledged tradition that nuclear weapons are different, their opportunistic use to be avoided. They are, to wit, not always recognized to be so.

It is asked if we see any crumbling of the conditions that, according to Gaddis's model, make for stability. In the period of détente, which established important rules of the game, no *institutions* were set up to preserve these rules, and there are reasons for fearing that the absence of an institutional structure tends to undermine their effectiveness.

It is questioned whether the talk about *self-regulating mechanisms* might give a false impression of the systemic interrelationship between the different factors that, according to Gaddis, make for stability. They are obviously self-regulating in very different ways, and it is not quite clear how they are related to each other. There may also be elements of circularity in the argument, notably in the discussion of behavioral self-regulating mechanisms. It appears misleading to say that, e.g., ideological moderation and the tendency not to exploit weaknesses, are self-regulating mechanisms accounting for stability, as these "mechanisms" simply *are* stability—stability does not exist outside them.

6

Patterns of Armed Conflict in the Third World*

SOEDJATMOKO

The urge to classify, to construct taxonomies, is a basic intellectual response to chaos. The record of armed conflict in the Third World since the end of the Second World War does, at first glance, give an impression of chaos. The vast majority of the more than 150 wars[1] that have been fought in the last forty years have been fought in the Third World, many with the direct or indirect participation of external powers.

There are at least three conclusions that might emerge out of an attempt to discern patterns in the apparent chaos. One is that armed conflicts in the Third World are a cluster of isolated instances, each unique in its causes, circumstances and possible solutions. A second possible conclusion is that armed conflicts in the developing countries are expressions of a common condition and therefore require generalized approaches toward and on the part of the countries involved. The third possibility is that the interaction of Third World conditions with an unstable international environment implies a much more complex answer than either of the other two. The available evidence—and it is abundant—comes closest, in this writer's view, to supporting this third conclusion.

What do the diverse countries of the Third World have in common, apart from their location in Africa, Asia or Latin America, that makes "Third World armed conflicts" an inter-

*The author would like to thank Kathleen Newland for her valuable assistance in the research and writing of this paper. The views presented in this paper are those of the author and do not necessarily represent those of the United Nations University.

esting category for consideration? Most developing countries share the experience of colonial domination, though the nature and duration of it varies tremendously among them. Most of them are poor. Perhaps most importantly, most are engulfed in a process of very profound social and economic transformation that, though a necessary condition for development, is in itself a source of instability.

There is also a psychological sense of belonging to the Third World, which arises from the recognition that the international system is dominated by and directed for the primary benefit of countries that exclude the Third World from decision-making and a fair share of the benefits of interaction. The resulting sense of vulnerability and exclusion—and the often angry sense of injustice that accompanies it—is one factor that gives the countries of the Third World some sense of solidarity despite their great diversity and the considerable dissension among them.

The dislocations caused by rapid and extensive change make countries vulnerable to conflict arising from both internal and external sources. Adjustment to the developments of the late twentieth century is threatening enough to the equanimity of any society without the further challenge of trying to compress centuries of technological change and nation-building into the span of a few decades.

It is important to keep in mind, however, that the process of social transformation is by no means confined to the Third World. All countries are in some measure caught up in sweeping value changes that respond to new technologies and modes of organization, and to a pace and scale of change that is unprecedented in human experience. It is not only in the Third World that the re-examination of old and newer values has led to challenges to the state. The function, purpose, character and structure of the state encounter challenges from neo-conservatives and religious fundamentalists in the United States, from "green" parties in Europe, from minority nationalities in the Soviet Union, as well as from numerous social and political movements in the Third World.

Reference is often made, particularly in the context of the Islamic world, to a struggle between the twelfth and the twenty-first centuries—that is to say, between the Age of Faith and the

Space Age. It may be more honest to acknowledge that this is a struggle that engages all countries to some extent. Many of today's conflicts are products of the inability to manage change. Others have their roots in contradictory perceptions of and beliefs about change. The complexity of the interlinkages among problems creates in many minds a longing for simple, reductionist explanations, whose foundations in reality are so insecure that they have no capacity for tolerance of other approaches.

No region has quite mastered the dislocations of the twentieth century, with its dizzying growth of populations and massive movements of people, its instant communications, alienating technologies, shrunken spaces, and horrifying destructive power—and so all remain vulnerable to conflict. The category "Third World" is therefore a fairly arbitrary one on any grounds except geography and psychology. It would be difficult, for example to draw a clear distinction between the conflict in Northern Ireland and many of the ongoing conflicts in the Third World. Nonetheless, three of the widely shared qualities that have been mentioned—colonialism, poverty, and accelerated change—do give armed conflicts in the Third World some distinctive characteristics.

One further distinguishing characteristic should perhaps be mentioned: with the achievement of functional nuclear parity between the superpowers, and the virtually uncontested recognition of spheres of influence dominated by one or the other in the North, the Third World has become the only "safe" battleground for the contest between East and West. Neither side is yet willing to run a serious risk of direct nuclear confrontation, which is implied by any armed conflict between them in the industrialized world. Thus the Third World has become a theater, in both the military and the dramatic sense, of East-West competition. Of course this competition is not a factor in all armed conflicts in or among developing countries, but it has prolonged and intensified many of those in which it is not a prominent cause.

Patterns of armed conflict in the Third World can be constructed in a number of different ways—all of them, inevitably, somewhat arbitrary. Few if any disputes that erupt into sustained violence fall easily into a single category. However, a useful approach to the identification of patterns is to identify the kinds of issues that have commonly given rise to armed conflict. The present attempt has arrived at five categories, all of which overlap very considerably in the real world. They are: (1) conflicts over national borders, (2) conflicts with or among minority groups, (3) conflicts involving questions of self-determination, (4) distributive disputes within or among states or regions, and (5) systemic conflicts. The examples chosen to illustrate these patterns are neither comprehensive nor unequivocal. They are merely illustrative.

The majority of boundary disputes in the Third World are the legacy of colonialism, and they are primarily of three kinds. The arbitrary drawing of lines on the map has balkanized some nationalities, leading to irredentist claims such as that of Somalia to the Somali-inhabited parts of Ethiopia and Kenya. It has artificially amalgamated others—often traditional enemies such as the Ndeles and the Shona in Zimbabwe; the Sara, the Arab clans, and the Toubou in Chad; the upland and lowland peoples of Burma and parts of Indochina—whose long-standing enmities were suppressed but not resolved under colonial rule. Very often such ethnic divisions were compounded by religious divisions, as for example between the Muslim Fulani and the largely Christian Ibo in Nigeria. In these and many other such cases hostility re-surfaced after independence and burst into armed conflict.

A third and particularly tragic result of colonial division of territory has been the attempt to create homogeneous states out of ethnically diverse regions, contributing to some of the worst humanitarian disasters in the context of armed conflict experienced in the post-war period—for example the exhanges of population and blood between India and Pakistan at the time of partition, and the interminable and complex aftermath of the creation of the state of Israel. There are, of course, border conflicts in the Third World that go beyond the problems of colonial map-making. The Sino-Indian war, for example, seems to have had more to do with new accessibility and strategic importance of remote border regions that in earlier times were beyond control or concern.

Closely connected in many cases to the artificiality of boundaries are conflicts that arise from tensions between minority and majority groups, or among minorities. The minorities involved in disputes that lead to armed conflict may be one of four types. The first that come to the minds of most people are probably the oppressed minorities who demand equal treatment or greater autonomy. In such cases as those of the Tamils in Sri Lanka, the Miskitos in Nicaragua, the Muslims in the southern Philippines, and many indigenous people in Asia and Latin America, inertia or outright resistance to their demands leads some among them to accept violence as the only way of breaking the impasse. Once resorted to, violence enters an escalating spiral of repression, resistance and reaction.

Armed conflict may also be the end result of disputes with achieving minorites, as the situation of the Sikh community in India graphically demonstrates. Resentment against an achieving minority is particularly bitter in those cases where the achieving group was preferred, or used and rewarded, by a former colonial ruler. The British philosophy of "divide and rule" left many minority groups in an exposed position—notably the groups of Asian expatriates who were introduced into colonies as far-flung as British Guyana, Malaya and Uganda in order to function as commercial middlemen, minor bureaucrats and in some cases professionals to service communities of laborers of the same stock.

Similarly, the overseas Chinese communities throughout Southeast Asia were preferred to the native populations as commercial and financial collaborators with the colonizers. Unequal treatment gave indigenous or imported minority groups a toehold on the economic ladder which some of them managed to parlay into lasting achievements through hard work and community solidarity. But their success carries with it a legacy of resentment that can easily become violent, especially in times of general economic difficulty.

Competing minorities, too, may generate violent confrontation. The illegal entry of Salvadorans into Honduras in the period leading up to the 1969 war between those two countries is one example of competition for jobs, land and resources leading to border tensions and finally to military engagement. There have been repeated bloody clashes in the Indian state of Assam between the native Assamese and land-hungry immigrants from across the border in Bangladesh. Recently, relations between Nigeria and Ghana have been severely strained by the forcible expulsion of Ghanaian workers whose competition for jobs became increasingly unwelcome as the slipping price of oil caused Nigeria's economy to deteriorate. Fortunately, these two countries have not shown any inclination to fight over the issue, but it is clear that episodes of this kind can set the stage for armed conflict. In the future, the pressure of rapidly growing labor forces on severely strained economic bases is likely to exacerbate the risk associated with this source of tension.

Finally, there is the sort of armed conflict generated by an oppressor minority's attempt to defend its position of privilege against the demands for social justice of the majority. In this class, the most familiar example is that of the South African white minority. Another is the uprising of the Hutu majority against the dominant Tutsi minority in Rwanda in the 1960s, which ultimately reduced the Tutsi population of that country from 15 percent to only 9 percent of the total, through a combination of slaughter and mass exodus.[2]

It is often difficult to make a clear distinction between minority issues and issues of self-determination and sovereignty, since minority demands so often develop into demands for self-determination in the form of regional autonomy or even independent statehood. The separatist movements of the Moros, the Kurds, and the Sikhs grew out of their dissatisfaction with their relations as minorities with the state. Secessionist movements, however, often go beyond this dissatisfaction, to the conviction that, even if fairly treated, a people such as the Eritreans want and have a right to an independent state of their own. The clearest illustrations of this sentiment are those arising from colonization, and from this clarity flows the almost universal sympathy for the struggle of the people of Namibia, for example.

Cases of post-colonial (or non-European) imperialism should on the same principle attract opprobrium for the empire-builders and sympathy for the victims of their ambitions, but these situations seldom generate such unanimity. The Organization of African Unity (OAU) has been deeply divided over the question of who should govern the Western Sahara, and controversy continues about the establishment of Indonesian sovereignty over East Timor. Libya has effectively annexed the Aou-zou strip of northern Chad to the great consternation of its neighbors and the international community, and Vietnam's presence in Cambodia is entrenched though not approved. In short, well past the supposed end of the colonial era, issues of self-determination remain one of the primary causes of armed conflict in the Third World.

Disputes over the distribution of the wealth of a nation, or the fruits of development, are another of the major causes of conflict. While these, too, often follow ethnic, religious, or racial lines, such factors are commonly intertwined with class divisions, rural-urban divisions, or regional divisions. They may have inter-state dimensions as well, as when the disputed re-sources require regional management, or have special strategic significance. In early 1985, the Egyptian Minister of State for Foreign Affairs, Dr. Butros Butros Ghali, was quoted as saying, "The next war in our region will be over the waters of the Nile, not politics".[3] Whether his prediction comes true or not, it illustrates the sensitivity that attaches to vital natural resources.

The distribution of land is one of the most ubiquitous and volatile of the issues that generate violence between communi-ties and nations. In most of Central America, land reform is a prerequisite for an end to the threat or the fact of civil war. Officially sponsored settlement programs have provoked armed conflicts between settlers and tribal peoples in Bangladesh, In-donesia and Brazil, among other countries. And in the poorest countries, the groundwork for conflict is being laid as rapidly growing populations press upon an agricultural base whose potential is in some cases actually declining through neglect or abuse.

Conflicts over the distribution of resources between states encompass many of the more traditional forms of inter-state rivalry: some kinds of boundary disputes, land-grabs such as the Zairean attempt to annex oil-rich Cabinda province from Angola, arguments over the distribution of river-waters or aqui-fers, conflicts over fishing rights and other uses of territorial waters, and disputes concerning access to strategic minerals. Other, intangible resources might also be mentioned here, in-cluding navigational rights (e.g. the Suez and Panama Canals and the Shatt al Arab waterway) and access to strategic positions (the Golan Heights, for example). All of the preceding have contributed to the flare-up of armed conflicts.

Distributive disputes within and among states often veer toward the fifth pattern of armed conflict, which is that of a systemic nature. In the case of internal conflicts, the search for solutions to basic problems of distribution may itself lead to armed conflict, as ideological contention over economic strategies degenerates into violent confrontation. This is clearly one element of the disputes between the government and the armed opposition movements in El Salvador, Nicaragua, Angola and Mozambique.

Inter-state conflicts often take on a broader, systemic dimension when the disputed resource is seen as vital for the maintenance of one of the contending systems. The recent apparent attempt by South African commandos to attack the oil refinery in Cabinda underscores how crucial that facility is seen to be for the economic viability of the Angolan state—a perception that is shared by both the supporters and the opponents of the state system in Angola. The retention of the West Bank and the Golan Heights is seen by Israeli decision-makers as vital to the continuing existence of the state.

In general, systemic conflicts may be characterized as ideological in character (including religious ideology); as dedicated to the extension of certain regimes of force or of principles; or as defense of an existing balance of power, sphere of influence or alliance system. It is difficult to find pure examples of ideologically based armed conflict, though ideology is a factor in many cases such as the ones in Central America and Africa, mentioned above. Similarly, religious ideology is an important element in the Gulf war between Iran and Iraq, and in Iran's involvement in other armed conflicts throughout the region—though it is only one part of the struggle for leadership taking place against the complex background of Middle Eastern radical politics.

The use of armed force to further either a political project or a moral cause is a category that may seem to combine very disparate elements; yet it is often a matter of judgment and perspective as to which pole of this classification is closer to a given conflict. The Cuban presence in Angola is presented by the Cuban government as a contribution to the historical process of self-determination and the defense of Angola's national sovereignty. It is portrayed by the US government, however, as a simple extension of Soviet power in the region.

Libya's various attempts at coalition and conquest in North Africa are seen by some as crude expressions of hegemonial ambitions, but presumably by Colonel Q'addafi as attempts to realize the dream of a greater and purer Islamic Maghreb. The Tanzanian invasion of Uganda, the Vietnamese invasion of Kampuchea, and the Indian invasion of East Pakistan are three examples of military action that put an end to situations of grave injustice and violation of accepted humanitarian norms. But in all cases, the regional political aspirations of the invading state were also served. The continuing conflicts of the front-line states with South Africa are less ambiguous, in that all pay a severe military and economic price for their efforts to put an end to the system of apartheid.

The third form of systemic conflict is that in which armed force is used to maintain, at the regional or global level, a balance of power, sphere of influence, or alliance system. The wars of the last thirty years in Indo-China, though they contain elements from virtually every other category, are perhaps dominated by factors from this category: the effort to maintain the French colonial empire; the US attempt to prevent the countries of the region from escaping the western sphere of influence; and Vietnam's establishment of domination over Laos and Kampuchea, which has led it into confrontation with Thailand and China. The US involvement in Central America is another example of system-maintenance as a motivation for armed conflict, as is the Soviet intervention in Afghanistan—though the two conflicts are quite different in scale, depth of involvement, and a number of other dimensions.

In general, systemic conflicts tend to be among the most bitter and intractable, since the parties involved often see themselves as fighting for their very existence—not only for their lives but for the continuation in the future of the principles, beliefs and structures for which they have lived.

The problem with classifications is that they are essentially static. The patterns of armed conflict in the Third World today are imbedded in an historical process that exposes all developing countries to tremendous turmoil and fragmentation. In some cases, as was pointed out, this turmoil is part of the struggle to throw off the remnants of colonial structures and power relationships. But in many others, the end of the colonial era has been followed in short order by a new period of violent contention as mechanisms for political representation and civic participation have failed to take hold.

In a number of countries, the state apparatus has been captured by one class or ethnic group, which has used it exclusively for its own advancement. But even without the willful appropriation of state power, the development process itself generates tensions and inequalities that a representative government must mediate. Mediation, however, requires strong political, economic, and legal institutions, which are lacking in much of the developing world. All too often, therefore, states have failed in or abandoned their mediating roles and substituted repression for social management.

In many instances, Third World states have compounded the error by inviting external military assistance to help them deal with the violent reactions engendered by developmental and distributive failures. Their opponents have of course responded in kind—or perhaps initiated the process to begin with. Thus in many cases Third World governments and opposition movements alike have lost control of the duration and intensity of their conflicts. The less successful they are in dealing with internal disputes through the exercise of persuasion, negotiation and accomodation, the more vulnerable they become to external interference—often, ironically, by invitation.

The volatility of a world that is going through a period of fundamental transformation creates a tinderbox effect in which conflict cannot easily be avoided or contained. The range of combustible materials is vast. One of the flaws of modern political science is perhaps a tendency to reduce the causes of conflict to rather bloodless assessments of the interests or organizational imperatives of various actors. It is terribly difficult to capture in this kind of framework the tremendously powerful forces that underlie much of the armed conflict in the Third World. The passions that lead people to kill and die for often intangible attachments—to a mother tongue, to a religion, to recognition of certain rights, to recovery or establishment of identity—are not within the power of governments to control, though governments and opposition movements often attempt to manipulate them.

The frequency with which these passions are misread, misinterpreted or simply overlooked is such as to tempt one to define a sixth class of armed conflict: war by miscalculation, or war by underestimation. One can scarcely begin to count the number of armed conflicts that have been based on faulty perceptions of the monolithic nature of Communism, of the power of independent nationalism, or the depth of ethnic passions; on the overestimation of the pacifying power of prosperity or on the underestimation of religion as a motivating force in politics.

Two current instances of armed conflict in the Indian subcontinent illustrate the ease with which deep currents of feeling are overlooked. The Indian Punjab has been repeatedly cited as one of the great success stories of the region for its great strides in agricultural productivity leading to remarkable economic growth. In a similar manner Sri Lanka has been cited for its success in achieving a high quality of life and a relatively egalitarian distribution of income even under the constraints of poverty. Both have been taken as exemplary cases of kinds of developmental success that have been widely supposed to innoculate an area against violent conflict. Yet today both are in flames, for very complex reasons. The depth of Sikh and Tamil feelings of grievance were not reckoned on, nor was the powerful backlash of majority communities.

Perhaps the most spectacular recent example of this sort of failure to perceive the powerful currents of feeling that channel the course of history was the Islamic Revolution in Iran. Waves of Islamic activism have flowed from its success to a number of different parts of the world.

These powerful currents that emanate from within the Third World play themselves out in the context of an unstable international system characterized by a number of dynamic currents. One is the progressive weakening or disintegration of less viable states such as pre-1972 Pakistan, and perhaps today's Lebanon or Chad. A second is the consolidation or attempted consolidation of new power configurations under regional hegemonic powers such as Libya in North Africa or India in the subcontinent. A third and related trend is the emergence of new econ-

omic and political centers of power, such as the newly industrialized countries (NICs) of East Asia as well as, of course, China.
A fourth is the interpenetration of traditional spheres of influence in a context of persistent or even heightened East-West
polarization. In this setting, the demand for self-determination
is sometimes an integrating and sometimes a disintegrating
force.

East-West and North-South issues have become even more
inextricably intertwined as the superpowers have symmetrically
and strongly committed themselves to a global projection of
force. The mere fact that one of the superpowers is arming and
otherwise supporting one party to an armed conflict is reason
enough for the other to back its opponent—though not without
restraint. The Soviet Union, for example, has been extremely
circumspect about its material support for Nicaragua; and in a
similar way the US has been careful about direct involvement
with the Afghan resistance. In neither case is one power in any
doubt about the desires of the other, but neither displays an
appetite for direct confrontation in the other's backyard. This
is of course a profound relief, but its effect on armed conflicts
in the Third World has been, in many cases, to inject an element
of proxyism that, as mentioned earlier, prolongs and intensifies
conflict. It has also made the position of former buffer states
such as Kampuchea and Afghanistan untenable, and subjected
them to a complete loss of autonomy.

The commitment to global force projection has drawn a
number of Third World countries very closely into the strategic
networks of the superpowers, because of the importance of
forward basing-areas for rapid deployment forces, ports for
blue-water navies, and air bases. It is thus all but impossible
for armed conflicts over issues of modernization, national integration and political succession in countries such as the Philippines and Afghanistan to be resolved according to a purely
internal logic.

The volatility of alliances between Third World states and
major powers has been amply demonstrated. In the Horn of
Africa, for example, Somalia has switched from Soviet to
American patronage while Ethiopia has made the opposite
exchange. The self-interests of the major powers are consistently
given priority over the interests of relatively weaker client states.

Pressures from domestic and bureaucratic rivalries within the big powers may work for or against various parties to Third World conflicts, but the Third World's ability to influence the direction of such pressures is in most cases very limited.

The role of superpower client, which is supposed to offer a strong degree of protection to the client, also carries with it a constant exposure to the risk of interference, of external support for internal dissenters, of destabilization. It is this realization, presumably, that has led Johan Galtung to recommend, as three of the four central elements of a more effective and independent security policy, that countries decouple their vital interests from the superpowers, arm themselves with defensive weapons only, and cultivate friendly and productive relations with countries at all points on the political spectrum.[4]

Dr. Galtung's fourth recommendation is that countries do everything in their power to build up their "internal strength", a recognition that instability creates the opportunity for armed intervention by external powers.[5] This is not to suggest that countries that are subject to intervention always bring it on themselves by a failure to keep their own houses in order. It is nonetheless true that injustice, lack of participation and a festering sense of unresolved grievance are breeding grounds for violence that may easily lead to armed conflict.

The foregoing may seem a truism, but it is frequently argued that the preservation of peace may require the acceptance of an unjust status quo.[6] The evils of armed conflict are weighed against the evils of the less-than-perfect reality and found heavier. So, for example, the member states of the OAU operate on the principle of respect for existing boundaries, though they themselves condemn the manner in which carelessly drawn boundaries violate the ethnic geography of the continent. Clinging to the status quo is seen as the only way to avoid bloody struggles in which no state or people could be sure of winning.

The idea that a flawed peace is preferable to almost any war is compelling in many circumstances, but there are two characteristics of contemporary armed struggle that rob the argument of its logic. One is the easy availability and vastly increased destructive power of modern weapons. The second is the willingness, discussed above, of external powers to supply and support armed resistance within states or armed conflict between states in pursuit of their own political or strategic objectives.

The increased sophistication and portability of weapons, the ease of manufacture of explosives, the eagerness of arms manufacturers of both the public and the private sectors to sell their wares, all mean that even very small groups can inflict enormous damage—enough to keep a society in chaos and effectively derail its development efforts. In earlier times, it would hardly have made sense to speak of the activities of fifteen people as "armed conflict". Yet a cell of only fifteen rightists uncovered by the Argentine authorities in May, 1985, was found to be equipped not only with small arms and military uniforms but also with high-powered explosives, sophisticated transmitting equipment and napalm-carrying warheads.[7]

The effectiveness of small groups in armed conflict is illustrated by the history of mercenary involvement in successful and near-successful coups in Africa in the post-colonial period. The 1975 coup that installed Ali Solih as president of the Comoro Islands was accomplished by a total force of eight men. The coup that removed Solih from power in 1978 and re-installed his predecessor was carried out by 45 mercenaries under the same leader who directed the 1975 coup.[8] Very small states with weak military forces and highly centralized (often in one person) power structures are particularly susceptible to the small, mercenary strike-force. The number of tempting targets for mercenary action is likely to grow with the importance of small states in politically volatile and strategically sensitive regions.

The ease with which serious violent disruption can be sustained by small groups if they are well armed, well financed and well trained has reduced the cost of interference in the internal affairs of another country and raised its pay-off. An adversary, or an adversary's client, can be kept off balance through the prolongation of armed conflict of the hit-and-run variety. This pattern is usually referred to as terrorism, though much of it is sporadic by virtue of limited means rather than a philosophy of unpredictability.

In order to operate successfully even at a fairly low level of intensity, armed groups need some base of local sympathy in order to conceal their activities and evade detection. Unresolved grievances and the persistence of an unjust status quo nurture the sympathy that the guerrilla and, to a lesser extent, the terrorist rely upon. The New People's Army of the Philippines is said even by the Philippine army to control or at least have friendly access to 20 percent of the villages in the country,[9] and is thus virtually indestructible by conventional military means. The spread of terrorism, and its growing sophistication as a means of political struggle, has also been encouraged by the failure to find solutions to protracted conflicts.

The function of the local base may also be filled by the adjacent sanctuary, if bordering states have populations or governments willing to harbor opposition forces. Sri Lankan negotiations with India in mid-1985 were a recognition of the fact that unless Tamil separatists operating from bases in the Indian state of Tamil Nadu could be prevented from crossing into Sri Lanka, no military solution to the conflict could be attained.

Since any group with a grievance and a domestic power base can find potent means—if necessary from outside—to disturb if not destroy the peace, it follows that the acceptance of unjust situations is not an alternative to armed conflict but a recipe for it. The only real alternative is political accommodation with the aggrieved groups. This, obviously, is easier to achieve before the resort to arms rather than after violent confrontation has heightened and polarized sentiments, and weakened the will to compromise.

In a context that makes resort to violence so easy, the peaceful management of conflict requires a great capacity for political innovation. There is no formula that can be applied across the board, although there are many valuable examples. There is, for example, the internal peace treaty negotiated by the Government of Colombia with the main domestic guerrilla movements there in 1984, and the unilateral amnesty declared in 1980 by Thailand toward domestic Communist insurgents who agreed to lay down their arms and re-enter Thai society.[10] The regional conflict-resolution effort of the Contadora group is innovative both in its proposals and its methodology. The Contadora method involves all parties in thorough exploration of the issues and discussion of negotiable positions before the process of formal negotiation begins. The group's most recent proposals

deal with domestic political issues as well as international security issues of concern to the Central American states.[11]

Highly innovative and constructive proposals will not, however, change the pattern of armed conflict in the Third World
or elsewhere without some commitment to their implementation. The Contadora process seems to be stalled, one hopes
temporarily, on this reality.

Virtually every failed proposal for constructive change
founders on this question of political will. Changing the current
destructive patterns of armed conflict in the Third World, however, does not require the wholesale adoption of new policies
or negotiating formulae. It requires something that is perhaps
a little easier to achieve: restraint.

The needed restraint has two major dimensions, one internal
to the decision-making structures of parties to Third World
conflicts, and one to be exercised by external powers. The first
of these applies chiefly to the ways in which actors in the
developing countries express and pursue the very real disputes
among themselves. All have a stake in the peaceful resolution
of conflicts, limits on the production and importation of arms,
and the vigorous application and extension of humanitarian
law.

Above all, it is in the interest of the developing countries to
wean themselves from external military support and involvement, for two compelling reasons. One is that external involvement almost always increases the scale and destructiveness of
conflicts, by providing weapons that multiply the number of
casualties (especially, in recent decades, civilian casualties) and
do considerable damage to the social and economic infrastruc-
ture of the area of conflict. For example, US military aid to El
Salvador, which more than doubled from 1983 to 1984 to reach
a level of $ 196.5 million, was invested in part in a dramatically
increased capacity for aerial bombardment. US-supplied combat helicopters increased from 15 to as many as 50 from the
one year to the next; gunship helicopters and at least one C-47
"airborne fire-support platform" were also supplied. As a result,
according to the Institute for Strategic Studies, "this caused
such an increase in civilian casualties that widespread concern
forced President Duarte in September to promise a tightening
of the rules for bombing".[12]

When one party to a dispute turns to outsiders for support, its adversaries are encouraged to do the same, thereby subjecting the country or region to the expression of rivalries and antagonisms in which it has no direct stake. External military aid is often the trigger for region-wide arms races, which drain the resources and heighten the tension level of the countries involved. The external patron may discourage client governments or factions from entering into negotiations or seriously pursuing negotiations that do get started. It may prefer to continue an armed conflict that costs it relatively little but is an effective source of discomfiture to its rivals. The current stalemate of the Contadora effort, for example, seems to owe much to the United States' reluctance to see the Sandinista regime in Nicaragua come to terms with its challengers.

The second compelling reason to forego external assistance is that such assistance undermines the autonomy of the recipient to such an extent that even the winner of a battle for control of a state may end up with a Pyrrhic victory. Measured against the loss of political independence and the danger of re-subjugation to the interests of external powers, the political or ideological goals of the combatants must be reassessed. Furthermore, the acceptance of external aid often entails a serious sacrifice of legitimacy, as the American-backed regimes in South Vietnam, the Soviet-backed regimes in Afghanistan, and the Vietnamese-backed regime in Kampuchea have discovered to their own and their patron's frustration. The legitimacy of UNITA in Angola and FROLINAT in Chad are similarly tainted by South African and Libyan patronage, respectively.

For the sake of limiting the destructiveness and the duration of armed conflicts, as well as to protect claims to legitimacy, restraint in seeking external military assistance is a serious consideration for all parties to armed conflict in the Third World. But such a regime of self-restraint is unlikely to hold up without a symmetrical restraint on the part of the external powers themselves. In increasing numbers of armed conflicts in the Third World, the external intervenor is not one of the superpowers nor one of the former colonial powers but rather one of the more powerful Third World states—such as India, Libya, Vietnam, and Tanzania, to name just a few. Therefore, any code of conduct that might be devised to discourage interference in armed conflicts will have to be negotiated on an inclusive basis, though regional organizations are often promising venues for initiating such discussions.

Restraint on the part of potential interventionist states has a powerful potential for limiting the scope of armed conflict in the Third World, given that few developing countries have sophisticated arms industries of their own. Only Brazil, China, India, Israel, South Africa and Taiwan have significant arms manufacturing capacity. Few other developing countries even approach self-sufficiency, and although the arms imports of the Third World countries as a whole have increased dramatically in the last twenty years, many of the non-oil exporting states are dependent upon military aid or credit.

Lest a regime of restraint in supplying Third World countries with the weapons to cripple each other be thought utterly utopian, it is worth recalling the considerable progress that was made in the late 1970s in one effort to negotiate such an agreement in a strategically very sensitive part of the world. The negotiations on transfer of conventional weapons involving the major countries of Latin America as well as consultations with the United States, the Soviet Union and other major arms-exporting countries did make substantial strides toward an agreement to lower the influx of weapons into that troubled region.[13] The deterioration of détente in the aftermath of the Soviet invasion of Afghanistan, and the advent of a more conservative US administration with little predilection for arms control, were among the factors that derailed those negotiations. But the progress made sets a valuable precedent that can be applied in other regions and, one hopes, revived in the region where it began.

A more demanding form of restraint on the part of external parties requires a narrow interpretation of the kinds of political developments that constitute threats to their national interests. Demanding as this is, however, it is not the same as insisting that states subordinate their national interests to higher principles such as respect for self-determination—for this, the realist must admit, is not likely to be accepted by powerful states in the near future.

Restraint in defining one's legitimate national security interests requires making a distinction between developments that are threatening and those that are merely distateful. The accession to power of a leftist regime in Nicaragua is certainly profoundly distasteful to the current US administration, but it is difficult to convince most of the community of nations that Nicaragua is a genuine threat to the security of the United States. Ironically, it becomes more of one the more it is forced to rely on the Soviet Union and its allies in order to protect its independence against US intervention. Perhaps the most valuable immediate effect of the Contadora effort has been to prevent the isolation of Nicaragua and the stark clientism that would almost certainly result.

The United States is showing a remarkable absence of restraint in defining threat in Central America—seeming almost to equate any degree of foreign policy independence or any social movement opposed to the social and economic status quo with a threat to US interests. Yet the US relationship with Mexico amply demonstrates that an independent foreign policy can be pursued even by a close neighbor without compromising security. A more plausible threat to US national security is in fact the persistence of the status quo in Central America. As Robert S. Leiken puts it, "Moscow's chief strategic asset in Central America is the United States' long backing of reactionary oligarchies and the legacy of anti-Yankeeism".[14]

A similar lack of restraint in perceiving threats may be seen in the Soviet decision to invade Afghanistan. In this case the realism of the Soviet fear of domestic contagion from Islamic fundamentalism is difficult to assess, but Soviet determination to consolidate a hold on a state it regards as belonging to its own sphere of influence shows a grave lack of restraint. One extremely important aspect of restraint that is negatively illustrated here concerns the role of buffer states. What is needed is a mutually acceptable definition of the internal power configurations and external policies that a buffer state can adopt and still be left alone by its more powerful neighbors.

Governments and non-governmental actors are motivated to observe restraints either because they recognize a moral imperative shored up by the approbation of the international community, or because they calculate the utilitarian value of reciprocal restraint on the part of adversaries. Any state that chooses to ignore restraints must calculate that its willingness to do so will inevitably encourage others to do the same; its calculations of self-interest must weigh the short-term advantages that might be gained in a particular conflict against the cost of achieving its objectives in an environment made more dangerous and difficult by a generalized lack of restraint.

The primary obstacle to restraint is desperation, and in that the Third World abounds. To reduce the sources of armed conflict there, as in the North, will call upon the deepest reserves of political innovation that governments and other political actors can command. The task is obviously not one for the Third World alone, given how closely its turbulence is tied to that of the international system as a whole.

Just as the countries of the North have a stake in reducing the occurrence of armed conflict in the South, the South has a direct stake in the restoration of East-West détente. This stake goes beyond the obvious one of avoiding the Third World War and the probability of a dreadful nuclear winter to follow. Superpower competition threatens a virtual recolonization of the Third World; it also assures a diversion of their scarce resources into military confrontations beyond their power to control. Détente is almost a prerequisite for peaceful and autonomous development in the Third World. The Third World, therefore, cannot afford to remain passive, but must actively involve itself in the struggle to restore détente and see that the concept extends beyond Europe and North America.

The patterns of armed conflict in the Third World are more like a kaleidoscope than a patchwork quilt: the patterns are constantly shifting. Unlike a kaleidoscope, the variations are not predictable, and the elements of change are not contained within a finite system. The volatility of the interactions between the Third World and the international system and among the developing countries themselves cannot be overestimated. The foreign policy priorities of the present superpowers are unpredictable; even more so the future course of Chinese foreign policy and that of other emerging powers. The stability of alliance systems, regionally and globally, cannot be taken for granted. The precarious economic situation of many developing countries raises serious questions about their ability to achieve or maintain political stability.

In the light of this extremely unsettled context, the prospect of nuclear proliferation in the Third World is terrifying. Yet it is very likely that new and existing tensions will lead countries, and possibly even some non-state actors, to an all-out effort to acquire nuclear weapons. The most powerful incentive for any nation to do so is the assumption that its opponents are planning to do the same, or have actually embarked upon the process. This vicious spiral is already underway: between India and Pakistan, Brazil and Argentina, South Africa and the front-line states, Israel and Iraq.

The growth of the nuclear power industry raises the risk of proliferation in two ways. The diversion of weapons-grade uranium and plutonium from conventional reactors has been constrained in large part by suppliers' and manufacturers' safeguards. However, the current economic crisis in the nuclear power industry has turned the reactor business into a buyers' market. There is a danger of a consequent bidding-down of safeguards by countries that are in a position to buy reactors. Secondly, the spread of nuclear power is beginning to put such quantities of plutonium into circulation that preventing the diversion of the tiny amount needed to construct a small weapon begins to seem a Herculean task. The development of the breeder reactor, even if it operates only in the industrial countries, promises greatly to aggravate this problem.

If there has never before been a sufficiently compelling reason for nations to cooperate in managing conflicts and attempting to eradicate their causes, the prospect of one or two or half a dozen more Hiroshimas—to say nothing of the risk of larger conflagrations and the risk of general escalation—should be enough to force a reconsideration.

DISCUSSIONS

K. Subrahmanyam

There is very little in Dr Soedjatmoko's presentation with which I am in disagreement. My comments will therefore be by way of supplementing certain aspects in his presentation which may help towards a fuller understanding of the conflicts in the developing world.

It has been pointed out often enough that since the end of the Second World War barring a few most of approximately 150 major instances of inter- and intra-state violence have taken place in the developing world. But what is often overlooked is that in about two thirds of these conflicts there was intervention by the developed world, either direct or indirect. It has been computed that in these conflicts nearly 20 million people died. Half of these casualties were caused by the armed forces of the developed world in Korea, Indochina, Algeria and other anti-colonial wars. While there might have been peace in the territories covered by the developed nations it would be totally incorrect to conclude that the developed nations have ceased to be warlike. They have been fighting wars away from Europe and North America.

In spite of the increasing capacity to produce armaments in the developing world over 95 percent of the arms requirements of the developing world are supplied by the developed world—mainly by six major industrialized powers. Deplorable as it is in the prolonged war between Iran and Iraq what is noteworthy is that there has been no move to have a UN embargo on arms supplies to the two belligerents as there was during the Indo-Pakistan war of 1965. It is difficult to believe that when the two superpowers profess to have a policy of non-intervention it is still not possible for the Security Council to act to enforce an arms embargo.

In most of the Western strategic literature of late, a composite picture of the strategic situation of the developing world is drawn on the following lines. The developing world is generally turbulent and in the throes of conflict. The military expenditure of the developing world has gone up manifold. Increasing militarization is taking place at the cost of development. Particularly dangerous is the possibility of some developing nations acquiring nuclear weapons. Let us analyze this picture in some detail.

The turbulence in the developing world is largely the result of stresses and strains undergone during the process of nation-state building. During the three centuries the European and North American states were attempting to evolve into stable nation-states they saw religious wars, sectarian strifes, inter-state wars for various reasons, and two global wars. As mentioned above, they still continue to fight wars outside Europe and North America. The developing nations are under compulsion to telescope the developments of three centuries in Europe into a minor fraction of that period and simultaneously tackle problems of nation-state building, democratization and industrialization which were done sequentially in the European and North American context. The inter-state conflicts in the developing world still constitute a small fraction of the total number. Most are intra-state conflicts and are expected to continue for some time to come.

These conflicts, unfortunate as they are, can be contained and their impact on international peace and security minimized if the major powers of the world, especially the superpowers, would exercise restraint.

Unfortunately this is not happening. According to a recent American study the US has demonstrated force without war from 1946 to 1982 on 259 occasions. The figure for the Soviet Union is somewhat less. Most of these demonstrations of force related to the developing world. This is one of the major causes underlying the sense of insecurity in the developing world. Besides the demonstration of force without war, interventionism occurs in the form of support to dissidents, arms supplies to insurgents, material support to a developing country in dispute with a neighbor and, above all, arms supplies on a selective basis. In some cases the developing countries themselves have invoked the support of superpowers to further their parochial interests. Often unpopular and unrepresentative regimes have sought to use the security relationship with one or the other superpower as an insurance to ensure the regime security—the foremost example of this type being the Shah of Iran.

The superpowers maintain dedicated instrumentalities for intervention. Mr William Colby, the former CIA director, justified the policy of interventionism on the ground that the President had to have various intermediate options ranging from sending a protest note to landing the marines.

The increasing interventionism in the developing world is an offshoot of the Cold War. Nuclear weapons legitimized by the Non-Proliferation Treaty are treated as a currency of power in international relations. Since the Helsinki Accord and the high stakes of the superpowers in preserving the status quo in Europe have stabilized the situation there, the credibility of the deterrent impact of the rival nuclear arsenals is being tested in the moves and counter-moves of the superpowers in the developing world, where the stakes are not high. When pressed hard, a superpower can disentangle itself without loss of face. Hence, as also pointed out by Dr Soedjatmoko, the second Cold War is being fought out in the developing world where all major crisis points lie today.

Dr Brezezenski has written that SALT II lay buried in the sands of Ogaden. Successive US Secretaries of State have maintained that the main issue with the Soviet Union is its non-cooperation in maintaining the US oriented world order—especially in the developing world. The linkage thesis argued that Soviet proclivities to intervene increasingly in the developing world were linked to their achieving nuclear parity with the United States and, according to some, even surpassing it. It is therefore unrealistic to compartmentalize the conflicts in the developing world and the developed world.

Reference was made earlier to the rise in defense expenditure of the developing countries from around 1.5 percent in the early fifties it has shot up to 16 percent in the early eighties. When viewed in a disaggregated manner, however, this perspective distorts the true state of affairs. Firstly, in those thirty years, some 100 new sovereign nations have emerged. Earlier the colonial powers were responsible for their *defense* and presently they have assumed this responsibility themselves. Therefore what was earlier included in the defense expenditure of erstwhile colonial powers is now shown as independant defense expenditure of developing nations. Secondly, a sovereign nation requires a basic security expenditure, and the larger the number of sovereign nations the larger the basic expenditure itself is as a percentage of global military expenditure. If Sweden and Switzerland, which have not seen wars at all for the last 150 years, need more than 3 percent of GNP in terms of defense expenditure, it is difficult to argue that the developing nations beset with problems of nation-building and insecurity should not spend some 3 percent of GNP on defense.

The high profile of defense spending by developing countries is largely due to excessive spending by those developing countries which are close to superpowers in their assessment of threat perceptions. They are rich and can afford to indulge in high defense expenditure. Half of the military expenditure of the developing world is incurred by the Middle East and North African states which export oil; a quarter of the military expenditure of the developing world is incurred by other high-income developing nations, mostly in East and Southeast Asia. Around 90 developing nations of the world, including such large nations as India, Indonesia, Pakistan, and Bangladesh, incur only 4 percent of global military expenditure.

Even this expenditure would not be incurred by them were it not for insecurities created by interventionism, demonstrations of use of force, and selective arms supplies in enormous quantities to the rich developing countries.

It is not contended that without the interventionism of the superpowers the developing world would be peaceful. For the reasons outlined by Dr Soedjatmoko it will continue to be turbulent. A policy of restraint by the superpowers would reduce the risks of war arising out of their interventions, reduce the scale of casualties in wars in the developing world and reduce their sense of insecurity.

On one issue I have major differences of opinion with Dr Soedjatmoko, namely, nuclear proliferation in the developing world. This fear is highly exaggerated and has a certain racist bias. Today, the nuclear weapon powers treat the so-called Non-Proliferation Treaty as a license to unlimited proliferation. Nuclear weapons are shared with allies to whom they will be made available when needed, and these crypto nuclear weapon nations style themselves as non-nuclear nations. The non-aligned nations have been moving a resolution in the UN General Assembly repeatedly that the use of nuclear weapons should be declared a crime against humanity and outlawed. One hundred and twenty-six nations including China and USSR have voted for the resolution. Only 17 nations—15 members of NATO (Greece excepted) and Australia and New Zealand—have been voting against it. These nations insist that they rely on nuclear deterrence and need nuclear weapons for their security. If one set of nations need nuclear weapons for their security—especially those who boast that they have been at peace for the last four decades—it should not be surprising, that others who are often victims of the interventionism of the nuclear weapon powers also feel the need to have nuclear weapons to deter their interventionism. It has been stated that nuclear arsenals operate like the roaring highway traffic; everyone takes note of it and feels deterred from stepping on the highway. If that is the logic, then a few more vehicles on the highway will not make all that much difference.

The danger today is not so much from a few developing countries acquiring a few weapons, but from the horizontal proliferation of nuclear weapons taking place within the Armed Forces of the nuclear weapon powers and their allies. Every nuclear missile submarine is a sovereign decision-making entity in regard to launch of nuclear weapons, since the submarine missiles cannot be kept electronically locked by the national command authorities. The quick reaction alert weapons, which cannot be locked, are a source of risk for terrorist diversion. The unsafeguarded nuclear fissile material facilities of nuclear weapon powers constitute grave risks and there is at least one documented case of diversion of weapon grade enriched uranium from the NUMEC facility in Apollo, Pennsylvania from which Israel was reported to have diverted hundreds of kilograms of enriched uranium in the 1960s.

Earlier, attention was drawn to the fact that nearly half of the 20 million casualties in the wars in the developing world were caused by intervention of the armed forces of the developed world. Carpet bombing and city busting, etc., are part of the Western military strategic tradition. Following this tradition, more than 5 million tons of bombs (more explosives than manufactured in history up to that point of time) were dropped on three countries of Indo-China. Use of nuclear weapons is a continuation of this tradition. It is ironic when these are the facts that questions are raised whether nuclear weapons are safe in the hands of a Khomeini or Qaddafi. If the weapons can be trusted with an unstable and alcoholic Nixon, a senile Mao Tse Tung, a dying Brezhnev or a drugged and sedated Pompidou, why should one worry about leaders of the developing world? Hitler and Mussolini outdid Idi Amins and Qaddafis.

People self-righteously shudder to think about what would have happened if Iran and Iraq had nuclear weapons. Applying the logic advocated by the strategists of the Western world, in that case there would have been no Iran-Iraq war. Stable deterrence would have prevailed.

In the last twenty years no new nation has declared itself explicitly as a nuclear weapon power. Israel and South Africa, which are believed by the developing world to be in possession of nuclear weapons, have been declared by the US and its allies as being non-nuclear. Pakistan has been given a waiver under the US Non-Proliferation Act and the US proclaims that Pakistan has not achieved nuclear weapon status. India has conducted a nuclear explosive test but has not built up an arsenal. All installations of Brazil are under safeguards. Argentina is discussing a mutual inspection arrangement with Brazil. In these circumstances it is obvious that horizontal proliferation of the conventional type is a total non-issue. The real issue is the sky-rocketing proliferation of nuclear weapons by the nuclear weapon powers, the new arms races (the Strategic Defense Initiative and Deep Strike Strategy), and the increasing interventionism of the major powers in the developing world.

General discussion

Although discussion centers around the question of linkages between superpower relationships and Third World disorders, it is very wide-ranging, touching upon a large number of important issues. Discussants also point out that Third World problems have been unduly neglected.

The discussion partly revolves around the question of the combustibles in the unstable Third World situation, i.e. the debt crisis, the population explosion, energy problems, and religious fundamentalism within the context of soft and penetrable states. Several discussants also touch the problems of militarization within the Third World and the flow of arms promoted by the industrialized countries. The latter question is taken up from widely different perspectives; on the one hand, it is seen as a drag on economic development, while on the other it is emphasized that Third World armaments expenditure is quite low compared to that of the developed world.

Discussants largely agree on the identification of conflict

issues in the Third World, and on the elements of instability in the present situation. They differ widely, however, both in their approach to the question of linkages, and as to the causes of Third World conflicts. A number of discussants are mainly preoccupied with the projection of superpower interests in Third World regions, and, as a consequence, of the prevalence of soft states, with the possibility for penetrating the spheres of influence of the opposite party.

Other discussants question the whole concept of superpower-induced conflicts and wars by proxy. An explanation of the mechanisms is thought to be required. A less radical critique of the emphasis on superpower policies is offered by those advocating a counterfactual argument. If one could insulate Third World conflicts from the policies of the developed world, which confrontations would then remain? There is considerable interest in trying to isolate those conflicts that might be considered endemic.

There is, nevertheless, considerable support for the idea that tensions inherent in the superpower rivalry within the developed world might have been eased by a transfer of conflicts to Third World regions. The possibility of repercussions of Third World conflicts upon the developed world is also taken up. Third World leaders have frequently taken advantage of superpower conflicts and looked for opportunities for exploiting their quite predictable behavior. The conflicts in Iraq and Somalia are considered cases in point. Third World instability is thus thought to put additional strain on the superpower relationship.

While regional confrontations, wars by proxy, and power projection into the Third World claim most attention, the sheer magnitude of some Third World problems is emphasized in itself as a future destabilizer on a global scale. The population explosion and the probable, massive transfer of people from the Third to the First World is singled out for particular attention; the energy problem and growth in religious fundamentalism are also recurrent themes.

The discussion focusses on the analysis of Third World problems and superpower involvement rather than on the modalities for changing or improving the situation. Regional solutions to Third World conflicts can be considered a possible avenue, the United Nations and the Security Council thus being bypassed.

The superpowers could be considered to have disqualified themselves as far as conflict resolution is concerned, since they have shown more interest in power projection and very little respect for international law.

The discussion on conflict resolution and the containment of conflicts leads into a prolonged debate on the problems of mutual understanding between the developed and the Third World. The debate touches on the questions of universal social science methodology and the development of national traditions of social science research. From a different point of view it is maintained that lack of knowledge or understanding is not a major stumbling block in the relationship between the Third World and the developing world, certainly not as far as the academic and scientific communities are concerned. It is proving much harder to change attitudes than to get the facts right. Fanaticism on both sides is deeply disturbing, as is the difficulty of making Third World countries and institutions accept reform proposals generated by outsiders.

7

Problems of Crisis Management and Crisis Avoidance in US-Soviet Relations

ALEXANDER L. GEORGE*

In their contributions to this volume Michael Howard, Lawrence Freedman, and John Gaddis have enriched our understanding of why and how the United States and the Soviet Union have managed to avoid war in the past forty years.

Yet, however, valid the explanatory model they put forward to account for the avoidance of the Third World War in the past, it cannot be taken as a reliable or adequate model of the conditions for maintaining peace between the superpowers in the future.

It is commonplace to observe that the superpowers have been more successful in managing war-threatening crises than in avoiding them. One can find no basis in the historical record for confidence that the United States and the Soviet Union have now learned to manage their global rivalry without plunging periodically into dangerous confrontations; or for expecting that they will be able to exert sufficient influence and control over an increasingly fragmented and violence-prone international system to avoid being drawn into regional conflicts by their allies and other actors.

In brief, without being able to predict the time and circumstances we must expect to see the superpowers drawn into dangerous war-threatening crises in the future as in the past. There are several reasons for pessimism in this respect. Crisis avoidance, it must be recognized, is for the superpowers a more

*The author is pleased to acknowledge support from the Carnegie Corporation of New York and the Center for International Security and Arms Control at Stanford University for the research on which this chapter is based.

amorphous objective than crisis management; moreover, it is not an objective to which the two superpowers are equally committed in every situation or capable of achieving even when they wish to do so. There are different kinds of diplomatic crises in US-Soviet relations, some more dangerous than others. Not only are some crises more acceptable (to one side if not both) because they are thought to carry a lesser, controllable risk of war; in the era of thermonuclear weapons some crises have become a substitute for war. That is, some diplomatic crises (e.g. the Berlin Blockade of 1948) may be deliberately initiated by one side in the hope of catalyzing desired changes in the status quo or preventing undesired changes. Other crises (Cuba, 1962) escalate to dangerous levels as a result of miscalculation. The United States and the Soviet Union are drawn into still other crises (for example, those occasioned by the Arab-Israeli conflict) because one or the other superpower knowingly supports a regional ally's resort to military action, acquiesces in it, or fails to exert strong pressure to prevent it.

Nor can the possibility be excluded that war-threatening crises could erupt in Europe in the future. In his insightful and generally reassuring analysis of the conditions which favor continued stability and peace in Europe, Freedman recognizes that profound threats to stability and peace in Europe could nonetheless emerge if either alliance system began to disintegrate. He concludes that "the cohesion of the alliance systems in Europe is as vital for the stability of East-West relations" as is a stable military relationship between the two blocs. Indeed, many thoughtful observers believe that while a war between NATO and the Warsaw Treaty Organization appears quite unlikely in the foreseeable future, should such a war occur it will likely grow out of major political-economic turmoil in East Europe that raises urgent questions in the minds of Soviet leaders as to their ability to maintain even minimal control of East Europe.[1]

The current nuclear relationship between the two superpowers, as Freedman suggests, may well prove to be "extraordinarily stable", capable of withstanding all kinds of weapons developments and the pressures of new diplomatic crises. But this, of course, cannot be taken for granted. It may indeed be difficult to imagine a highly plausible context or scenario in which an inadvertent or deliberate nuclear war occurs in Europe. Efforts to sketch plausible scenarios of this kind invariably lead sophisticated analysts to respond, in effect, with the observation that such a hypothetical set of events is most improbable. History, however, is replete with seemingly improbable occurrences. Hardly anyone, for example, expected that the assassination of Archduke Ferdinand of Austria-Hungary in July 1914 would escalate into a world war. More recently, few would have regarded it as likely that President Truman's decision in late June 1950 to employ American military forces in defense of South Korea would lead to a major war with Communist China before the year was over.

In other words, history warns us that hypothetical future developments that seem quite implausible as well as highly improbable beforehand do occur sometimes in real life and with catastrophic consequences. Accordingly, one need not assign substantial probability to the danger of nuclear war in order to justify efforts to study ways in which it might come about so that prudent measures can be taken to further reduce its likelihood.[2]

Crisis Instability and the Danger of Inadvertent War

Concern over the danger of inadvertent or accidental war has mounted in recent years in response to developments in military technology and changes in force postures. Increased missile accuracies, deployment and forward basing of highly accurate strategic systems that reduce warning time, and developments in warning and alert systems raise the possibility of so-called "decapitation" strikes against vulnerable political and military command posts. As a result of these developments in the strategic military environment in which deterrence has to operate, both American[3] and Soviet[4] analysts express increasing concern over the heightened danger of crisis instability.

Moreover, the prospect of crisis instability is heightened in the European context because, given differences in NATO and WTO force postures and doctrines, Soviet and American military leaders operate with different perspectives and logics in designing political-military strategy. Without a better shared understanding of these differences, the two sides may misinterpret the significance of each other's military alerts in an escalating crisis and over-react. The danger that one side's actions and intended signals will be misinterpreted by the other side is increased by the fact that the United States and the Soviet Union do not have identical views about the types of force deployments and actions that pose threats to crisis stability.[5]

It should be noted in this connection that the history of major Soviet defeats early in the Second World War has led to an emphasis in Soviet military doctrine on pre-emption if war appears inevitable.[6] It is not surprising, therefore, to detect in some Soviet discussions of crisis instability tacit recognition of, and grave concern over the possibility that in a tense crisis either side's military leaders might urgently recommend a preemptive strike of some kind to their top-level political authorities. This possibility is, as would be expected, articulated more openly by Western analysts, for example by John Steinbruner: "If war should ever appear unavoidable, military commanders on both sides charged with executing their assigned missions would inevitably seek authority to initiate attack, whatever prior security policy may have been ... The pressures on political leaders at that point would be extreme ..."[7]

Other analysts, as well, have expressed concern over the danger of "inadvertent" nuclear war. This term is employed to characterize a scenario in which nuclear war begins not accidentally (as through false warning of a nuclear attack) but as the result of a deliberate decision to initiate military action that is taken most reluctantly by top political authority during a crisis that has escalated out of control.[8] In this scenario, contrary to the expectations of either side in the early stages of a diplomatic crisis, the interaction between the two sides creates a situation in which one or both conclude that there is no alternative but to initiate use of nuclear weapons. Such an agonizing decision might be "forced" on a reluctant political leader in Washington or Moscow if the escalating crisis interaction generates the following three beliefs simultaneously in his mind, *whether or not these beliefs are valid*:

1. A belief that the crisis is out of control, that cooperation in crisis management has broken down and cannot be restored;
2. A belief that war has become virtually inevitable and that it

is time-urgent to decide whether to initiate a pre-emptive strike of some kind oneself or to accept a virtually certain pre-emptive strike by the opponent;

3. A belief that, however costly a war will be, there is a premium on going first.

Thus far, no US-Soviet crisis has developed to a point at which all three of these beliefs emerged in the consciousness of a desperate American or Soviet leader. However, several of these beliefs did begin to enter President Kennedy's mind during the course of the Cuban missile crisis in 1962. On Saturday, October 27th, the crisis reached its most dangerous point. The President feared that the confrontation was getting out of hand, that his efforts at crisis management were jeopardized, and that he might soon be confronted by irresistible pressures to authorize air strikes against the missile sites in Cuba that might trigger, in turn, a Soviet military response against US forces or horizontal escalation via pressure against West Berlin. These beliefs and the accompanying fear that the crisis was at the threshold of uncontrollable escalation led Kennedy reluctantly to decide upon an ultimatum to Khrushchev, coupled with the offer of a quid pro quo, in the hope that this would lead to a quick, mutually acceptable termination of the crisis.[9]

Threats to Effective Crisis Management

Given their shared fear of thermonuclear war that dates back to the early years of the Cold War, American and Soviet leaders can be counted upon to be powerfully motivated to manage and terminate any new diplomatic crises that entail the threat of war between them. Indeed, policy-makers on both sides intuitively grasped the essential requirements for crisis management from the very beginning of the Cold War, and they have succeeded in dealing with a series of war-threatening crisis in Berlin, Cuba, the Middle East, and Asia without engaging in any kind of shooting war, however limited in scope and weapons. The general principles of crisis management and the operational requirements that go with them are not only well understood but are now more explicitly articulated than in the early crises of the Cold War. There can be no guarantee, however, that the two superpowers will be successful in avoiding war in future crises that may arise. Mere awareness of the principles of crisis management and a desire to meet them by no means ensures that they will be, or can be, effectively implemented. While the general requirements of crisis management remain roughly the same in every confrontation, the challenging and often difficult task facing policy-makers is to find ways of adapting their behavior to meet those requirements in the specific, idiosyncratic configuration of each new crisis situation.

Detailed studies of past crises and realistic simulations of hypothetical ones have enhanced our understanding of the various *threats* to effective crisis management. While US and Soviet policy-makers have effectively avoided or defused these threats in all past confrontations, similar threats to effective management of crises are certain to arise again in future confrontations. In the space available, only brief discussion of four major threats to crisis management is possible.[10]

The first of these threats arises from the tension that exists between some of the requirements of prudent crisis management and the military measures one side might decide to take during a crisis to enhance coercive pressure on the other side. During a diplomatic confrontation, one side often feels obliged to threaten force in order to deter the other side from escalating the crisis, to induce the other side to curtail harmful actions, or to terminate the crisis on acceptable terms. The use of military measures to enhance coercive bargaining can easily conflict with the following three established principles of crisis management:

1. Each side shall slow down the tempo of military movements and, if necessary, deliberately create pauses in the momentum of the crisis in order to provide time for assessing the situation, making decisions, exchanging diplomatic signals and communications, and preparing proposals.
2. Each side shall avoid military movements and threats that give the mistaken impression that it is about to resort to large-scale warfare, thereby forcing the other side to consider pre-emption.
3. Each side shall select diplomatic proposals and military moves that leave the other side a way out of the crisis that is compatible with its fundamental interests.[11]

Adherence to these principles of crisis management may be eroded if, in order to optimize coercive pressure, one side (as did President Kennedy in the Cuban missile crisis) sets a time limit or creates a sense of urgency for compliance with its demands and backs its demands with threats of escalation. Because one side may deem such pressure essential in order to avoid an unfavorable outcome or to secure a favorable one, the temptation to strengthen coercive pressure upon the other side may be difficult to resist. However, violation of these principles of crisis management, either deliberately or unwittingly, may have an effect opposite from that intended and lead to escalation.

Another threat to crisis management and escalation control arises from the ever-present possibility that one side will misperceive and exaggerate the intentions of the other side as a result of misreading the significance of its military moves and alerts. It is necessary to question whether crisis management concepts will be robust enough to withstand the possibly destabilizing and escalatory consequences of the military alert measures that the two superpowers may take during a war-threatening crisis.[12] In order to hedge against the possibility that efforts to manage and terminate the crisis may fail, each side is likely to regard it prudent to take measures to reduce the vulnerability of its military forces and to increase their readiness. However, because intentions are not free of ambiguity, one side's alerting measures are likely to be perceived by the other side as threatening. Such a situation demonstrates a particularly acute and dangerous version of the fundamental *security dilemma* in international relations: the actions one side undertakes to enhance its security may be judged by the other side as endangering its security. Thus, an initial misperception by one side of the other's motives for alerting its military forces can trigger an action-reaction cycle that can contribute to a breakdown of mutual efforts to manage a crisis.[13] A fourth principle of crisis management warns against and attempts to avoid this manifestation of the security dilemma:

4. Each side shall ensure that military alerts and force movements undertaken to reduce vulnerability, increase readiness, and signal resolve are consistent with its limited diplomatic

objectives in the crisis; and, correspondingly, it shall avoid military moves that may send conflicting or incorrect indications of its intentions.

Another threat to crisis management arises from the difficulty top-level political authorities may experience in controlling their military forces as a crisis unfolds. Citing several possible examples of President Kennedy's inability during the Cuban missile crisis to coordinate and synchronize actions of US military forces with overall crisis management imperatives, John Steinbruner concludes:

Though there is reason to be concerned about the implications of these incidents, they cannot be explained away simply as unusual mistakes or aberrant behavior on the part of a few individuals. *They reflect rather the sort of thing that might be expected to happen when high crisis strikes the very complicated, inevitably decentralized, very large organizations that constitute modern strategic forces.* ... Once military command channels perceive that actual combat may be in prospect, there are a large number of organizational preparations which must be made. *It is not possible for the President or any single individual to control or even be informed of all aspects of this activity.* In order for the complex organizational system to work at all a great deal of authority to make preparations necessarily resides at low levels of the command structure. *This very basic fact unfortunately provides ample means for the events of a crisis to exceed the control of central political authorities and the decisions they make.*[14]

The problem Steinbruner identifies relates to the *rules of engagement* under which combat forces operate in a crisis. In developing contingency plans for dealing with possible crises, military planners formulate provisional *standing orders* consisting of (a) actions that may be taken in specified circumstances at the discretion of different levels of command unless negated by countermanding orders of higher command or by political authorities (i.e. *command by negation*) and (b) actions that may be taken by military units only if expressly authorized by higher command or by political authorities at some point in the development of the crisis (i.e. *positive command*). Together, actions controlled via command by negation and positive command constitute the rules of engagement under which military forces operate in a crisis.

The ability of top-level political authorities to maintain control over military moves would be jeopardized by the exceedingly large number and complexity of standing orders contained in the rules of engagement that would come into effect at the onset of and during a crisis. It is not easy for political authorities to have full and timely knowledge of the multitude of existing standing orders. As a result, they could fail to coordinate some critically important standing orders with overall crisis management strategy. Similarly, lacking adequate sophistication and experience in military matters, political authorities could fail to understand the military rationale for some standing orders or the possible harmful consequences of altering them for the ostensible purpose of managing the crisis.

The problem is compounded by virtue of the fact that important changes in authorized rules of engagement go into effect as higher levels of alert are declared by the national political authorities. Some alert-induced changes in rules of engagement are pre-programmed with general crisis requirements in mind and would not necessarily be sensitive to the special characteristics of a particular crisis. Accordingly, elements of pre-programmed rules of engagement triggered by successively higher alerts could be dysfunctional for a particular crisis and, therefore, in need of timely alteration.

Awareness that this type of threat to effective escalation control may arise emphasizes the importance of adherence to two additional principles for crisis management:

5. Top-level political authorities must maintain knowledge and informed control over the selection and timing of military alerts, movements, and actions.
6. Top-level authorities must carefully coordinate movements of military forces and force options with diplomatic actions as part of an integrated strategy for pursuing crisis objectives at acceptable cost-risk levels.

A fourth threat to effective crisis management arises from the possibly harmful effects that psychological stress of the kind experienced by policy-makers during a tense confrontation can have upon performance of critical decision-making tasks. As is well known,[15] up to a point situationally-induced stress can lead to improvement in performance of various tasks. If it increases beyond a certain magnitude and duration, however, stress can begin to markedly impair the ability of decision-makers and their staffs to make realistic assessments of the situation and to exercise good judgment in dealing with it. Several characteristics of international crises can arouse acute anxiety and other strong emotional feelings, such as fear, anger, and aggressiveness. In the first place, by its very nature an international crisis poses a major threat to national interests that top-level decision-makers are responsible for safeguarding. Much is at stake in a crisis not only for the country but for the political leader—will he prove equal to the challenge; be able to deal with the crisis in ways that will safeguard his sense of personal worth, assure him the esteem and respect of others, protect his own and his party's political interests?

Second, crises often erupt unexpectedly and the resulting shock and surprise can have harmful effects on a policy-maker's ability to assess the situation calmly and to exercise good judgment. A third stress-inducing characteristic of many crises is that they require—or are perceived by policy-makers, sometimes perhaps erroneously, as requiring—quick decision. Short response-time can impose an additional psychological burden on decision-makers and their advisers. Fourth, and finally, there is the factor of cumulative emotional strain and physical fatigue that a prolonged confrontation imposes on policy-makers and staffs. A crisis imposes intense demands on the energies and emotions of the participants and, at the same time, there are limited opportunities for rest and recuperation.

The literature on American policy-making during the Cuban missile crisis offers testimony on the adverse effects crisis-induced stress can have on the functioning of policy-makers. Theodore Sorensen, a participant in President Kennedy's circle of advisers during the crisis, subsequently made the cryptic statement that he had seen at firsthand, "during the long days and nights of the Cuban crisis, how brutally physical and mental fatigue can numb the good sense as well as the senses of normally articulate men."[16] A similar observation was made by

Robert Kennedy in his memoir of the Cuban crisis.[17] Details as to what happened were lacking for many years. In 1984 a high official in the Kennedy administration told the author, without revealing their names, that two important members of the president's advisory group had been unable to cope with the stress, becoming quite passive and unable to fulfill their responsibilities. Their condition was very noticeable, however, and others took over their duties. Inability to cope with crisis-induced stress has been reported for other leaders as well. Stalin evidently suffered a temporary depression after the Nazi invasion of the Soviet Union in 1941. Prime Minister Eden reacted to the failure of the Suez invasion in 1956 with a near physical and emotional collapse. At one point in the prolonged crisis leading to Israeli initiation of war against Egypt and Syria in June 1967, Israeli Army Chief of Staff Yitzhak Rabin became so visibly overstressed that he was temporarily relieved of his duties.

In all the cases cited here the dysfunctional effects of stress on the policy-maker were highly visible and could be easily recognized by others, thus providing opportunities for timely intervention and compensatory action. But undue stress can also have less visible but nonetheless insidious effects on the performance of decision-makers. A great deal is known about the ways in which acute psychological stress degrades performance of cognitive and judgmental tasks of the kind that policy-makers must discharge in a crisis. The following is a brief summary of major types of effects that have been noted:

1. *Impaired attention and perception*: (a) important aspects of the crisis situation may escape scrutiny; (b) conflicting values may be overlooked; (c) the range of perceived alternatives is likely to narrow but not necessarily to the best alternatives; and (d) "search" for relevant information and options tends to be dominated by past experience, with a tendency to fall back on familiar solutions that have worked in the past whether or not they are appropriate to the present situation.
2. *Increased cognitive rigidity*: (a) impaired ability to improvise and reduced creativity; (b) reduced receptivity to information that challenges existing beliefs; (c) increased stereotypic thinking; and (d) reduced tolerance for ambiguity, which

results in a tendency to cut off information search and evaluation and to make decisions prematurely.
3. *Shortened and narrowed perspective*: (a) less attention to longer-range consequences of options; (b) less attention to side effects of options.
4. *Shifting the burden to the opponent*: the belief that one's own options are quite limited and that only the other side has it within its power to prevent an impending disaster.[18]

One of the most challenging and difficult tasks facing those responsible for crisis management is to find ways of designing and managing the policy-making process in order to reduce the likelihood and consequences of these dysfunctional effects of stress.[19]

Since effective control and management of crises usually requires some degree of US-Soviet cooperation, it is important for Soviet and American specialists to discuss together problems of crisis stability, to identify types of force postures and movements of military forces that may aggravate crisis instability, and to consider remedial measures. Preliminary discussion of some of these matters early in the START talks proved abortive; it needs to be revived and pursued in some appropriate forum. Similarly Moscow and Washington need to assess the desirability and feasibility of one or another variant of the proposal for a joint US-Soviet crisis control center and, if it seems to provide a useful supplement or extension of existing channels for crisis communications, begin discussions for possibly establishing a center of this type.[20]

Avoiding US-Soviet Crises

It was noted at the outset of this essay that the incentives of American and Soviet policy-makers for avoiding diplomatic crises are significantly weaker than their incentives for managing and terminating such confrontation without war. The occurrence of crises from time to time is an inherent risk—some would say an unavoidable one—given the global rivalry of the two superpowers within the "anarchic" international system. Avoiding US-Soviet crises, therefore, is best viewed as part of the larger task of adjusting conflicts between the two superpowers' conception of their security requirements and the related task of moderating and managing their global competition for influence.

While the relationship between the superpowers will continue to be a competitive one, both sides have a strong interest to find ways of cooperating or adjusting to one another in order to limit the costs and risks of their rivalry. Accepting this as a starting point, many observers view the task of developing a more constructive, stable, and peaceful US-Soviet relationship as requiring the superpowers to develop mutually acceptable norms of competition and norms of cooperation. According to this view, a mixed "competitive-collaborative" relationship is distinctly preferable to a "competitive-confrontational" one. Indeed, the Nixon-Brezhnev experiment with détente in the early 1970s aimed at increasing the scope of collaboration and reducing the incidence of confrontation. The effort of the two leaders to develop a mixed competitive-collaborative relation proved abortive for various reasons. As Breslauer puts it in his detailed analysis of the experiment with détente, "It failed because each side tried to define the terms of competition, and the terms of collaboration, in ways geared toward maximizing unilateral advantage than toward expanding the mutual interest in institutionalizing the relationship".[21] Whatever the merits of explanations that blame the United States, the Soviet Union, or both for the demise of détente, explanations at this level of analysis need to be linked to more fundamental factors such as the structure of the international system and differences in ideology. We turn, therefore, to a brief discussion of "the basic security dilemma" in the international area and how it is exacerbated by ideological differences between the superpowers and the way in which they have operationalized strategic nuclear deterrence.

The concept of "security dilemma" was introduced into international relations theory in the early 1950s by Professor John Herz (but with antecedents in earlier writings of political philosophers). Herz called attention to the fact that the "anarchic" nature of the international system creates conditions in which the self-help efforts of individual states to attend to their security needs tend to aggravate the insecurity of other states. Thus, the measures State A takes to strengthen its security are often perceived by State B as posing threats to its security; therefore State B feels obliged to take additional defensive measures of its own. State B's actions, in turn, may be perceived by State A as posing additional threats that require further strengthening of its security posture. Even when all such measures are defensively motivated and do not reflect aggressive intensions or hegemonic aspirations, a vicious cycle of interaction can be set into motion that may feed the arms race and frustrate either side's ability to stabilize achievement of security for itself. The competitive search for greater security may result, paradoxically, in no improvement in security for either side and, at times, creates a sense of greater insecurity in both.

The general phenomenon described here is, as many observers have noted with dismay, an apt characterization of the way in which the relationship between the two superpowers has developed. The dynamics of the security dilemma in US-Soviet relations would be difficult to bring under control under the best of circumstances. It is much accentuated by ideological differences, the way in which the two sides have operationalized strategic nuclear deterrence, and the rapid and continuing revolution in military technology.

John Gaddis is correct in observing that however profound the ideological differences between the United States and the Soviet Union, this factor has not kept them from avoiding war with each other. But this is not to deny that ideological differences have made it more difficult to bring the arms race under better control and have also hampered efforts, such as in the détente of the early 1970s, to develop a more constructive relationship that would reduce the need to rely solely on mutual deterrence in order to keep the peace.

Ideology exacerbates the malignant dynamics of the basic security dilemma in US-Soviet relations insofar as it creates on both sides an idealized self-image and an invidious image of the opponent. That such perceptions can severely exacerbate conflicts of interests between two parties was aptly conveyed in the observation made many years ago by the famous American jurist, Oliver Wendell Holmes. In any argument between two persons, Holmes remarked, six persons are actually involved: the two persons as they actually are; each of the two as he sees himself, a self-image which may bear little relationship to what he actually is; and each of the two as he sees the other, a perception which is quite different from the other's image of himself. No wonder, Holmes exclaimed, that two persons engaged in a dispute talk past each other and that mediation of their heated argument by third parties becomes so difficult.

By accentuating the basic security dilemma, ideology has generated additional suspicion and distrust in US-Soviet relations. It has severely complicated efforts at arms control by raising the threshold for verification of compliance with agreements. And by reinforcing doubts about the opponent's longer-range intentions, ideology has increased the difficulty of getting agreements that effectively control the technological component of the arms race since neither side believes it to be prudent to forego promising weapons technology opportunities in view of the possibility that to do so may have highly damaging consequences for one's security position in the future.

The basic security dilemma has been magnified also by the way in which the two sides have implemented their strategic deterrence postures and policies. Deterrence itself may be essential for keeping the peace but, ideally, deterrence should be achieved in ways that increase one's own sense of security without adding to the opponent's sense of insecurity.[22] But in fact both superpowers have all too often chosen weapons, deployments, and policies for purposes of deterring each other that exacerbate each other's sense of vulnerability to a counterforce first-strike and, hence, have augmented each other's insecurity. What has evolved is a strategic balance which, while it may provide for mutual deterrence under ordinary peacetime conditions, is fraught with latent crisis instability. This condition will not be easily corrected.[23] This sobering fact makes it all the more urgent for the superpowers to avoid getting into dangerous confrontations.

Cooperation Under the Security Dilemma

Let us briefly take note of some research efforts that have attempted to consider how the basic security dilemma might be alleviated and how cooperation in the face of it might nonetheless be achieved. Unfortunately, the concept of security dilemma has received limited theoretical development in the international relations literature. Much of the insight we have gained has come from the work of game theorists studying the "Prisoner's Dilemma". The Prisoner's Dilemma can be described as a mixed-motive game, where the players have a mix of shared and conflicting interests. It has been a source of continual study by game theorists because it describes a situation in which the logic of individual action defeats the logic of collective action. The Prisoner's Dilemma is analogous to the security dilemma, thus, in the sense that when each player acts unilaterally so as to increase his own welfare, both sides may end up worse off than they might have been, had they been able to cooperate.

Until recently game theorists were unable to identify conditions or strategies which might permit independent, self-interested actors to achieve cooperative outcomes in the Prisoner's Dilemma. Recent work by Robert Axelrod, however, has demonstrated that under certain restrictive conditions, a strategy of "tit-for-tat" (cooperate on the first round, and thereafter do whatever the adversary did on the previous round) can lead to stable cooperation.[24] While Axelrod's study offers stimulating ideas of possible relevance to US-Soviet relations, efforts to transfer the simplistic, game-theoretic strategy of tit-for-tat to the complex environment of international relations have encountered the familiar problem of external validity. Axelrod's theoretic contribution will require significant elaboration and refinement before its potential contribution to US-Soviet cooperation can be evaluated.

More directly relevant to the real world has been the work of Robert Jervis, who has refined and elaborated the concept of security dilemma in an attempt to identify variables that can either exacerbate or alleviate it in the context of specific historical and political realities.[25] In addition Jervis has posed the question as to whether the US and the Soviet Union might be able to create a security "regime" (a set of norms and principles regulating behavior in the security area) analogous to the regimes that have evolved in economics and other non-security issue-areas of international relations.[26] The concept of regime is valuable for present purposes because it moves the discussion away from the narrow focus on moves and strategies for solving a Prisoner's Dilemma game. The regime literature shifts attention to the development of mutually acceptable norms and

principles for regulating competition and enhancing cooperation in areas of mutual interest. The acceptance of norms may
eventuate in the creation of institutions which, while not binding
on the participants, do serve to "decrease transaction costs",
making it less costly and less risky to conclude cooperative
agreements when both sides judge such agreements to be in
their self interest.[27]

In developing the concept of security regime for application
to US-Soviet relations, it would be advisable to start with the
sober expectation that a *comprehensive* security regime, one that
covers most if not all aspects of the competition between the
United States and the Soviet Union, is probably not feasible
given the complexities of the superpower relationship. Nonetheless, the two states may be successful—indeed, they have already
been successful to a degree—in developing norms and principles
to regulate behavior in a certain subset of security issues. The
"rules" of crisis management discussed earlier may be seen as
the foundation of a "Crisis Management Regime" which has
evolved over time. It is useful, thus, to regard the security
dimension of the superpower relationship as comprising a number of separate issue-areas which can be decoupled and dealt
with (either in theory, or by the actors themselves) separately.

What is needed at this time is a better understanding of the
mixed record of successes and failures of the superpowers in
developing cooperative arrangements in the various aspects of
the security dimension of their relationship. Such a study should
attempt to identify the conditions, policies, and superpower
interactions that have led to different types of cooperative security arrangements and should not be confined solely to the area
of arms control. A study of this kind should also analyze failed
and flawed efforts of this kind in order to understand better
the obstacles to cooperation and provide "contrast" cases for
comparison with instances of success.[28]

Successful US-Soviet cooperation includes, but is not limited
to, negotiated formal agreements covering a variety of security-
related problems.[29] Achievement of successful cooperation may
also take the form of tacit or even fortuitous US-Soviet "cooperation" emerging from informal coordination of unilateral policies. One may cite in this connection the evolution of an informal "satellite reconnaissance intelligence regime" whereby both

powers have tacitly accepted and benefited from the development of each other's national intelligence capabilities for monitoring force developments, deployments, and readiness.[30] Charles Lindblom's concept of "partisan mutual adjustment" is suggestive in this respect in reminding us that avoidance and management of potential conflicts can sometimes be achieved through mutually adaptive moves taken by actors without necessarily communicating with each other.[31]

Not all of the rich experience of the last forty years can be neatly compartmentalized into discrete cases of "successful" and "unsuccessful" cooperation. US-Soviet efforts to deal with security problems—as in the case of test bans, avoiding militarization of space, preventing nuclear proliferation—often continue over a period of years and progress may be uneven, fitful or cumulative. The problem of a security regime is as much one of management as it is one of creation. An examination of security regimes should include attention to "missed opportunities" as well as efforts that were either overly ambitious, perhaps feasible but inadequately conceptualized, unskillfully pursued, poorly timed or that floundered because of unfavorable contextual conditions and events not easily anticipated or controlled by US and Soviet leaders.

Moderating US-Soviet Global Rivalry: Some Approaches and Lessons

Only a brief summary is possible here of the "lessons" derived by some specialists, in and outside the US government, with regard to how the two superpowers might better manage their global competition for influence so as to avoid diplomatic crises, whether these be of a war-threatening nature or lesser confrontations that inflict serious damage on the overall US-Soviet relationship. The objective of crisis avoidance can be pursued in a variety of ways: reliance on deterrence strategy; policies aimed at increasing the internal stability and security posture of weak allies; use of third parties to mediate regional disputes that might otherwise lead to superpower intervention; creation of neutral or buffer states; recognition of spheres of influence, etc. These options for moderating superpower rivalry have been and will remain of considerable importance but will not be given further attention here. Instead, we consider the feasibility of another option—namely, superpower cooperation in developing general principles, a "code of conduct", "ground rules", norms of competition, or patterns of restraint by means of which to regulate and moderate their global rivalry.

The "general principles" approach, imbedded in the Basic Principles Agreement (B.P.A.) and the Agreement on Prevention of Nuclear War (A.P.N.W.), that were signed by Nixon and Brezhnev at their summit meetings in 1972 and 1973, was quickly called into question by subsequent events. Given the generality and ambiguities of these principles, the fact that they were given different interpretations by the two sides and were not self-enforcing, and that Moscow and Washington did not set up procedures for their clarification and implementation, it is not surprising that the circumstances surrounding the outbreak of the Arab-Israeli war in October 1973, subsequent developments in the Middle East, and the Angolan crisis in 1975 provoked charges and counter-charges of non-fulfillment of the crisis avoidance provisions of the B.P.A. and the A.P.N.W.

Despite this unsatisfactory experience interest in the possibility of developing a "code of conduct", "rules of the game", or "norms of competition" to limit and regulate superpower involvement in regional affairs has persisted. Various efforts have been made to encourage efforts of this kind. A particularly ambitious, far-reaching proposal for a US-Soviet non-intervention agreement encompassing most so-called Third Areas was set forth by the American Committee on East-West Accord in 1982.[32]

The possibility of formulating general principles, guidelines, or "rules" for regulating superpower competition in Third Areas has also been discussed by American specialists and Soviet academicians in recent years in several meetings of the Dartmouth Conference Task Force on Regional Conflicts and in meetings of the Harvard-Soviet group on Prevention of International Political Crises. Some progress has been made in clarifying the difficulties this approach encounters. At one meeting of the Task Force several years ago the Soviet and American delegations each formulated a new set of principles but the two drafts had little in common. Thereupon members of the Task Force agreed to examine a number of actual and potential crisis situations to see how such general principles or guidelines might apply in concrete cases. At subsequent meetings of the Task Force, however, the discussion turned to efforts to identify the respective interests of the United States and the Soviet Union in specific areas. The two delegations also attempted to assess how threatening to its interests each superpower would regard a variety of actions the other superpower might take in a given country or region, and how it might respond to different threatening actions.

Members of the Dartmouth Conference Task Force appear to share the belief that, while the general principles approach need not be abandoned, the shift in focus to specific situations is necessary and worthwhile from an analytical point of view, even though the two delegations have not agreed on how best their governments ought to deal with the specific crises and flashpoints that have been discussed. Particularly the members of the American delegation favor the alternative of a case-by-case approach that focuses on the relative interests of the two sides while members of the Soviet group continue to approve the general principles of the kind set forth in the B.P.A. and the A.P.N.W. although recognizing the need for their additional development and elaboration.[33]

Underlying the Nixon-Brezhnev effort to develop general principles and subsequent efforts by others to consider alternative approaches is the assumption that existing international law does not provide a sufficient or reliable basis for regulating and moderating superpower involvement in Third Areas.[34] The pursuit of state interests in a harshly competitive relationship such as that characterizing US-Soviet relations often leads to circumvention, if not actual violation, of the constraints which existing formal statements of international law seek to impose.

Given the limited applicability and efficacy of formal international law, several other modalities for regulating competition may be resorted to from time to time by members of the state system and, indeed, by the two superpowers. Thus, states may act to limit the scope of their competition and avoid harmful conflicts by entering into specific, ad hoc agreements or explicit understandings. There are many examples of this in US-Soviet relations, some of them mentioned earlier in this paper: the Second World War agreement on occupation zones and administration of Germany; the Austrian State Treaty of 1955; the agreement on neutralization of Laos in 1962; the Quadripartite Agreement on Berlin in 1971. In addition there are understandings of the kind that emerged during the Ogaden war between Soviet- and Cuban-backed Ethiopia forces and Somalia when the United States requested and received assurances from the Soviet Union that Ethiopian forces would not move into Somalia after "liberating" Ogaden.

In addition to explicit, formal agreements of this kind that are analogous to contract law, cooperation in regulating potentially conflictful competition may take the form of understandings of a wholly tacit or partly verbalized character. That is to say, norms of competition may emerge from previous experience or, rather, from the shared interpretations and lessons derived from earlier experiences. Sometimes experience yields a fairly explicit norm that may even take the form of a quasi-agreement. An example of this is the quid pro quo agreement between Kennedy and Khrushchev that ended the Cuban missile crisis. Kennedy agreed that the United States would not invade Cuba in the future in return for Khrushchev's withdrawal of the missiles and a pledge not to reintroduce offensive weapons into Cuba. This case illustrates the interesting possibility that the terms on which the superpowers terminate a crisis may constitute, as it were, a tacit crisis-avoidance agreement for the future. The quid pro quo ending the missile crisis indeed provided the reference point for settling a superpower disagreement that arose in 1970 over the construction of a Soviet submarine base in Cuba.[35]

Similarly, twenty years of superpower competition in the Middle East appear to have led to the development of certain tacit norms, or at least recognizable patterns of restraint, though these are not as well defined or as explicitly formulated as in the Cuban case. If the United States and the Soviet Union have not always wanted to cooperate, or have not been able to cooperate effectively to prevent the resort to force by parties to the Arab-Israeli conflict, the superpowers have nonetheless come to recognize that it is to their mutual interest that each should prevent its local allies from dragging the superpowers into war with each other. Part of the learning experience derived by the superpowers from repeated outbreaks of warfare between their regional allies in the Middle East is the lesson that they must cooperate, if necessary, to bring about a timely cease-fire before either the Arab side or Israel is threatened with a devastating defeat. Of a piece with this is the shared, though tacit, understanding that each superpower will provide as much assistance to its side in Arab-Israeli conflicts as needed, including the possibility of direct military intervention, to enable it to avoid a military catastrophe.[36]

An Enhanced Role for Diplomacy

To urge that the superpowers undertake timely, serious diplomatic discussions to clarify their interests in a particular area and to identify actions by the other side that they would regard as threatening those interests is to do no more than to enjoin US and Soviet leaders to make greater use of traditional diplomatic practices. Indeed, Washington and Moscow have made sporadic efforts of this kind, some successful and others not, for many years. The question is how to institutionalize such practices and to make them more effective.

Nor is the suggestion advanced here a novel one. It is often said, with considerable justification, that the United States and the Soviet Union can reduce the risk of confrontations by timely clarification and communication of their interests in particular areas and situations. If we were to systematically examine the history of US-Soviet relations from this standpoint, however, we would find many episodes in which they failed to do so. Some of these failures might be attributed to oversight, human error, technical communication difficulties of a kind that could be rather easily avoided in the future.

Other failures to define and communicate one's interests effectively cannot be so easily explained and are rooted in causes that cannot be so readily eliminated. One root cause has to do with *difficulties of diplomatic signaling and communication* – e.g. a failure to convey what one's interests and intentions are in a timely, clear manner that is comprehensible and credible to the opponent; or a failure of the recipient to attend properly to serious communications directed towards him and to interpret them correctly. There are various constraints on the ability of the superpowers to communicate effectively with each other that deserve the most careful study. Indeed, this is a common problem that could greatly benefit from joint US-Soviet analysis of past failures. But there is also a more fundamental root cause of failures to convey one's interests on a timely basis—namely, *the difficulty superpowers often experience deciding what their interests are in a timely and reliable way*—that needs much more attention than it has yet received.[37]

Given the difficulties American and Soviet leaders experience from time to time in determining their own and each other's interests in various geographical areas and in foreseeing how each other's actions might be viewed as threatening those interests, it is all the more necessary that they make serious efforts to discuss these matters in diplomatic channels. The superpowers would do well to commit themselves to reviving and making greater use of the traditional diplomatic practice of frequent, timely consultations to clarify and adjust, if possible, their interests in specific geographical areas.

A useful step in this direction was taken by President Reagan in his address to the United Nations on September 24, 1984, in which he proposed a series of Soviet-American regional discussions to alleviate tensions. Shortly thereafter the idea of discussing the Middle East in detail was proposed by President Reagan to Foreign Minister Andrei Gromyko when they met in Washington and later discussed with Gromyko by Secretary of State Shultz. Subsequently US and Soviet delegations met for two days in Vienna on February 9-10, 1985, to discuss Middle East issues. The talks were restricted to an exchange of already familiar views and were primarily of symbolic importance. Evidently no effort was made to develop a more ambitious agenda for a subsequent meeting or indeed to schedule a second meeting.[38]

Thus far, therefore, only quite limited progress has been made in developing and institutionalizing a procedural mechanism for bilateral discussions of regional problems on a frequent and timely basis. To move such talks from a symbolic level to serious discussion and negotiation aimed at clarifying, narrowing and possibly resolving substantive disagreements each side will have to prepare thoroughly and to minimize publicity. To this end representatives of the two sides should attempt to achieve a mutual clarification of the specific configuration of the case at hand—i.e. what was at stake for each side in the area in question; what actions by each side would be regarded as threatening by the other side and as requiring some response; what was the danger of unwanted escalation; whether other external actors were or might become involved and how this could be avoided; what development and outcome of the local situation would and would not be acceptable to each of the superpowers; whether diplomatic solutions could be worked out.

An important advantage of the case-by-case approach proposed here is that it would bring the two superpowers together in the most serious kind of diplomatic conversations at an early stage in the development of a local situation before it got out of hand. Even if the efforts of the United States and the Soviet Union to devise an ad hoc understanding covering a specific situation proved abortive or only partly successful, the timely diplomatic exchanges between them could have the useful result of mutual clarification of interests engaged by that situation; it could offer the possibility of correcting misperceptions of each other's intentions and activities that might otherwise result in escalation of mutual involvement; it could lead to encouragement by the superpowers of efforts by third parties or the United Nations to deal with the local situation before the Soviet Union and the United States were drawn in more actively.

While the difficulties standing in the way of US and Soviet efforts, taken unilaterally or cooperatively, to moderate their global rivalry will remain formidable, it is possible to be too pessimistic on this score. The various ways in which the international system can be reformed, which Michael Walzer discusses in his contribution to this volume, should surely include the possibility that the superpowers may redefine and delimit their global aspirations. In fact, both the United States and the Soviet Union are drawing and may be expected to continue to draw sober lessons from their experiences in the Third World. For a variety of reasons, both superpowers have ample cause to come to a better understanding of the limits of military power and of their economic resources for maintaining and extending their global positions.

This process of learning is not confined to the United States, where the earlier impact of the Vietnam experience on public and policy views on foreign policy has by no means dissipated.[39] For a variety of reasons the Soviet elite, too, has ample cause to reassess its policies and aspirations. Careful study of Soviet statements indicates the existence of a policy debate that reflects important differences regarding priorities and cost-benefit evaluations of Soviet investment in extending influence in the Third World. Moreover, visitors to the Soviet Union have reported a new tendency on the part of some of their contacts to entertain second thoughts about the wisdom of the assertive Soviet policies of the mid- and late-1970s in parts of the Third World that, they now acknowledge, helped to undermine support for détente in the United States and led to a marked deterioration in the overall US-Soviet relationship.[40] There is recognition, too, that the trend toward even greater turbulence and instability (to which Dr. Soedjatmoko calls attention in his chapter) will confront *both* superpowers, not just the United States, with the prospect of declining influence and control in the Third World.

In view of these developments and prospects, the analyst of US-Soviet relations might well venture the prediction that the issue of what global "equality" of the two superpowers means will be displaced in the future by the necessity both the United States and the Soviet Union will experience to redefine and shrink their conception of what kind of global role remains a viable goal for the superpowers. Not only will this task be difficult and painful; it could also accentuate the competitiveness and instability of the superpower global rivalry, especially if one side attempts to exacerbate, and gain advantages for itself, from the difficulties the other is experiencing in maintaining positions of influence in the Third World. Hopefully, however, it might also enhance superpower incentives for mutual restraint and tacit cooperation in reducing their involvements abroad.

8

The Reform of the International System

MICHAEL WALZER

I

There is hardly a contemporary writer on international politics who has a good word to say for the state system as we know it and experience it today. The need for reform is widely recognized. Projects for reform abound, defended sometimes in apocalyptic, sometimes in prudent and measured tones. Who indeed would say that this world, scarred by injustice and threatened with mass destruction, is the best of imaginable worlds? And yet the way to reform seems radically barred: for the only possible agents of reform, at least as reform is usually conceived, are also the crucial objects of reform. All the available projects that would move us toward global solidarity or economic redistribution, all of them, in one way or another, call the present standing and capacity, the legitimacy and power of the sovereign state into question. This is what the reformers propose: that states act upon themselves, to their own detriment. Hence reform looks like an impossible enterprise, at once necessary and wildly impractical.[1]

Perhaps I shall not succeed in making it look any less impractical. But I do have a somewhat different view than that held by most reformers of what is necessary. And I have some examples to offer of a kind of success (though not of intentional success, not the success of a *project*). What is commonly said is that we must move beyond the state system, that we must transcend or escape the idea of sovereignty. Sovereignty is the villain, at least local sovereignty, since many reformers imagine a kind of global sovereignty as the endpoint of their activity. Kant described this endpoint in negative terms: "a global, soulless despotism".[2] One might think his description plausible, however, and still want to move beyond the state system; and I shall argue that we should do that, at some point, in some (limited) ways. But that isn't the first argument that needs to be made. Indeed, it is a great paradox that this yearning for the "beyond" should so dominate reformist thinking in an age that has seen the steady proliferation of sovereign states and of demands for statehood. One might say that the actual reformist enterprise of the period since the Second World War has not been the transcendence but the expansion, the full development, the universalization of the state system. That process is still incomplete; much of the violence in the world today is connected to it—not so much a consequence of sovereignty as an accompaniment of the efforts to achieve sovereignty or to resist or postpone that achievement. It does not seem likely that we will find our way beyond the sovereign state until we put this process behind us.

In other words, the state system won't be transcended until it has been completed. I don't say this out of some metaphysical belief that historical forms of organization must exhaust their possibilities before they disappear. There is a clearer and more plausible proposition, ethical rather than metaphysical in character, that I would prefer to defend: the gains that some people have made by acquiring states of their own must become gains for everyone. In any case, men and women subjected to imperial or colonial rule will not willingly forego such gains. It is not an accident that the vision of a world beyond the sovereign state is attractive chiefly to citizens of sovereign states, while the state system is most strongly defended by people who don't yet have, or who have only just come into possession of, states of their own.[3] Conceivably, at least, neither of these groups is mistaken; their differing views reflect different experiences, the product of uneven development on a global scale. And this raises the most serious doubts as to the possibility, or desirability, of a single agenda for international politics.

Those of us in secure possession of statehood may forget why it was that we, or our ancestors, once sought that security. So I shall repeat what is for us a nineteenth-century argument. One can readily find it, though not in quite the form I give it here, in writers like Mazzini or John Stuart Mill. It is an argument in three parts, resting on three claims about the world. First, the prudential claim: that we and our fellows, members of a people or historical nation, can only guarantee our physical survival, our long-term existence as individuals or as a coherent group, through the medium of sovereign power. We can be sure of no one's protection but our own. I have called this a nineteenth-century argument, but obviously it has taken on new force in the twentieth century—even if sovereignty has turned out to be no guarantee. It is undeniable that Armenians and Jews, to take only the easiest examples, would have been better off with states (and with bureaucrats, policemen, and soldiers) of their own. But wouldn't they have been better off still if they had not had states and if Turks and Germans had not had states either? Maybe; but power would still have rested somewhere, and groups of people would still require protection against its possibly malevolent use.

Second, the expressive claim: that we and our fellows have the same right that every other historical nation has to organize our life together so as to give expression to our values, cultural understandings, sense of ourselves. Of course, the modern state is only one way, not the only way, of organizing a common life. Vis-à-vis the great multinational empires, however, it was (and, insofar as imperial rule persists, still is) the available alternative. The need for expression, and the national culture that is to be expressed, are both of them artifacts, the product of a political and economic mobilization that also constituted a mass awakening. Given that awakening, statehood seems an inevitable claim; the likely alternative is repression in someone else's state.

Third, the internationalist claim: that we and our fellows, and others like us, are disturbers of world peace only insofar as we are denied the protective and expressive powers of sovereignty. Hence the vindication of this critical principle, *for every nation its own state*, would open the way to an international settlement. This argument was first put forward with regard to religious toleration and ecclesiastical self-government. "The establishment of this one thing," wrote John Locke in his *Letter on Toleration*, "would take away all ground of complaints and tumults upon account of conscience ..." The case for independence is the same: that it will take away all ground of complaints and tumults upon account of culture and nationality. A strong claim, obviously, but it rests upon an even stronger one without which domestic peace and international settlement would be vain hopes. Thus Locke: "There is only one thing which gathers people into seditious commotions, and that is oppression."[4] The parallel argument is that oppression is the sole cause (more weakly and plausibly: one of the chief causes) of all the wars of national liberation and national unification that have plagued the modern world and provided so many occasions for great power intervention. Peace will come when conscience is quiet and nationalism satiated.

The quiet conscience is, I suppose, easier to imagine than the satisfied nation. Indeed, we have some experience of consciences at peace; liberal states have made Lockeian toleration an every-day political reality, and the results have been very close to what Locke predicted. Disagreement and conflict persist, insofar as religion continues to be a serious concern of liberal citizens, but the sorts of tumult that characterized the seventeenth century have been surpassed, and it would seem decisively surpassed, wherever religious persecution has been given up as a state policy. Would a similar result follow if every form of national subjugation were renounced? But the two renunciations cannot be made effective in the same way. Any number of religious groups can be tolerated on the same territory, while each nation requires territory of its own if it is to form a sovereign state in accordance with the claims for security and cultural expression. National independence requires physical space while ecclesiastical self-government does not. And the necessary space is not instantly available or naturally (or divinely) marked out. It must be appropriated in one way or another, and the appropriation will often be contested—not only by imperial powers but also by other nations similarly claiming security and expression. So complaint and tumult don't end; one nation's freedom is, often, another nation's oppression.

Men and women caught up in struggles of this sort, however, are not usually led to forego the hope of statehood and sovereign power. Indeed, the dangers of the struggle may well serve to intensify the hope. Nor are the struggles in principle endless and irremediable. There are historical examples of vindicated claims to security and expression (the separation of Norway from Sweden makes a useful case), and vindication does seem to bring, if only locally, something like the peace that the Lockeian argument promises. Good borders make good neighbors. Separation, secession, partition, liberation—all for the sake of statehood—point the way toward a kind of international settlement. The way itself is bloody enough, and there probably are cases where people from different nations are so radically entangled on the same piece of territory that a "good border" is virtually inconceivable. Still, the completion of the state system is a reform worth pursuing. Various national movements and parties will of course pursue it, but established states should pursue it too, sometimes helping, sometimes (when they threaten to over-reach themselves) constraining the movements and parties. The goal is a world of states within relatively secure borders, from which no sizable group of people is excluded. Is this a utopian program? Yes, in the sense that such a world exists "nowhere"—no, in the sense that the achievement of statehood by one nation after another is an actual and visible process. That the process is uneven, that it is violent, that it produces anomalies along the way (states without nations, nations with more than one state): none of these is a reason for backing away from it.

A few years ago, the American political scientist Michael Doyle published a long article entitled "Liberal Legacies", in which he made a startling claim: in the years since 1800, no wars have been fought between or among states with liberal (republican, democratic, social democratic) regimes.[5] As the number of such states has expanded, from eight in the period 1800-49, to 29 in the period 1900-45, to 49 in the period since 1945, they have created, without ever planning the creation among themselves, what Doyle, following Kant, calls "a pacific union". Liberal states have fought wars with illiberal states and also, significantly, with national liberation movements in their imperial territories and spheres of influence, but not with one another. Doyle suggests a number of liberal and Kantian reasons for the existence of this zone of peace in an otherwise warlike world, and each of his reasons seems plausible enough, though the sum of reasons doesn't, it seems to me, quite account for the phenomenon. I would add one more: within this world of liberal states, the ground of complaints and tumults on account of nationality has been largely eliminated. The pacific union is a union of satisfied nations. That satisfaction may have something to do with their liberalism; it also has something to do with the peace that marks their coexistence.

Unfortunately, national liberation does not necessarily make for liberal politics or a peaceful foreign policy. Not for liberal politics because the political culture of many nations, after as well as before liberation, does not support the individual activism and institutional independence that liberalism requires. Not for a peaceful foreign policy because new states sometimes claim more territory than their nation inhabits. They are still insecure, still defending themselves, and now with sovereign power; or, the nationalist fervor generated by the struggle for liberation overflows its proper borders. Moreover, new states are sometimes internally so unstable that they invite external interventions. But the existence of a zone of peace suggests that none of these outcomes is inevitable or permanent. One can hope for further developments, toward liberalism, perhaps, or more immediately, toward the international equivalent of toleration. It is worth remembering that the first achievement of religious liberty for dissenting sects—the American Puritans, for example—did not lead these sects to tolerate what might be called the religions that came next. The logic of the process pointed nevertheless toward a generalized tolerance. Similarly, the logic of national liberation points toward, what is therefore worth working for, a completed, universalized state system.

II

Having said that, I want to add immediately that this completion is not any sort of historical endpoint. Precisely because of the difficulties encountered along the way, further processes are set in motion that are not similarly constrained by the idea of sovereignty. These processes are of two sorts. The first is a process of devolution that creates autonomous regions and provinces within the state; the second is a process of alliance that creates federations and economic unions among states. Neither has gone very far in the contemporary world; there have been many false starts, few successes. The results are partly visible, mostly imagined, but insofar as they generate, or insofar as they might generate, loyalties like those generated in the past by statehood, they point toward what Hedley Bull has called "a new medievalism".[6] They suggest a movement beyond sovereignty by way of a kind of regression. At the same time, both devolution and alliance respond to contemporary needs; they represent alternative fulfillments, fulfillments without statehood, of the claims for security and cultural expression.

Devolution is best understood as a way of meeting the needs of ethnic or religious minorities that have maintained some territorial integrity—they are not yet a dispersed population—but are no longer so differentiated from the bulk of their fellow citizens as to require a full independence. Some degree of autonomy is sufficient to their purposes, at least as most of them define their purposes. There are often more radical groups among them that demand secession and statehood, but the frequency with which these groups resort to terrorist tactics is an index of their lack of popular support. Devolution of sovereignty, rather than its entire appropriation, suffices in these cases for the defense of group identity and the encouragement of cultural expression. Or, better, one can plausibly imagine that it would suffice. The test is more likely to come in old and established states than in new ones—autonomy for the Welsh or the Basques, say, rather than for the Ibos or the Baluchis (whose needs may well be greater). The hard work of state-building makes new political elites suspicious of devolution, unwilling to share the power they have so recently, and with such high hopes, acquired. Older elites are more likely to surrender some of their power in order to hold the rest with less trouble.

Something similar could be said about the process of alliance. The United Arab Republic and the East African economic union are typical false starts, noble or at least ambitious efforts at political and economic federation undercut by the greater urgency of a national interest newly served by a nation-state. The EEC is a more likely model, and one that will probably be adapted, sooner or later, to other times and places. For the exercise of sovereignty is a way of accumulating power, but limits are fixed to the accumulation by the size and resources of the state, and the limits are often severe. Alliance with neighboring states promises an escape from those limits—more resources, more power, a stronger and therefore safer position in international affairs.[7] And alliance can support cultural expression also, since religion, or a way of life, or a civilization (like "European civilization") is often shared across state borders, even if a more particular sharing goes on within them.

Devolution and alliance create new units, the exact status of which is still radically uncertain; it's not yet clear what they will amount to, what authority they will wield, what sorts of loyalty they will generate. But sovereignty divided, downwards and outwards, as it were, offers some remedy for the inadequacies of sovereignty-in-itself, which are more and more likely to be realized as the first flush of independence wears off. If this realization is widely shared, then we may hope that the division of sovereignty will bring an end to its seemingly endless multiplication—with autonomy replacing statehood at the micro-level and alliance replacing it at the macro-level. Professor Bull has speculated that a new medievalism of this sort, a pattern of political units of indeterminate and probably contested authority within and above the state, might well bring with it the same sort of endemic disorder and violence that we associate with the original medievalism.[8] That is certainly one possibility but not the only one. It is equally possible that devolution and alliance might steady the state system, as extra wheels steady a bicycle for an unsure rider. In the Middle Ages the results of devolution and alliance were arbitrary from a political point of view, determined by the power, sometimes the mere whimsy, of local feudal dynasties. Now, though power will never be irrelevant, they will be determined in part at least by the actual wishes of whole populations—and sustained by the satisfaction and security they generate.

III

Here, then, are two sorts of international reform: the completion and then the complication of the state system. But neither of these, it might be said, addresses the greatest danger posed by the sovereign state, namely, the capacity of political leaders wielding sovereignty, making unilateral decisions, to destroy the world. There lie the threats that reformers must address: the exhaustion of resources, the pollution of the environment, the use of nuclear weapons. I shall argue later on that completion and complication do help, or could help, to diminish these threats, but it is true that neither reform speaks directly to them.

The threats are posed primarily by the great powers, and the great powers, by virtue of their greatness, successfully resist the effects of reform. This is the most obvious example of the dilemma with which I began.

It is worth noticing, though, that the power of the great powers would in fact be reduced by the completion of the state system. The Soviet Union faces the greatest risk, having reconstituted the multinational empire of the Romanovs and so saved it from the fate of all the other empires with which it once coexisted—Ottoman, Hapsburg, French, and British. Were reform an entire success, the Russian empire would finally, belatedly, meet that fate. But a world of truly independent nation-states, no nation without its state, would be a world in which all the great powers would be significantly less great, diminished in size and resources, or unable to dominate their spheres of influence as they now do. The effects of devolution and alliance would be similar, weakening the larger states from within or confronting them with federations and economic unions of smaller states. Right now, the great powers shape the alliance system to the requirements of their own competition, but one can readily imagine alliances among truly independent states aimed precisely at balancing the great powers and complicating the competition between them. In the economic sphere, the EEC is already effective in these ways. For the moment, however, significant political complications are not available, and that is why reformers, driven by the urgency of the threats we all face, look for some authority beyond the sovereign state—which really means beyond the United States and the Soviet Union.

But no such authority could possibly be constituted without the agreement of those same two states, and no such agreement seems even remotely likely. There are real political forces working, if often unsuccessfully, for the completion and complication of the state system, but no forces working for its transcendence. When we focus on the particular problems posed by great power rivalry, then, we have no choice except to search for remedies within the scope of that rivalry itself. The first remedy is the balance of power, the policy of mutual deterrence. Since mutual deterrence is the keynote of the international system whose reform I am supposed to be discussing, I shall note here only that deterrence is better than the failure of deterrence: hence reformers must attend to the stability of the balance even while they try to alter its fundamental character. The second remedy is the negotiation of specific conflicts. This is also a commonplace of the state system, and even successful negotiations do not amount to systemic reforms. Nevertheless, it is a mistake for reformers, intent upon transcending the system, to underestimate the value of specific negotiations. The same mistake is made, for different reasons, by cold war ideologists who view the rivalry of the great powers as a conflict of world views, even as a war of good and evil—as if we stood at Armageddon (when, indeed, the state system will have been transcended). The conflict of world views is real enough, but it is only part of the story. The United States and the Soviet Union have distinct interests, and conflicts over these interests, though not entirely unrelated to one another, are also not merely aspects of one grand struggle; they are available for specific negotiation. A series of successes in negotiations of this sort would make for a kind of peace-in-pieces, and would reduce the dangers of the ideological war. So it is important to press for what might be called negotiation without linkage, even if this means acknowledging the reality of the state system.

The third remedy is communication generally: hot lines, summit conferences, diplomatic routines, cultural exchanges, scientific meetings, tourism, and commerce. Reformers sometimes speculate that this sort of thing, carried to the nth degree, might make for mutual dependency and a strong sense of shared interests and even shared values. Carried to the nth degree, it might; but then, by definition, not at any point short of that. In fact, communication of these sorts—talk and trade, official and unofficial—is a common feature of the state system and has often persisted right up to some catastrophic breakdown of relations and a savage war. Still, it is a good thing to talk and trade and sometimes, at least, these two will provide reasons for or occasions for negotiated settlements of particular disputes. Another form of great power communication, this one more likely to be undervalued, is espionage, which makes for a sharing of information about new weapons systems and recent troop deployments and so, perhaps, reduces the risks such things involve.

The fourth remedy is of a somewhat different sort: the exposure of great power policies to domestic and global scrutiny. This is not a common feature of the state system. States crave secrecy and often manage to maintain it (hence the importance of espionage). But democratic decision-making, mass politics, and instant communication have begun to ensure a kind of visibility. International organizations focused on civil liberties, environmental issues, problems of development, and so on, regularly describe the concrete impact of great power (and other power) decisions. Television cameras record the conduct of military interventions; reporters write about the "covert" politics of counter-insurgency and subversion. All this works, of course, only where there is a free press—and freedom also to protest against the particular policies whose effects the press reveals. These freedoms make Western governments considerably more vulnerable than other governments to their own populations and even to the populations of neighboring or allied (democratic) states. But it is not the case that other governments are entirely invulnerable. For political elites across the globe learn about the world, directly or indirectly, from the free press of the West. One reads the *New York Times* to find out what is happening, *Pravda* only to find out what the Soviet authorities want their people to think about what is happening. So both great powers know that the world knows, more or less well, what they are doing. And while this knowledge is at this moment only a marginal constraint, it could take on greater importance.

I am inclined to say that it would take on greater importance given the completion and complication of the state system. The more great power decision-making takes place in a world of independent states and of independently allied states, the more the decisions made will be publicized, scrutinized, condemned, and resisted. This is not in any obvious sense a program for global harmony, but the conflicts likely to arise ought to be more diffused and less dangerous than those we currently live with. Publicity and resistance may also provide a way of coping with dangers unrelated or only tangentially related to great power rivalry. Consider for a moment the dispute between the United States and Canada over acid rain. I consider myself better represented in this dispute by the Canadian government, which aims narrowly at protecting its environment and its people, than by my own. And I would be even better represented by a stronger, more determined, and more independent Canadian government. It is possible, of course, to imagine a world state that would act authoritatively to impose restraints on American industry for the sake of Americans and Canadians alike. But a more independent Canada is (somewhat) easier to imagine. So other states can become surrogates for the world state dreamt of by reformers.

A range of surrogate activities might, in combination, impose significant constraints upon the great powers. If independent states and alliances of states limit the deployment of nuclear weapons on their territory; if they protest the incursion of nuclear submarines into their territorial waters; if they insist on some control over the use of the ocean's resources; if they mediate local conflicts and oppose great power interventions; if they extend foreign aid for reasons unconnected to the Cold War; if they sponsor scientific studies of ecological dangers and actively publicize the results—then they act, though in their own interests, in ways that benefit us all. I can see no other source of such benefits. International agencies, as they are now constituted, work effectively only when they are worked, that is, used, by states and alliances. They are not likely to work in any other way, barring an extensive usurpation of sovereign power. It would have to be a usurpation, for consent is not and won't be forthcoming—and usurpation lies far beyond the compass of organizations like the UN or any of its more specialized adjuncts. But other states, acting in the ways I have described, would merely be claiming their rights, and they would be doing that within a system whose legitimacy even the great powers themselves must recognize.

IV

It is a mistake to think that there is or could be a single agenda for international reform. Given the uneven development of the state system, and the uneven distribution of power among existing states, we need a set of proposals and programs adapted to different stages of state-building and self-determination and to different levels of "greatness". In many parts of the world, the completion of the state system is the first requirement—if only because its incompletion, and the festering discontent of stateless peoples, is one of the prime causes of violence, war, and great power confrontation. Not the only cause, but sufficiently important so that it compels our attention. The conflict of nationalisms may be endless, but no particular conflict is necessarily endless, and each particular solution reforms even as it expands the state system and improves the chances for a general peace. Devolution and alliance might bring additional improvements. These two are experimented with throughout the world, but they are probably most feasible in states with a strong sense of their independent standing and inner cohesiveness—in older states, chiefly, rather than in states still building the machinery of power, still struggling for security and cultural expression. But this is no reason to discourage the experiments wherever they occur. They might well make sovereignty easier to bear or easier to defend in new as well as old states, and so inhibit the resort to insurrection and war.

With regard to the great powers, we can hope only for balance and détente and a (slowly) growing responsiveness to world opinion. Détente holds the stage, as it were, until new actors, satisfied nations and free alliances of nation-states, can begin the construction of a pacific union. That's not a project likely, ever, to be finished; in important ways it will always be at the mercy of the great powers (which are by definition unsatisfied: "greatness" can never be satisfied). Still, it seems to me a project more worthy of pursuit than the transcendence of sovereignty through the construction of a world state. That last is a reform of the international system that would effectively eliminate international politics, while all that the pacific union involves is a series of political reforms. And politics is something we know, an activity in which we are engaged, more or less disastrously, more or less successfully. We serve our interests, and we can reasonably hope that somewhere in a reformed state system our interests would be served. A world state, by contrast, is like the withering away of the state or the administration of things or the millennial kingdom or the end of time: we can imagine it in any way we please; it is an empty vision; it provides no practical guidance. Its advocates promise solutions to all our problems. The only problem they cannot solve is the political problem of creating, once and for all, this omnipotent source of solutions. The completion and then the complication of the state system invite a more concrete politics and promise only what they might actually deliver—the permanence of international politics.

DISCUSSIONS

David Watt

The program that Professor Walzer has put before us I would prefer to call Wilsonian rather than Mazzinian; perhaps because the drawbacks of the system were more apparent in the aftermath of President Woodrow Wilson than of Mazzini. But there is no doubt that what Professor Walzer is saying is basically what both Mazzini and Wilson said: the festering discontent of stateless people is one of the prime causes of war and great power confrontation.

As Professor Walzer himself agrees, the Wilsonian model has been modified by him in two important respects. First of all, he concedes that it will have to be adapted on the one hand towards alliance diplomacy and the other hand towards further devolution from the level of the State to smaller sub-units of the State. These last can either be a kind of safety valve to the State system or, as he seems to say in some parts of the paper, they can be regarded as being good things in themselves.

The second modification he makes to the Wilsonian Model is that the role of the superpowers—the Big Two, of course, rather than Wilson's Big Four—is much better defined. The great flaw in the Wilsonian Model, as John Gaddis points out in his paper, was the fact that in asserting the right to self-determination of the nations that had gone to make up the Habsburg Empire, the vital interests of Germany and Russia were ignored; and these were reasserted, in their turn, with absolutely catastrophic results in the 1930s. Professor Walzer deals with this by suggesting more open relations between the superpowers and by hoping that the "completed" state system, to use his word, will help to keep the superpowers in order, partly by making their lives more complicated and partly by exposing them to the pressure of world opinion.

I have a good deal of instinctive sympathy with Professor Walzer's position particularly in so far as it is predictive, rather than prescriptive, though I would add as a sort of preliminary comment on his paper that he does seem to me to shift between the predictive and prescriptive attitudes, sometimes implying "this is what is going to happen anyway, and we better put up with it", and at others saying "this is highly desirable objective which we should work for". I would agree with him that World Government is chimerical and that this kind of approach, like various other imposed solutions whether they are imperial or not, causes more trouble for us all. The nation-state is a nice convenient unit of account; people on the whole believe in it, and they are prepared to work and even to cooperate through it.

Why, then, should not we take its "perfection" as a starting point? I can think of a number of reasons why not. The most fundamental is the theoretical problem of knowing what "completion" could actually mean. This is another way of saying "how far down the devolutionary scale do you go?" Professor Waltzer tries to draw a line somewhere in his scale of devolution, but I don't believe that he is very precise about it—and for a good reason. It is almost impossible to draw that line with precision because, as he says himself, one man's nation is another man's oppression. One side says that the Biafran War was won by a government that was asserting a legitimate nationality for Nigeria; the other side says that is was caused by a gallant assertion of the rights of a subunit that ought to have been a nation.

Another difficulty is that nationalism, as we all know, has its dark and chaotic side. Professor Walzer seems to assume, as Mazzini or Wilson would, that we are talking about a beneficent liberal State system that is simply waiting to come into being, if only we could release it. This has not, I fear, always been our experience—Idi Amin, Bokassa, Pol Pot, Duvalier, Galtieri, the Derg—you can go on making a very long list of illiberal regimes, illiberal in the highest and most disgusting degree, which have come to power, at least in part, as a result of rampant nationalism. One can say that these are aberrations and deformations, but they are worth mentioning because they indicate that we cannot expect that the norms of interstate behavior as they have been evolved in Europe since the treaty of Westphalia, are necessarily going to be accepted in the Third World or indeed that those norms would be accepted in practice by first and second world countries far more liberal in theory than the ones that I have just mentioned. You can't banish greed, fear and envy from the international scene by such simple means. Professor Walzer obviously recognizes this, but I don't think he quite faces the fact that these forms of behavior arise inevitably as a concomitant of the proliferation of interests. The fissiparous systems that he is describing are bound to cause enormous trouble not only for those countries and their neighbors, but also grave inconvenience and often serious damage to the interests of the superpowers.

The third reason why I take a less optimistic view about the perfection of the State system than Professor Walzer is the fact that in the present system the nation-state is actually being undermined in many ways. Obviously this process hasn't caused the nation-state to disappear, but it is worth mentioning some of the ways in which it is being attacked. First of all these are internal social, economic and ethnic factors of one sort or another. Secondly there are international economic factors. The multinational corporation is itself a challenge to the authority of the nation-state (and I would say in passing that another general criticism that one could make of Professor Walzer's paper is that there is very little economic dimension in it). Again, religious fundamentalist movements—Islamic and other—cut across the State system. The communications revolution has profound effects on states' ability to control their exchange rates and their reserves as well as their ability to control what appears on their television screens—as the East German government constantly complains. And, finally, there is the question of lower level violence and terrorism. In all these ways, the omnipotence of the state is being brought into question, and while we can't forecast how far the assault will actually get in the long run, it would certainly cause very considerable problems for anyone pinning his hopes centrally on the idea of the nation-state and its "completion".

Where does all this point? One could argue, and indeed some people in the present free market style and fashion do argue, that the best thing is to simply take one's hand off the steering wheel. At the superpower level Professor Schelling has suggested perhaps a little whimsically that we should not aim too hard for arms control agreements, but go in for unilateral tacit understanding; and we could carry that thought further in relation to the Third World. There are many people on the right in British politics for instance who are fanatically opposed to the whole idea of economic aid to underdeveloped countries because they think it actually makes things worse. To them Africa is a sort of black hole which we had better avoid getting sucked into; there is nothing to be done except let the Africans sort out their own affairs. I believe there are too many risks associated with that strategy. We are talking here about change—all sorts of economic, social and technological change—and we must attempt, as best we can, to manage it. But on the whole we must try to do it with, rather than against, the grain of the present system. How is this to be achieved? I would argue with Professor Walzer that we should recognize that the nation-state is not finished, and that we have to deal with and through it. We must also recognize that the great powers will continue to take a geo-political view of their interests and that they will interpret those interests in a way that will oblige them to take an interest, and occasionally to intervene, in the affairs of the second and third world. What we need, it seems to me, is better rules of the game, and more, acceptance of a common standard of international behavior. This implies accepting what Professor Hinsley has called for—a new comity of nations, a substitute in the twentieth century for a set of rules which worked reasonably well in the nineteenth century but which has not yet been adapted to the twentieth century state system.

What would be the elements of this? So far as superpower rules of the game are concerned, I think that I would accept John Gaddis's list as being a pretty good account of what we might hope for. The essential question here concerns spheres of influence. I think that the objection to spheres of influence is understandable but mistaken. Superpowers have their uses in this world of ours. West Europe needs the United States not simply to protect itself against the other superpower, but also to help solve some of its internal regional problems including a possible resurgence of Germany. And on the other side, as George Kennan is constantly pointing out, if the Soviet Union's East European Empire didn't exist we should probably see some of the post-Habsburg troubles reappearing in the old form. Those are not, of course, conclusive arguments in favor of either of those situations, but they illustrate the point that it is an illusion to suppose that people invariably wish to give up their client status at the earliest possible opportunity. Another entertaining example of the same point—and one that Professor Walzer has raised himself—the question of acid rain. He says that he, as an American, is very glad of the existence of Canada which takes enlightened view about the pollution problem. But it seems clear that if the roles were reversed, and if it was the United States that was on the right side and Canada on the wrong side of his argument, then he would be delighted at the power of the United States to impose a more enlightened regime on the Canadians.

On regionalism, which Professor Blackaby brought up, I think some regional elements of control and management ought to be part of any stable system. But what is the role of institutions? Some difficulties arise from the fact that institutions are in a situation which reflects the power position immediately after war, and does not reflect the real position today. The G.A.T.T., the I.M.F., the World Bank and a number of other institutions need reform in order to try and make them less objectionable to people who may be driven, as OPEC was, to moves that turn out to be against their own interest as well as everybody else's. Power is still going to be the determining factor in international organizations and one cannot get away from that, but I believe that they ought to be made more adaptable than they are now. Finally, I think we must extend the scope and acceptance of international law. That is long, arduous and tortuous, but it is part of the process that I have described, the process of trying to induce people to accept that international affairs is not simply a zero-sum game.

To conclude, I am optimistic. We have only been 40 years in our present situation, and less in the situation in which the proliferation of states and interdependence on a grand economic scale have actually come into being. We are learning by error as much as by trial, but the longer we can survive, the better chance that we have. And on the whole I think we are surviving.

Øyvind Østerud

Michael Walzer argues that "completion of the state system" is both instrumental to peace and order, and a moral value in itself. Possession of statehood is a legitimate aspiration for dissatisfied nations because it provides security and protection, because it satisfies the need for self-expression and self-determination, and because it is a condition for peace. Walzer here asserts that national oppression and denial of sovereignty produce disturbers of world peace. Universalizing the gains of those peoples who have acquired status is a necessary step towards transcending the state system.

Walzer acknowledges certain problems and anomalies with this general idea (for instance cases where one nation's freedom is another nation's oppression, or cases with national rivalries over the same territory), but "completion of the state system" is still put forward as an important reform.

The proposition is very nearly identical to a classical idea from the mid-nineteenth century, the so-called *principle of nationality*, by which each nation should have a state and each state should be a nation. Walzer supplements this principle with the Kantian idea that democratic republics don't fight each other. His global solution is a world of liberal states, with satisfied national aspirations for statehood.

It seems reasonable to call this a neo-Wilsonian program, quite close to a replica of Woodrow Wilson's formula for a more peaceful world. Walzer adds that "the logic of national liberations points toward ... a completed state system".

Is this really so? There are reasons for doubting it. Much heavier stress should probably be put on difficulties which Walzer is aware of *en passant*.

The principle of nationality is intrinsically ambiguous and unclear. Sir Ivor Jennings once stated that "the doctrine of self-determination was in fact ridiculous, because the people cannot decide until someone decides who are the people". The "nation" is equally problematic. Liberation movements do not oppose an anti-national establishment view of society, they oppose an *alternative* view of the identification and delineation of the proper collective unit. Is the "nation" an historical entity? Is it a subjective fellowship? Is it a given political unit? Is it a racial or ethnic or religious or linguistic group? Is it a combination of all of these, or does it allow for a variation among them? The answer is all the way *yes*; a nation is any of these alternatives.

Take a look at contemporary Africa, where there are at least three fundamentally different views on national criteria. First, we find the *political nation*. Respect for the political boundaries drawn up by the colonial powers was a basic axiom for the new independent states, written into the Charter of the Organization for African Unity. Numerous struggles for national liberation had these purely political boundaries as their own delimitation.

Secondly, there is the *historical nation*. In some parts of Africa independent states have argued for inclusion of territories which were held together by pre-colonial bonds of allegiance. They have been arguing for a restoration of some pre-colonial greater kingdom transformed into a modern nation-state.

Thirdly, we find ideas of the *ethnic nation*. In some parts of the continent claims for independent statehood, or for irredentist rectification, are made on tribal or ethnic grounds, or from group identity across state boundaries or within sections of states. Countries like Mauritania and Somalia have been cases in point.

The most intensive and intricate national conflicts arise when these conflicting criteria and claims arise over the same territory, as we have seen happen for instance in the struggle about the Western Sahara. The principle of nationality as such is thus no clue to satisfied aspirations for statehood. In this perspective there is no uniform logic of national liberation.

There were different types of critique of the Wilsonian formula for national liberation during and immediately after the First World War. The disappointed liberals pointed to the gaps between ideals and reality: the double standards, the inconsistencies, the compromises, the selective and biased employment of the doctrine. It was pointed out that Wilson and the victorious powers betrayed their own ideals and explicit goals —in Ireland, in South Tyrol, in North Bohemia, in the colonies overseas. Harold Nicolson probably became the most articulate spokesman for this perspective—the restoration of the ideal. The neo-Wilsonianism in Michael Walzer's paper is quite close to this purified version.

The alternative perspective did not say that a sacred ideal was betrayed, but that the ideal itself was intrinsically ambiguous and utterly unrealistic: a recipe for instability, chaos, rebellion, utopian hopes, insoluble rivalries, dismemberment of any organized state. The US Secretary of State, Robert Lansing, confessed such complaints to his diary already in Paris in 1918. He had his diary published three years later, after his dismissal.

There is one strong point in this realist anti-Wilsonianism. If there *is* a logic of national liberation, it does not point just towards a completed state system, but equally well towards an unlimited secession from established states, with no uncontroversial criteria for nationhood. The process towards "completion of the state system" also produces conflicting national claims, trapped minorities within the new units, increased vulnerability and a reduced resource base for remaining groups. These possible prospects are not an argument against national liberation, but an argument against the principle of nationality as a universal clue to a more peaceful world order. The principle endorsed by Walzer does not give the necessary criteria for completion of the state system. Nationhood on ethnic criteria, for instance, might produce several thousand states, and not only the break-up of the Soviet Union.

The second major point in Walzer's paper is a double idea about modification of sovereignty. In a plea for stabilization of the state system, he argues for subnational devolution on the one hand and international alliance on the other. The hypothesis is that completion *and complication* of the state system will weaken the larger states from within (by devolution), confronting them with powerful federations and economic unions of smaller states (by alliance). This is supposed to stabilize the system of states.

The argument here is not convincing. Devolution might equally likely—or more likely—weaken the smaller states with less solid central authority; and alliance might equally likely—or more likely—increase the domination of large states. Walzer himself admits this possibility, but he nevertheless seems to dismiss it without further consideration.

We are thus left with two big question marks to the argument of the paper. One concerns the implications of the principle of nationality, due to its intrinsic ambiguity. The other concerns the effects of devolution and alliance on the international power structure, where a counter-hypothesis to Walzer's argument has been suggested.

Nevertheless, these comments are made in profound sympathy with the aim and scale of the propositions put forward in the paper. The acceptance of state sovereignty and the rejection of easy globalism are well placed. There is no reason to quarrel with the more modestly internationalist propositions presented. Two of the basic ideas of the paper, however, are less convincing.

General discussion

Much attention is given to the concepts of nation and nation-state, and criteria of *nationality*. It is argued that the way in which the nations of Europe—especially Eastern Europe—developed in the nineteenth century, indicates that pure chance played a considerable part in determining the extent to which self-proclaimed nations became effective political entities. Success depended on the most fortuitous processes; for example, whether or not a people developed an elite which was influential within their country, or whether or not they produced effective lexicographers who were able to exhume a language for them from the remote past. If nations were not thus fortunate, they did not make it. Other states, like Belgium, have made it because it was convenient for other nations to create them. There is, in other words, something inherently unstable about nations as such. They are artefacts, not real things. By contrast, behind the ideal of Mazzini—which to some extent is echoed in Walzer's paper—lies the idea of nation-states as a finite number of, so to speak, ontologically defined units waiting to be born.

Now it is clear that Walzer's argument does not presuppose the existence of some criterion by which one may recognize nations that are deserving recipients of statehood. It assumes, rather, that the borders between states will be drawn by a whole series of political and military struggles. The outcome of these struggles will be, in a certain sense, arbitrary from a moral point of view—some nations will not be fortunate enough to create their own states, and there is no remedy for that.

The merits and demerits of this particular proposal for *reform* of the international system may be assessed if it is related to other cognate proposals. Around the turn of the century, a peace program that has become known as "moderate internationalism" was important in European politics. The international system was to remain one of independent states whose freedom of action was constrained by international law, international organizations and economic interdependence. This program later became part of the foreign policy ideology of a number of small West European states. It is, moreover, a vision of a better world that has been tried to a considerable extent. It has failed, however, to lead to a significantly more peaceful and orderly world. There also appears to be an increasing backlash on the part of many states to these various moderate internationalist measures, as is evident, for example, in strong protectionist tendencies. This experience indicates perhaps some of the difficulty in organizing a system of independent states in a satisfactory manner.

A more specific problem is how to make the transition from the condition of *superpower rivalry*, which we have known for the last 40 years, to a situation in which reform of the entire international order might be feasible. To explore the prospects of transition, one must first ascertain what the Cold War is actually about. It has been contended that many of the original sources of conflict are no longer live issues. It is doubtful whether spheres of influence, ideology or the overall balance of power continue to be major sources of disturbance. Today attention focuses largely on arms and the arms race, which is more of a reflection than a cause of the Cold War. In view of this, the Cold War may seem to feed on habit, tradition and lack of imagination. Thus it is important when thinking about reform of the international system to consider how one might break through this habit and momentum of the Cold War.

Is a proposal for international reform in which *self-determination* is a crucial ingredient, a recipe for rebellion, endless conflict and permanent instability? This depends to a great deal on how one conceives of the social and political world within which self-determination is worked out. It is argued that the Lockean argument that it is only oppression that makes for tumult, is wrong as a single proposition about tumult, but certainly right as a proposition about a great deal of the tumult in the world. Still, it is conceivable that conditions of peace may presuppose the acceptance of situations that are widely held to be unjust.

Notes

CHAPTER 1 (Howard)

1 Karl von Clausewitz, *On War* (Princeton University Press, 1976).
2 James Joll, "The Unspoken Assumptions", in H. W. Koch, (ed.), *The Origins of the First World War* (London: 1972).
3 Arno Mayer, *The Persistence of the Old Regime* (London: 1981).
4 Hedley Bull, *The Anarchical Society* (London: 1977).
5 Michael Howard, "Weapons and Peace", in *The Causes of Wars* (London: 1983), p. 151.

(Waltz)

1 Quoted by Stephen Walt, "Alliance Formation and the Balance of World Power", *International Security*, Spring 1985, p. 7.
2 Letter to Lord Lytton, June 15, 1877. Quoted in Lady Gwendolyn Cecil, *Life of Robert Marquis Salisbury* (London: Hodder & Stoughton, 1921), v. 2, p. 153.
3 Quoted by Jim Hoagland in "'Star Wars': A Dim French View", *Washington Post National Weekly Edition*, November 12, 1984.

CHAPTER 2 (Singer)

1 J. David Singer & Melvin Small, "Foreign Policy Indicators: Predictors of War in History and in the State of the World Message", *Policy Sciences* 5/3 (September 1974), pp. 271-296.
2 Ernest R. May, *Lessons of the Past: The Use and Misuse of History in American Foreign Policy* (New York: Oxford University Press, 1973), p. xi.
3 James Lee Ray, *Global Politics* (Boston: Houghton Mifflin, 1983).
4 J. David Singer & Melvin Small, "National Alliance Commitments and War Involvement, 1815-1945", *Peace Research Society, Paper*, 5 (1966), pp. 109-140; Melvin Small & J. David Singer, "Alliance Aggregation and the Onset of War, 1815-1945" in J. David Singer (ed.), *Quantitative International Politics: Insights and Evidence* (New York: Free Press, 1968).
5 James Lee Ray, "The Measurement of System Structure" in J. David

Singer (ed.), *Correlates of War II: Testing Some Realpolitik Models* (New York: Free Press, 1980).

6 For polarity indicators, see Bruce Bueno de Mesquita, "Measuring Systemic Polarity", *Journal of Conflict Resolution* 19/2 (1975), pp. 187-216; for alliance aggregation indicators, see J. David Singer & Melvin Small, "National Alliance Commitments", op. cit., 1966; for structural clarity indicators, see J. David Singer & Sandra Bouxsein, "Structural Clarity and International War: Some Tentative Findings" in Murray (ed.), *Interdisciplinary Aspects of General Systems Theory*, 1975, pp. 126-135.

7 Charles Gochman & Zeev Maoz, "Militarized Interstate Disputes, 1816-1976: Procedures, Patterns, and Insights", *Journal of Conflict Resolution* 28/4 (December 1984), pp. 585-616; Melvin Small & J. David Singer, *Resort to Arms* (Beverly Hills, California: Sage, 1982).

8 For political integration indicators, see Quincy Wright, "The Mode of Financing Unions of States as a Measure of their Degree of Integration", *International Organization* XI (Winter 1957), pp. 30-40; for economic interdependence indicators, see Karl Deutsch & Alexander Eckstein, "National Industrialization and the Declining Share of the International Economic Sector, 1890-1959", *World Politics* 13 (1961), pp. 267-299; for international tension indicators, see Kjell Goldmann, *Tension and Detente in Bipolar Europe* (Stockholm: Scandinavia University Press, 1974); and for inter-state behavior patterns, see Russell Leng & J. David Singer, "Toward a Multi-Theoretical Typology of International Behavior", in Bunge, Galtung & Malitza (eds.), *Mathematical Approaches to International Relations* (Bucharest: Romanian Academy of Social and Political Sciences, 1977).

9 Jean de Bloch, *The Future of War* (New York: Doubleday & McClure, 1899); Lewis F. Richardson, *Mathematical Psychology of War* (London: UK Copywright Library, 1919; Pitirim Sorokin, *Social and Cultural Dynamics* 3 (New York: American Book Co., 1937); Quincy Wright, *A Study of War* (Chicago: Chicago University Press, 1942).

10 Karl Deutsch, *The Nerves of Government* (New York: Free Press, 1963).

11 Klaus Knorr & James Rosenau (eds.), *Contending Approaches to International Politics* (Princeton, N. J.: Princeton University Press, 1968).

12 On these points, see Zeev Maoz, *Paths to Conflict: International Dispute Initiation, 1816-1976* (Boulder, Colorado: Westview, 1982); Russell J. Leng, "Coercive Bargaining in Recurrent Crises", *Journal of Conflict Resolution* 27 (1983), pp. 379-420 and "Reagan and the Russians: Crisis Bargaining Beliefs and the Historical Record", *American Political Science Review* 78 (June 1984), pp. 338-355.

13 J. David Singer (ed.), *Human Behavior and International Politics: Contributions from the Social-Psychological Sciences* (Chicago: Rand McNally, 1965).

14 P. C. Asbjørnsen & J. Moe, *Norwegian Folk Tales* (Oslo: Dreyers Forlag, 1960).

15 J. David Singer & Sandra Bouxsein, op. cit., 1975.

16 Dina Zinnes, *Contemporary Research in International Relations* (New York: Free Press, 1976).

17 J. David Singer, Stuart Bremer & John Stuckey, "Capability Distribution,

Uncertainty, and Major Power War, 1820-1965" in Bruce Russett (ed.), *Peace, War, and Numbers* (Beverly Hills, California: Sage, 1972).

18 J. David Singer, "Military Preparedness, National Security, and the Lessons of History", in Huldt (ed.), *Swedish Yearbook of International Affairs* (Stockholm: 1985).

19 On this point, see Will Durant & Ariel Durant, *The Lessons of History* (New York: Simon & Schuster, 1968) and Ernest R. May, op. cit., 1973.

20 Frank Wayman, J. David Singer & Gary Goertz, "Capabilities, Allocations, and Success in Militarized Disputes and Wars, 1810-1976", *International Studies Quarterly* 27 (1983), pp. 497-515.

21 Joseph A. Schumpeter, *Imperialism and Social Classes* (New York: Kelley 1919 and 1951; Harold Lasswell, "The Garrison State", *American Journal of Sociology* 46 (1941), pp. 455-468.

22 Paul Diehl & Gary Goertz, "Trends in Military Allocations Since 1816" (Athens, Ga: University of Georgia, mimeo, 1985).

23 Leon Festinger, *Conflict, Decision, and Dissonance* (Stanford, California: Stanford University Press, 1964).

24 Stuart Bremer, "National Capabilities and War-Proneness" in J. David Singer (ed.), *The Correlates of War II: Testing Some Realpolitik Models* (New York: Free Press, 1980).

25 Frank Wayman, J. David Singer & Gary Goertz, op. cit., 1983.

26 Quincy Wright, "Project for a World Intelligence Center", *Journal of Conflict Resolution* I (1957), pp. 93-97; J. David Singer & Michael Wallace, *To Augur Well: Early Warning Indicators in World Politics* (Beverly Hills, California: Sage, 1979); J. David Singer & Richard Stoll, *Quantitative Indicators in World Politics: Timely Assurance and Early Warning* (New York: Praeger, 1984).

27 For a badly organized international system, see Hedley Bull, *The Anarchical Society* (New York: Columbia, 1979); also F. H. Hinsley, *Power and the Pursuit of Peace* (Cambridge: Cambridge University Press, 1963) and Kenneth Waltz, *Man, the State, and War* (New York: Columbia, 1959); for a weak sense of global ethics, see Michael Howard, *The Causes of War* (Cambridge, Mass.: Harvard University Press, 1984), also Michael Walzer, *Just and Unjust Wars* (New York: Basic Books, 1979).

CHAPTER 5 (Gaddis)

1 Geoffrey Blainey, *The Causes of War* (London: 1973), p. 3.

2 Jack S. Levy, *War in the Modern Great Power System, 1495-1975* (Lexington: 1983), p. 1. Other standard works on this subject, in addition to Blainey, cited above, include: Lewis F. Richardson, *Arms and Insecurity: A Mathematical Study of the Causes and Origins of War* (Pittsburgh: 1960);

Quincy Wright, *A Study of War*, 2nd ed. (Chicago: 1965); Kenneth N. Waltz, *Man, the State and War: A Theoretical Analysis* (New York: 1959); Kenneth Boulding, *Conflict and Defense: A General Theory* (New York: 1962); Raymond Aron, *Peace and War: A Theory of International Relations*, translated by Richard Howard and Annette Baker Fox (New York: 1966); Robert Gilpin, *War and Change in World Politics* (New York: 1981); Melvin Small and J. David Singer, *Resort to Arms: International and Civil Wars, 1816-1980* (Beverly Hills, California: 1982); and Michael Howard, *The Causes of Wars*, 2nd ed. (Cambridge, Massachussetts: 1984). A valuable overview of conflicting explanations is Keith Nelson and Spencer C. Olin, Jr., *Why War? Ideology, Theory, and History* (Berkeley: 1979).

3 The classic example of such abstract conceptualization is Morton A. Kaplan, *System and Process in International Politics* (New York: 1957). For the argument that 1945 marks the transition from a "multipolar" to a "bipolar" international system, see Glenn H. Snyder and Paul Diesing, *Conflict Among Nations: Bargaining, Decision Making, and System Structure in International Crises* (Princeton: 1977), pp. 419-420; and Kenneth Waltz, *Theory of International Politics* (Reading, Massachusetts: 1979), pp. 161-163.

4 I have followed here the definition of Robert Jervis, "Systems Theories and Diplomatic History," in Paul Gordon Lauren (ed.), *Diplomacy: New Approaches in History, Theory, and Policy* (New York: 1979), p. 212. A more rigorous discussion of the requirements of systems theory, and a critique of some of its major practitioners, occurs in Waltz, *Theory of International Politics*, pp. 38-78. Akira Iriye is one of the few historians who have sought to apply systems theory to the study of international relations. See his *After Imperialism: The Search for a New Order in the Far East, 1921-1931* (Cambridge, Massachusetts: 1965); and *The Cold War in Asia: A Historical Introduction* (Englewood Cliffs, New Jersey: 1974).

5 See, on this point, Robert Jervis, *Perception and Misperception in International Politics* (Princeton: 1976), pp. 58-62. Jervis points out that "almost by definition, a great power is more tightly connected to larger numbers of other states than is a small power ... Growing conflict or growing cooperation between Argentina and Chile would not affect Pakistan, but it would affect America and American policy toward those states ..." [Jervis, "Systems Theories and Diplomatic History,", p. 215.]

6 "A future war with the Soviet Union", retiring career diplomat Joseph C. Grew commented in May, 1945, "is as certain as anything in this world". [Memorandum of May 19, 1945, quoted in Joseph C. Grew, *Turbulent Era: A Diplomatic Record of Forty Years, 1904-1945* (Boston: 1952), II, 1446.] For other early expressions of pessimism about the stability of the post-war international system, see Walter Lippmann, *The Cold War: A Study in US Foreign Policy* (New York: 1947), pp. 26-28, 37-39, 60-62. "There is, after all, something to be explained—about perceptions as well as events—when so much that has been written has dismissed the new state system as no system at all but an unstable transition to something else." [A. W. DePorte, *Europe Between the Super-Powers: The Enduring Balance* (New Haven: 1979), p. 167.]

7 Karl W. Deutsch and J. David Singer, "Multipolar Power Systems and International Stability," in James N. Rosenau (ed.), *International Politics and Foreign Policy: A Reader in Research and Theory*, Rev. Ed. (New York: 1969), pp. 315-317. Deutsch and Singer equate "self-regulation" with "negative feedback': "By negative—as distinguished from positive or amplifying—feedback, we refer to the phenomenon of self-correction: as stimuli in one particular direction increase, the system exhibits a decreasing response to those stimuli, and increasingly exhibits the tendencies that counteract them." See also Jervis, "Systems Theories and Diplomatic History", p. 220. For Kaplan's more abstract definition of stability, see his *System and Process in International Politics*, p. 8. The concept of "stability" in international systems owes a good deal to "functionalist" theory; see, on this point, Charles Reynolds, *Theory and Explanation in International Politics* (London: Martin Robertson, 1973), p. 30.

8 I have followed here, in slightly modified form, criteria provided in Gordon A. Craig and Alexander L. George, *Force and Statecraft: Diplomatic Problems of Our Time* (New York: 1983), p. x, a book that provides an excellent discussion of how international systems have evolved since the beginning of the eighteenth century. But see also Gilpin, *War and Change in World Politics*, pp. 50-105.

9 See, on this point, Waltz, *Theory of International Politics*, pp. 180-181; also DePorte, *Europe Between the Super-Powers*, p. 167.

10 Waltz, *Theory of International Politics*, pp. 73-78; Gilpin, *War and Change in World Politics*, pp. 85-88.

11 "... [S]tructure designates a set of constraining conditions ... [It] acts as a selector, but it cannot be seen, examined, and observed at work ... Because structures select by rewarding some behaviors and punishing others, outcomes cannot be inferred from intentions and behaviors." [Waltz, *Theory of International Politics*, pp. 73-74.]

12 Harold Nicolson, *Peacemaking 1919* (New York: 1965), pp. 30-31.

13 Bernadotte E. Schmitt and Harold C. Vedeler, *The World in the Crucible: 1914-1919* (New York: 1984), p. 470. "Mr Evelyn Waugh's view, that what began as a crusade turned into a tug of war between indistinguishable teams of sweaty louts, is idiosyncratic. Most of us [in World War II] did not feel like that. But it is evident that by the end of the First World War a large number of intelligent people did; and ten years later their doubts had become general". [Michael Howard, *Studies in War and Peace* (New York: 1970), p. 99.]

14 Nicolson, *Peacemaking 1919*, pp. 26-29. See also Lawrence E. Gelfand, *The Inquiry: American Preparations for Peace, 1917-1919* (New Haven: 1963).

15 Quoted in John Morton Blum, *Woodrow Wilson and the Politics of Morality* (Boston: 1956), p. 161. The most convenient overview of Wilson's ideas regarding the peace settlement can be found in N. Gordon Levin, Jr., *Woodrow Wilson and World Politics: America's Response to War and Revolution* (New York: 1968), esp. pp. 123-251; and Arthur S. Link, *Woodrow Wilson: Revolution, War, and Peace* (Arlington Heights, Illinois: 1979), pp. 72-103.

16 See, on this point, Gelfand, *The Inquiry*, pp. 323-326; Schmitt and Vedeler, *The World in the Crucible*, pp. 474-475; and Klaus Schwabe, *Woodrow Wilson, Revolutionary Germany, and Peacemaking, 1918-1919: Missionary Diplomacy and the Realities of Power* (Chapel Hill: 1985), pp. 395-402.

17 Winston Churchill's is the classic indictment of this decision. See his *The Gathering Storm*, Bantam ed. (New York: 1961), pp. 9-10.

18 Craig and George, *Force and Statecraft*, pp. 87-100; see also Howard, *The Causes of Wars*, pp. 163-164. "... [T]he victors at Versailles ... failed ... because, as if lulled by their own rhetoric, they continued to assert morality while they neglected armaments." [Blainey, *The Causes of War*, p. 163.]

19 See, on Germany, Tony Sharp, *The Wartime Alliance and the Zonal Division of Germany* (Oxford: 1975), and John H. Backer, *The Decision to Divide Germany: American Foreign Policy in Transition* (Durham: 1978); on Austria, William Bader, *Austria Between East and West, 1945-1955* (Stanford: 1966), and Sven Allard, *Russia and the Austrian State Treaty: A Case Study of Soviet Policy in Europe* (University Park, Pennsylvania: 1970); on Korea, Charles M. Dobbs, *The Unwanted Symbol: American Foreign Policy, the Cold War, and Korea, 1945-1950* (Kent, Ohio: 1981), and Bruce Cumings, *The Origins of the Korean War: Liberation and the Emergence of Separate Regimes, 1945-1947* (Princeton: 1981). For useful comparative perspectives on the issue of partition, see Thomas E. Hachey (ed.), *The Problem of Partition: Peril to World Peace* (Chicago: 1972).

20 Lynn Etheridge Davis, *The Cold War Begins: Soviet-American Conflict Over Eastern Europe* (Princeton: 1974); Eduard Mark, "American Policy toward Eastern Europe and the Origins of the Cold War, 1941-1946: An Alternative Interpretation", *Journal of American History*, LXVIII (September, 1981), pp. 313-336; and, for first-person accounts from American diplomats, Thomas T. Hammond (ed.), *Witnesses to the Origins of the Cold War* (Seattle: 1982).

21 See, on this point, John Lewis Gaddis, "The Emerging Post-Revisionist Synthesis on the Origins of the Cold War", *Diplomatic History*, VII (Summer, 1983), pp. 181-183. For a perceptive discussion of post-World War II American "imperial" expansion, see Tony Smith, *The Pattern of Imperialism: The United States, Great Britain, and the Late-Industrializing World since 1815* (Cambridge: 1981), pp. 182-202.

22 Robert H. Ferrell (ed.), *The Autobiography of Harry S. Truman* (Boulder, Colorado: 1980), p. 120; David S. McLellan, *Dean Acheson: The State Department Years* (New York: 1976), p. 116.

23 Hans J. Morgenthau, *Politics Among Nations: The Struggle for Power and Peace* (New York: 1949), p. 285. For the transition from bipolarity to multipolarity, see the 1973 edition of *Politics Among Nations*, pp. 338-342; also Waltz, *Theory of International Politics*, p. 162. For an eloquent history of the Cold War that views it as the product of the polarization of world politics, see Louis J. Halle, *The Cold War as History*, (New York: 1967).

24 Among those who have emphasized the instability of bipolar systems are Morgenthau, *Politics Among Nations*, pp. 350-354; Wright, *A Study of War*, pp. 763-764. See also Blainey, *The Causes of War*, pp. 110-111.

25 "... [W]hat *was* dominant in their consciousness," Michael Howard has

written of the immediate post-Second World War generation of statesmen, "was the impotence, almost one might say the irrelevance, of ethical aspirations in international politics in the absence of that factor to which so little attention had been devoted by their more eminent predecessors, to which indeed so many of them had been instinctively hostile—military power." [Howard, *The Causes of War*, p. 55.]

26 Henry Kissinger has written two classic accounts dealing with the importance of individual leadership in sustaining international systems. See his *A World Restored* (New York: 1957), on Metternich; and, on Bismarck, "The White Revolutionary: Reflections on Bismarck," *Daedalus*, XCVII (Summer, 1968), pp. 888-924. For a somewhat different perspective on Bismarck's role, see George F. Kennan, *The Decline of Bismarck's European Order: Franco-Russian Relations, 1875-1890* (Princeton: 1979), esp. pp. 421-422.

27 Waltz, *Theory of International Politics*, p. 176. On the tendency of unstable systemic structures to induce irresponsible leadership, see Ludwig Dehio, *The Precarious Balance: Four Centuries of the European Power Struggle*, translated by Charles Fullman (New York: Knopf, 1962), pp. 257-258.

28 See, on this point, Roger V. Dingman, "Theories of, and Approaches to, Alliance Politics," in Lauren (ed.), *Diplomacy*, pp. 247-247.

29 My argument here follows that of Snyder and Diesing, *Conflict Among Nations*, pp. 429-445.

30 Waltz, *Theory of International Politics*, pp. 167-169.

31 Foster Rhea Dulles, *The Road to Teheran: The Story of Russia and America, 1781-1943* (Princeton: 1944), p. 8.

32 See, for example, Thomas A. Bailey, *America Faces Russia: Russian-American Relations from Early Times to Our Day* (Ithaca: 1950), pp. 347-349. A more recent discussion of these developments is in John Lewis Gaddis, *Russia, the Soviet Union, and the United States: An Interpretive History* (New York: 1978), pp. 27-56.

33 The argument is succinctly summarized in Nelson and Olin, *Why War?*, pp. 35-43. Geoffrey Blainey labels the idea "Manchesterism" and satirizes it wickedly: "If those gifted early prophets of the Manchester creed could have seen Chamberlain—during the Czech crisis of September 1938—board the aircraft that was to fly him to Bavaria to meet Hitler at short notice they would have hailed aviation as the latest messenger of peace. If they had known that he met Hitler without even his own German interpreter they would perhaps have wondered whether the conversation was in Esperanto or Volapuk. It seemed that every postage stamp, bilingual dictionary, railway timetable and trade fair, every peace congress, Olympic race, tourist brochure and international telegram that had ever existed, was gloriously justified when Mr Chamberlain said from the window of number 10 Downing Street on 30 September 1938: 'I believe it is peace for our time.' In retrospect the outbreak of war a year later seems to mark the failure and the end of the policy of appeasement, but the policy survived. The first British air raids over Germany dropped leaflets." [*The Causes of War*, p. 28.]

34 Waltz, *Theory of International Politics*, p. 138. For Waltz's general argu-

ment against interdependence as a necessary cause of peace, see ibid., pp. 138-160.

35 Melvin Small and J. David Singer, *Resort to Arms: International and Civil Wars, 1816-1980* (Beverly Hills, California: 1982), p. 102. The one questionable case is the Crimean War, which pitted Britain and France against Russia, but that conflict began as a dispute between Russia and Turkey.

36 Small and Singer identify 44 civil wars as having been fought between 1945 and 1980; this compares with 30 inter-state and 12 "extra-systemic" wars during the same period. [Ibid., pp. 92-95, 98-99, 229-232.]

37 Soviet exports and imports as a percentage of gross national product ranged between 4 and 7% between 1955 and 1975; for the United States the comparable figures were 7-14%. This compares with figures of 33-52% for Great Britain, France, Germany and Italy in the four years immediately preceding the First World War, and figures of 19-41% for the same nations plus Japan for the period 1949-1976. [Waltz, *Theory of International Politics*, pp. 141, 212.]

38 See, on this point, Herbert S. Dinerstein, *The Making of a Missile Crisis, October, 1962* (Baltimore: 1976), esp. pp. 230-238.

39 See Note 35, above. It is worth noting, in this connection, the striking tendency of American diplomats who have spent time inside the Soviet Union to become Russophobes. Comparable tendencies seem strikingly absent among China specialists in the Foreign Service. Compare, for the contrast, Hugh DeSantis, *The Diplomacy of Silence: The American Foreign Service, the Soviet Union, and the Cold War, 1933-1947* (Chicago: 1980); and E. J. Kahn, Jr., *The China Hands: America's Foreign Service Officers and What Befell Them* (New York: 1975). Whether Soviet diplomats who serve in the United States develop "Americophobic" tendencies is difficult to say, given currently available information.

40 Zbigniew Brzezinski and Samuel P. Huntington, *Political Power: USA/USSR* (New York: 1964), pp. 90-104. For a more recent assessment of the extent of public participation in the Soviet political system, see Jerry F. Hough and Merle Fainsod, *How the Soviet Union Is Governed* (Cambridge, Massachusetts: 1979), pp. 314-319.

41 For a useful brief review of this literature, see Nelson and Olin, *Why War?*, pp. 58-84; also Richard J. Barnet, *Roots of War* (New York: 1972), pp. 208-214.

42 See, most recently, Arno J. Mayer, *The Persistence of the Old Regime: Europe to the Great War* (New York: 1981), esp. pp. 304-323; and Paul M. Kennedy, *The Rise of Anglo-German Antagonism, 1869-1914* (Boston: 1980), esp. pp. 465-466.

43 Examples include Charles S. Maier, *Recasting Bourgeois Europe: Stabilization in France, Germany, and Italy in the Decade After World War I* (Princeton: 1975); Stephen A. Schuker, *The End of French Predominance in Europe: The Financial Crisis of 1924 and the Adoption of the Dawes Plan* (Chapel Hill: 1976); Michael J. Hogan, *Informal Entente: The Private Structure of Cooperation in Anglo-American Economic Diplomacy, 1918-1928* (Columbia, Missouri: 1977); Melvyn P. Leffler, *The Elusive Quest: America's*

Pursuit of European Stability and French Security, 1919-1933 (Chapel Hill: 1979); Frank Costigliola, *Awkward Dominion: American Political, Economic, and Cultural Relations with Europe, 1919-1933* (Ithaca: 1984).

44 For some recent—and sometimes contradictory—attempts to come to grips with this question, see John Lewis Gaddis, *Strategies of Containment: A Critical Appraisal of Postwar American National Security Policy* (New York: 1982), pp. 352-357; Ralph B. Levering, *The Public and American Foreign Policy, 1918-1978* (New York: 1978); William Appleman Williams, *Empire as a Way of Life* (New York: 1980); Cecil V. Crabb, Jr., *The Doctrines of American Foreign Policy: Their Meaning, Role, and Future* (Baton Rouge: 1982), esp. pp. 371-386; Robert Dallek, *The American Style of Foreign Policy: Cultural Politics and Foreign Affairs* (New York: 1983), esp. pp. xi-xx; Lloyd C. Gardner, *A Covenant with Power: America and World Order from Wilson to Reagan* (New York: 1984).

45 William Appleman Williams, *The Tragedy of American Diplomacy,* rev. ed. (New York: 1962). See also Charles A. Beard, *The Idea of National Interest: An Analytical Study in American Foreign Policy* (New York: 1934), and *The Open Door at Home: A Trial Philosophy of National Interest* (New York: 1934). Other important expressions of the Beard/Williams thesis include Gabriel Kolko, *The Roots of American Foreign Policy: An Analysis of Power and Purpose* (Boston: 1969); and Harry Magdoff, *The Age of Imperialism: The Economics of US Foreign Policy* (New York: 1969).

46 Charles S. Maier, "The Two Postwar Eras and the Conditions for Stability in Twentieth-Century Western Europe," *American Historical Review,* LXXXVI (April, 1981), pp. 327-352; Robert Griffith, "Dwight D. Eisenhower and the Corporate Commonwealth," ibid., LXXXVII (February, 1982), pp. 87-122; Michael J. Hogan, "American Marshall Planners and the Search for a European Neocapitalism," ibid, XC (February, 1985), pp. 44-72.

47 The best critiques of the "open door" model are Robert W. Tucker, *The Radical Left and American Foreign Policy* (Baltimore: 1971); Charles S. Maier, "Revisionism and the Interpretation of Cold War Origins," *Perspectives in American History,* IV (1970), pp. 313-347; Richard A. Melanson, "Revisionism Subdued? Robert James Maddox and the Origins of the Cold War," *Political Science Reviewer,* VII (1977), pp. 229-271, and "The Social and Political Thought of William Appleman Williams," *Western Political Quarterly,* XXXI (1978), pp. 392-409. Kenneth Waltz provides an effective theoretical critique of "reductionism" in his *Theory of International Politics,* pp. 60-67. There is as yet no substantial published critique of "corporatism", although the present author attempted an insubstantial unpublished one at a panel on "The Future of American Diplomatic History" at the American Historical Association annual convention, Chicago, December 30, 1984.

48 Williams, *The Tragedy of American Diplomacy,* pp. 43, 49 [emphases in original]. See also N. Gordon Levin's elaboration of this key point in *Woodrow Wilson and World Politics,* pp. 2-5.

49 Maier, "The Two Postwar Eras and the Conditions for Stability in Twentieth-Century Western Europe"; Hogan, "American Marshall Planners and the Search for a European Neocapitalism".

50 C. Wright Mills, *The Power Elite* (New York: 1956), p. 360.

51 Eisenhower "farewell address", January 17, 1961, *Public Papers of the Presidents of the United States: Dwight D. Eisenhower, 1960-61* [hereafter *Eisenhower Public Papers*] (Washington: 1961), p. 1038.

52 Fred J. Cook, *The Warfare State* (New York: 1962); W. Carroll Pursell, Jr. (ed.), *The Military-Industrial Complex* (New York: 1972); Bruce M. Russett and Alfred Stepan, *Military Force and American Society* (New York: 1973); Seymour Melman, *The Permanent War Economy: American Capitalism in Decline* (New York: 1974).

53 See, on the immediate postwar period, Warner R. Schilling, "The Politics of National Defense: Fiscal 1950," in Warner R. Schilling, Paul Y. Hammond, and Glenn H. Snyder, *Strategy, Politics, and Defense Budgets* (New York: 1962), pp. 1-266; on the 1970s, Lawrence J. Korb, *The Fall and Rise of the Pentagon: American Defense Policies in the 1970s* (Westport, Connecticut: 1979).

54 Vernon V. Asparturian, "The Soviet Military-Industrial Complex—Does It Exist?" *Journal of International Affairs*, XXVI (1972), pp. 1-28; William T. Lee, "The 'Politico-Military-Industrial Complex' of the USSR.," ibid., pp. 73-86; Andrew Cockburn, *The Threat: Inside the Soviet Military Machine* (New York: 1983), pp. 120-149.

55 Joseph S. Nye, Jr. (ed.), *The Making of America's Soviet Policy* (New Haven: 1984); I. M. Destler, Leslie H. Gelb, and Anthony Lake, *The Own Worst Enemy: The Unmaking of American Foreign Policy* (New York: 1984).

56 See, on this point, Seyom Brown, *The Faces of Power: Constancy and Change in United States Foreign Policy from Truman to Reagan* (New York: 1983), pp. 7-14.

57 Kennan to State Department, March 20, 1946, U.S. Department of State, *Foreign Relations of the United States: 1946* [hereafter FRUS], VI, 721. See also Kennan's famous "long telegram" of February 22, 1946, in ibid, pp. 696-709; and his influential "Mr. X" article, "The Sources of Soviet Conduct," *Foreign Affairs*, XXV (July, 1947), pp. 566-582. The circumstances surrounding the drafting of these documents are discussed in George F. Kennan, *Memoirs: 1925-1950* (Boston: 1967), pp. 292-295, 354-357.

58 Kennan has emphasized that the recommendations advanced in the "long telegram" and the "X" article applied to the Stalin regime. [See his *Memoirs: 1925-1950*, pp. 364-367.] But he does still see the role of institutionalized suspicion in Soviet society as making relations with the outside world unnecessarily difficult. [See, for example, George F. Kennan, "Letter to a Russian," *New Yorker*, LX (September 24, 1984), pp. 55-73.]

59 See, for example, Vernon V. Aspaturian, "Internal Politics and Foreign Policy in the Soviet System," in Aspaturian (ed.), *Process and Power in Soviet Foreign Policy* (Boston: 1971), pp. 491-551; William Taubman, *Stalin's American Policy: From Entente to Detente to Cold War* (New York: 1982), pp. 243-255; Seweryn Bialer, "The Political System," in Robert F. Byrnes (ed.), *After Brezhnev: Sources of Soviet Conduct in the 1980s* (Bloomington: 1983), pp. 10-11, 35-36, 51, 55; Adam Ulam, "The World Outside," in ibid., pp. 345-348.

60 On this point, see Gaddis, *Strategies of Containment*, pp. 34-35, 62, 74, 83-84.

61 The most conspicuous exception would appear to be the authors of NSC-68, the comprehensive reassessment of national security policy drafted early in 1950, who argued that when Soviet *capabilities* reached the point of being able to win a war, Soviet *intensions* would automatically be to provoke one. See NSC 68, "United States Objectives and Programs for National Security," April 14, 1950, *FRUS: 1950*, I, esp. pp. 251-252, 266-267.

62 See, on this point, Alexander L. George and Richard Smoke, *Deterrence in American Foreign Policy: Theory and Practice* (New York: 1974), pp. 527-530; also Patrick M. Morgan, *Deterrence: A Conceptual Analysis* (Beverly Hills: 1977), pp. 205-207.

63 Blainey, *The Causes of War*, p. 53. See also Howard, *The Causes of Wars*, pp. 14-15; Paul M. Kennedy, *Strategy and Diplomacy: 1870-1945* (London: 1983), pp. 163-177; and Richard Smoke's perceptive discussion on the role of expectations in escalation in *War: Controlling Escalation* (Cambridge, Massachusetts: 1977), pp. 268-277.

64 Kennan, *The Decline of Bismarck's European Order*, pp. 3-4.

65 See Michael Howard's observations on the absence of a "bellicist" mentality among the great powers in the post-war era, in his *The Causes of War*, pp. 271-273.

66 Small and Singer, *Resort to Arms*, pp. 167, 169.

67 For a persuasive elaboration of this argument, with an intriguing comparison of the post-1945 "nuclear" system to the post-1815 "Vienna" system, see Michael Mandelbaum, *The Nuclear Revolution: International Politics Before and After Hiroshima* (New York: 1981), pp. 58-77; also Morgan, *Deterrence*, p. 208; Craig and George, *Force and Statecraft*, pp. 117-120; Howard, *The Causes of War*, pp. 22, 278-279.

68 See, on this point, Mandelbaum, *The Nuclear Revolution*, p. 109; also the discussion of the "crystal ball effect" in Albert Carnesale, *et al.*, *Living With Nuclear Weapons* (New York: 1983), p. 44.

69 For a brief review of the literature on crisis management, together with an illustrative comparison of the July, 1914, crisis with the Cuban missile crisis, see Ole R. Holsti, "Theories of Crisis Decision Making", in Lauren (ed.), *Diplomacy*, pp. 99-136; also Craig and George, *Force and Statecraft*, pp. 205-219.

70 Gilpin, *War and Change in World Politics*, pp. 202-203. Geoffrey Blainey, citing an idea first proposed by the sociologist Georg Simmel, has suggested that in the past war was the only means by which nations could gain an exact knowledge of each others' capabilities. [Blainey, *The Causes of War*, p. 118.]

71 A useful up-to-date assessment of the technology is David Hafemeister, Joseph J. Romm and Kosta Tsipis, "The Verification of Compliance with Arms-Control Agreements", *Scientific American*, 252 (March, 1985), pp. 38-45. For the historical evolution of reconnaissance satellites, see Philip J. Klass, *Secret Sentries in Space* (New York: 1971).

72 The most recent assessment, but one whose analysis does not take into

account examples prior to 1940, is Richard K. Betts, *Surprise Attack: Lessons for Defense Planning* (Washington: 1982). See also, on the problem of assessing adversary intentions, Ernest R. May (ed.), *Knowing One's Enemies: Intelligence Assessment Before the Two World Wars* (Princeton: 1984).

73 For a summary of what the open literature reveals about the difficulties faced by American intelligence in the first decade after the Second World War, see Thomas Powers, *The Man Who Kept the Secrets: Richard Helms and the CIA* (New York: 1979), pp. 43-58; and John Prados, *The Soviet Estimate: U.S. Intelligence and Russian Military Strength* (New York: 1982), pp. 24-30.

74 On this point, see Michael Krepon, *Arms Control: Verification and Compliance* (New York: 1984), esp. pp. 8-13.

75 Prados, *The Soviet Estimate*, pp. 30-35, 96-110.

76 See, on this point, Wright, *A Study of War*, pp. 1290-1291; Aron, *Peace and War*, pp. 64-69; Reynolds, *Theory and Explanation in International Politics*, p. 176; also Murray Edelman, *Politics as Symbolic Action: Mass Arousal and Quiescence*, (Chicago: 1971), pp. 53-64.

77 Norman Rich, *Hitler's War Aims: Ideology, the Nazi State, and the Course of Expansion* (New York: 1973), pp. xxxvi-xxxvii, xlii-xliii, 3-10.

78 One thinks, in this connection, of the successful struggles of the Vietnamese and the Algerians against the French and of Portugal's African colonies against that country, of equally successful separatist movements within India and later Pakistan, and of the unsuccessful Biafran rebellion against Nigeria.

79 On the recent resurgence of religion as an influence on world politics, see Paul Johnson, *Modern Times: The World From the Twenties to the Eighties* (New York: 1983), pp. 698-710.

80 See, on this point, Halle, *The Cold War as History*, 157-160.

81 Adam B. Ulam, *Expansion and Coexistence: The History of Soviet Foreign Policy, 1917-73*, 2nd ed. (New York: 1974), pp. 130-131.

82 See, on this point, E. H. Carr, *The Bolshevik Revolution, 1917-1923* (New York: 1953), pp. 549-566; and Marshall D. Shulman, *Stalin's Foreign Policy Reappraised* (New York: 1969), p. 82. It is fashionable now, among Soviet scholars, to minimize the ideological component of Moscow's foreign policy; indeed Lenin himself is now seen as the original architect of "peaceful coexistence", a leader for whom the idea of exporting revolution can hardly have been more alien. [See, for example, G. A. Trofimenko, "Uroki mirnogo sosushestvovania", *Voprosy istorii*, #11 (November, 1983), pp. 3-7.] It seems not out of place to wonder how the great revolutionary would have received such perfunctory dismissals of the Comintern and all that it implied; certainly most Western students have treated more seriously than this the revolutionary implications of the Bolshevik Revolution.

83 For Stalin's mixed record on this issue, see Shulman, *Stalin's Foreign Policy Reappraised, passim.*; also Adam B. Ulam, *Stalin: The Man and His Era* (New York: 1973), esp. pp. 641-643, 654; and William Taubman, *Stalin's American Policy: From Entente to Detente to Cold War* (New York:

1982), pp. 128-227. It is possible, of course, that Stalin followed both policies intentionally as a means both of intimidating and inducing complacency in the West.

84 Herbert Dinerstein, *War and the Soviet Union: Nuclear Weapons and the Revolution in Soviet Military and Political Thinking* (New York: 1959), pp. 65-90; William Zimmerman, *Soviet Perspectives on International Relations, 1956-1967* (Princeton: 1969), pp. 251-252.

85 Nikita S. Khrushchev, *Khrushchev Remembers: The Last Testament*, translated and edited by Strobe Talbott (Boston: 1974), p. 529.

86 Zimmerman, *Soviet Perspectives on International Relations*, pp. 252-255.

87 Ibid., pp. 5, 255-259. See also *Khrushchev Remembers*, p. 530.

88 "... [P]layers' goals may undergo very little change, but postponing their attainment to the indefinite future fundamentally transforms the meaning of ... myth by revising its implications for social action. Exactly because myths are dramatic stories, changing their time-frame affects their character profoundly. Those who see only the permanence of professed goals, but who neglect structural changes—the incorporation of common experiences into the myths of both sides, shifts in the image of the opponent ('there are reasonable people also in the other camp'), and modifications in the myths' periodization—overlook the great effects that may result from such contextual changes." [Friedrich V. Kratochwil, *International Order and Foreign Policy: A Theoretical Sketch of Post-War International Politics* (Boulder: 1978), p. 117.]

89 John Lewis Gaddis, *The United States and the Origins of the Cold War, 1941-1947* (New York: 1972), pp. 56-62, 133-175.

90 See, on this point, Michael S. Sherry, *Preparing for the Next War: American Plans for Postwar Defense, 1941-45* (New Haven: 1977), pp. 52-53; Eduard Maximilian Mark, "The Interpretation of Soviet Foreign Policy in the United States, 1928-1947," (Ph.D. Dissertation, University of Connecticut, 1978), pp. 95-96, 326-329; and, for the Wilsonian background of this idea, see Levin, *Woodrow Wilson and World Politics*, pp. 37-45. For the ideological roots of "unconditional surrender", see Anne Armstrong, *Unconditional Surrender: The Impact of the Casablanca Policy Upon World War II* (New Brunswick: 1961), pp. 250-253.

91 See, for example, Hannah Arendt, *The Origins of Totalitarianism* (New York: 1951) and Carl Friedrich and Zbigniew Brzezinski, *Totalitarian Dictatorship and Autocracy* (Cambridge, Massachusetts: 1956); also Les K. Adler and Thomas G. Paterson, "Red Fascism: The Merger of Nazi Germany and Soviet Russia in the American Image of Totalitarianism, 1930's-1950's" *American Historical Review*, LXXV (April, 1970), pp. 1046-1064.

92 NSC 20/4, "U.S. Objectives with Respect to the USSR to Counter Soviet Threats to U.S. Security," November 23, 1948, *FRUS: 1948*, I, pp. 668-669. In an earlier version of this document, George F. Kennan had explained that "we could not hope to achieve any total assertion of our will on Russian territory, as we have endeavored to do in Germany and Japan. We must recognize that whatever settlement we finally achieve must be a *political* settlement, *politically* negotiated." [NSC 20/1, "U.S. Objectives

With Respect to Russia," August 18, 1948, in Thomas H. Etzold and John Lewis Gaddis (eds.), *Containment: Documents on American Policy and Strategy, 1945-1950* (New York: 1978), p. 193.]

93 The best brief review of early American war plans is in Gregg Herken, *The Winning Weapon: The Atomic Bomb in the Cold War, 1945-1950* (New York: 1980), pp. 195-303. A selection from these plans has been published in Etzold and Gaddis (eds.), *Containment,* pp. 277-381. The Soviet Union has yet to make any comparable selection of its post-war documents available.

94 NSC 68, "United States Objectives and Programs for National Security," *FRUS: 1950,* I, 242.

95 Kennan made the point explicitly in NSC 20/1 [Etzold and Gaddis (eds.), *Containment,* p. 191]; also in *The Realities of American Foreign Policy* (Princeton: 1954), p. 80.

96 On changing Soviet psychology as the ultimate goal of containment, see Gaddis, *Strategies of Containment,* pp. 48-51, 71-83, 98-99, 102-106.

97 See, for example, Hans J. Morgenthau, *In Defense of the National Interest: A Critical Examination of American Foreign Policy* (New York: 1951), pp. 31-33, 142-146. The critique of "unconditional surrender" can best be followed in Armstrong, *Unconditional Surrender,* pp. 248-262; and in Hanson W. Baldwin, *Great Mistakes of the War* (New York: 1950), pp. 14-25.

98 David Alan Rosenberg, "'A Smoking, Radiating Ruin at the End of Two Hours': Documents on American Plans for Nuclear War with the Soviet Union, 1954-55," *International Security,* VI (Winter, 1981/82, pp. 3-38, and "The Origins of Overkill: Nuclear Weapons and American Strategy, 1945-1960," ibid., VII (Spring, 1983), pp. 3-71. For more general accounts, see Fred Kaplan, *The Wizards of Armageddon* (New York: 1983), esp. pp. 263-270; and Gregg Herken, *Counsels of War* (New York: 1985), pp. 137-140.

99 Rosenberg, "The Origins of Overkill," pp. 8, 69-71; Kaplan, *Wizards of Armageddon,* pp. 268-285; Herken, *Counsels of War,* pp. 140-165; Stephen E. Ambrose, *Eisenhower: The President* (New York: 1984), pp. 494, 523, 564.

100 See, on this point, John Spanier, *Games Nations Play: Analyzing International Politics,* 5th ed. (New York: 1984), p. 91.

101 Gaddis, *The United States and the Origins of the Cold War,* pp. 23-31.

102 The United Nations, regretfully, cannot be considered an effective supranational authority.

103 My definition here is based on Paul Keal, *Unspoken Rules and Superpower Dominance* (New York: 1983), pp. 2-3. Other more generalized studies dealing with theories of games and bargaining include Kratochwil, *International Order and Foreign Policy, passim.*; Snyder and Diesing, *Conflict Among Nations,* esp. pp. 33-182; Anatol Rapaport, *Fights, Games, and Debates* (Ann Arbor: 1960); and Charles Lockhart, *Bargaining in International Conflicts* (New York: 1979).

104 On this point, see Geir Lundestad, *America, Scandinavia, and the Cold War, 1945-1949* (New York: 1980), esp. pp. 327-338. For the formation of spheres of influence, see Keal, *Unspoken Rules and Superpower Dominance,*

pp. 66-71, 80-84, 90-98; also John Lewis Gaddis, "The United States and the Question of a Sphere of Influence in Europe, 1945-1949," in Olav Riste (ed.), *Western Security: The Formative Years: European and Atlantic Defence, 1947-1953* (Oslo, 1985, pp. 60–91).

105 "In general terms, acquiescence in spheres of influence has taken the form of A disclaiming what B does and in fact disapproving of what B does, but at the same time acquiescing by virtue of effectively doing nothing to oppose B." [Keal, *Unspoken Rules and Superpower Dominance*, p. 115.]

106 For a good overview of this process of consolidation, see ibid., pp. 87-115.

107 George and Smoke, *Deterrence in American Foreign Policy*, pp. 523-526, 557-560.

108 Ibid., pp. 536-543.

109 For a discussion of the Hungarian, Czech, Cuban and Dominican Republic episodes, see Keal, *Unspoken Rules and Superpower Dominance*, pp. 116-158. There is no adequate comparative analysis of how the United States responded to the defections of Yugoslavia and China.

110 Coral Bell, *The Conventions of Crisis: A Study in Diplomatic Management* (London: 1971); Phil Williams, *Crisis Management: Confrontation and Diplomacy in the Nuclear Age* (New York: 1976). They have also managed successfully to control incidents at sea: see Sean M. Lynn-Jones, "A Quiet Success for Arms Control: Preventing Incidents at Sea," *International Security*, IX (Spring, 1985), pp. 154-184.

111 This analysis assumes, as do most scholarly examinations of the subject, that the North Korean attack could not have taken place without some form of Soviet authorization. The most thorough assessment of this admittedly unclear episode is Robert R. Simmons, *The Strained Alliance: Peking, Pyongyang, Moscow and the Politics of the Korean Civil War* (New York: 1975).

112 Which is not to say that the Soviet Union does not engage in covert operations as well; it is, however, somewhat more successful at concealing them. The best recent overview is John Barron, *KGB Today: The Hidden Hand* (New York: 1983).

113 The classic case, of course, is the amply-documented July, 1914, crisis, the implications of which have most recently been reassessed in a special edition of *International Security*, IX (Summer, 1984). But see also Richard Smoke's essays on how the Seven Years' War and the Crimean War grew out of a comparable failure of the major powers to limit the escalation of quarrels they did not initiate. [Smoke, *War: Controlling Escalation*, pp. 147-236.]

114 See Gaddis, *Strategies of Containment*, pp. 145-152; also Glenn H. Snyder, "The 'New Look' of 1953," in Schilling, Hammond and Snyder, *Strategy, Politics, and Defense Budgets*, pp. 379-524.

115 Henry A. Kissinger, *Nuclear Weapons and Foreign Policy* (New York: 1957). It should be added, in fairness, that Kissinger by 1961 had repudiated his earlier position on this point. See his *The Necessity for Choice: Prospects of American Foreign Policy* (New York: 1961).

116 For a summary of Soviet thinking on the subject, see Harriet Fast Scott

and William F. Scott, *The Armed Forces of the USSR* (Boulder: 1979), esp. pp. 55-56, 61-62.

117 John K. Emmerson to Dean Rusk, November 8, 1950, *FRUS: 1950*, VII, pp. 1098-1099. See also a memorandum by Paul Nitze, November 4, 1950, ibid., pp. 1041-1042; and Philip C. Jessup's notes of a meeting between Truman and Attlee at the White House, December 7, 1950, ibid., pp. 1462-1465. For a comprehensive policy statement on the use of atomic weapons in war, see the Department of State-Joint Strategic Survey Committee paper, "United States Position on Considerations Under Which the United States Will Accept War and on Atomic Warfare," August 3, 1951, *FRUS: 1951*, pp. 866-874.

118 Ambrose, *Eisenhower: The President*, p. 184. For examples of Eisenhower's refusal to authorize the use of nuclear weapons, see ibid., pp. 179, 206, 213, 229-230, 243, 274, 483-484. Eisenhower's "bullet" statement is from his March 16, 1955 press conference, *Eisenhower Public Papers, 1955* (Washington: 1959), p. 332.

119 With the exception of chemical weapons, for which there appears to be an even deeper aversion than to the use of nuclear weapons. See, on this point, Mandelbaum, *The Nuclear Revolution*, esp. pp. 29-40.

120 It is interesting to note that John F. Kennedy began his administration with what appeared to be a pledge never to initiate the use of nuclear weapons against the Soviet Union; after protests from NATO allies, though, this was modified into a promise not to initiate hostilities only. See Michael Mandelbaum, *The Nuclear Question: The United States and Nuclear Weapons, 1946-1976* (Cambridge: 1979), p. 75.

121 For a recent review of non-proliferation efforts, see the National Academy of Sciences study, *Nuclear Arms Control: Background and Issues* (Washington: 1985), pp. 224-273.

122 Dulles to certain diplomatic posts, March 6, 1953, *FRUS: 1952-54*, II, pp. 1684-1685. Contingency planning for such an effort had been underway for years, although Eisenhower complained that these had provided no clear conclusions. [Ambrose, *Eisenhower: The President*, pp. 67-68].

123 Eisenhower speech to the American Society of Newspaper Editors, April 16, 1953, *Eisenhower Public Papers: 1953* (Washington: 1960), pp. 179-188. For the origins of this speech, see Emmet John Hughes, *The Ordeal of Power: A Political Memoir of the Eisenhower Years* (New York: 1963), pp. 100-112.

124 See, for example, Lyndon B. Johnson, *The Vantage Point: Perspectives of the Presidency, 1963-1969* (New York: 1971), pp. 468-469; also Henry Kissinger, *Years of Upheaval* (Boston: 1982), pp. 287-288.

125 I have in mind here the long history of dynastic struggles in Europe up through the wars of the French Revolution; also, and much more recently, the way in which a refusal to acknowledge leadership legitimacy has perpetuated the Iran-Iraq war.

126 I am indebted to Ambassador Jack Matlock for suggesting this point.

127 See Carl Sagan, "Nuclear War and Climatic Catastrophe: Some Policy Implications," *Foreign Affairs*, LXII (Winter, 1983/84), pp. 257-292.

128 Paul Kennedy has pointed to the significance of the perception among

Germans, after 1900, that British influence in the world was increasing, while their own was not. [*The Rise of Anglo-German Antagonism*, p. 313.]

(Goldmann)

1 Bertil Nygren, *Fredlig samexistens: klasskamp, fred och samarbete. Om Sovjetunionens detente-doktrin* (Stockholm: Statsvetenskapliga institutionen, Stockholms universitet, 1984).

2 See, for example, Raymond Cohen, *International Politics: The Rules of the Game* (London/New York: Longman, 1982), and Christer Jönsson, *Superpower: Comparing American and Soviet Foreign Policy* (London: Frances Pinter, 1984).

3 For a consideration of what may go wrong with nuclear alerts see Scott D. Sagan, "Nuclear Alerts and Crisis Management," *International Security*, IX, 4 (Spring 1985), pp. 99-139. For data about one aspect of U.S.-Soviet crisis behavior see Barry M. Blechman and Stephen S. Kaplan, *Force without War: U.S. Armed Forces as a Political Instrument* (Washington, D.C.: Brookings, 1978), and Stephen S. Kaplan, *Diplomacy and Power: Soviet Armed Forces as a Political Instrument* (Washington, D.C.: Brookings, 1981).

4 This is considered in Kjell Goldmann, "Change and Stability in Foreign Policy: Detente as a Problem of Stabilization," *World Politics*, XXXIV, 2 (January 1982), pp. 230-266); and "Detente and Crisis," *Cooperation and Conflict*, XVIII, 4 (1983), pp. 215-232.

5 Patrick M. Morgan, *Deterrence: A Conceptual Analysis,* 2nd ed., Beverly Hills/London/New Delhi: SAGE 1983).

6 Morton A. Kaplan, *System and Process in International Politics* (New York: John Wiley, 1957), p. 9.

7 Several attempts have been made to map the fluctuations quantitatively. The most recent and important effort is Daniel Frei and Dieter Ruloff, *East-West Relations* (Cambridge, Massachusetts: Oelgeschlager, Gunn & Hein, 1983).

8. Quoted from Alexander L. George, *Managing U.S.-Soviet Rivalry: Problems of Crisis Prevention* (Boulder, Colorado: Westvien 1983), p. 148.

CHAPTER 6 (Soedjatmoko)

1 The difficulties of specifying what sort of conflict constitutes a war make this a very imprecise figure. Estimates range widely from about 100 upwards, including the count of 259 "wars or warface incidents" made by the historian of the US Joint Chiefs of Staff and the 307 "conflicts" counted by Dr. Nazli Choucri in *Population and Conflict: New Dimensions of Population Dynamics* (Cambridge, Massachusetts: M.I.T. Press, 1983).

2 John Paxton (ed.) *The Statesman's Year-Book, 1977/78* (London: The Macmillan Press Ltd., 1977).

3 Quoted in Lloyd Timberlake, *Africa in Crisis: the Causes, the Cures of*

Environmental Bankruptcy (London: International Institute for Environment and Development, 1985).

4 Johan Galtung, *There Are Alternatives! Four Roads to Peace and Security* (Nottingham: Spokesman Press, 1984).

5 Ibid.

6 See for example in this volume, Michael Howard, "The Causes of War".

7 Jackson Diehl, "Argentina Takes Steps Against a Rightist Paramilitary Group", *International Herald Tribune*, June 3, 1985.

8 Gerry S. Thomas, *Mercenary Troops in Modern Africa* (Boulder, Colorado: Westview Press, Inc., 1984).

9 Anthony Short, review of *Armed Communist Movements in Southeast Asia: Issues in Southeast Asian Security*, edited by Lim Joo-Jock and S. Vani, in *Survival*, XXVII, 2 (March-April, 1985)

10 Maria Elena Hurtado, "Colombia: So Who Writes to the Colonels?", in *South*, 58 (August, 1985); "CPT No Longer Poses a Threat to Thailand", in *Thailand Foreign Affairs Newsletter*, 15/84 (November, 1984).

11 "Central America: Revolution and Counter-Revolution", in *Strategic Survey 1984-85* (London: The International Institute for Strategic Studies, 1985).

12 Ibid.

13 Sergio Gonzaléz Gálvez, "The Arms Race as a Factor of Instability in Latin America", in *Security and Development* (Tokyo: United Nations University, forthcoming).

14 Robert S. Leiken, "Can the Cycle Be Broken?", in Robert S. Leiken (ed.), *Central America: Anatomy of Conflict*, (New York: Pergamon Press, 1984).

Further References

Al-Mashat, Abdul-Monem M., *National Security in the Third World*. Boulder: Westview Press, 1985.

Chege, Michael, "Conflict in the Horn of Africa". Paper presented in Addis Ababa at the United Nations University's Seminar on "Peace, Development and Regional Security in Africa", January 1985.

Gavshon, Arthur, *Crisis in Africa: Battleground of East and West*. Boulder: Westview Press, 1984.

Hansen, Emmanuel, "Peace and Regional Security in Africa: A State of the Art Report". Paper presented in Addis Ababa at the United Nations University's Seminar on "Peace, Development and Regional Security in Africa", January 1985.

Hewedy, Amin, "The Impact of the Middle East Crisis on African Security". Paper presented in Addis Ababa at the United Nations University's Seminar on "Peace, Development and Regional Security in Africa", January 1985.

International Institute for Strategic Studies, *Strategic Survey 1984–1985*. London: The International Institute for Strategic Studies, 1985.

Leiken, Robert S. (ed.), *Central America: Anatomy of Conflict*. New York: Pergamon Press, 1984.

Macfarlane, Neil, "Intervention and Regional Security" (Adelphi Paper No. 196). London: The International Institute for Strategic Studies, 1985.

Mandaza, Ibbo, "Conflict in Southern Africa". Paper presented in Addis Ababa at the United Nations University's Seminar on "Peace, Development and Regional Security in Africa", January 1985.

Nashif, Taysir N, *Nuclear Warfare in the Middle East: Dimensions and Responsibilities*. Princeton: The Kingston Press, Inc., 1984.

Ntalaja, Nzongola, "The National Question and the Crisis of Instability". Paper presented in Addis Ababa at the United Nations University's Seminar on "Peace, Development and Regional Security in Africa", January 1985.

Porter, Bruce D, *The USSR in Third World Conflicts: Soviet Arms and Diplomacy in Local Wars 1945-1980*. Cambridge/New York/Melbourne: Cambridge University Press, 1984.

Tandon, Yash, "Africa and the Global Super Power Struggle". Paper presented in Addis Ababa at the United Nations University's Seminar on "Peace, Development and Regional Security in Africa", January 1985.

Thomas, Gerry S., *Mercenary Troops in Modern Africa*. Boulder: Westview Press, 1984.

Treverton, Gregory F., "Latin America in World Politics: The Next Decade" (Adelphi Paper No. 137). London: The International Institute for Strategic Studies, 1977.

CHAPTER 7 (George)

1 This possibility was examined in a simulation conducted at Stanford University. See Alexander L. George, David M. Bernstein, Gregory S. Parnell and J. Philip Rogers, *Inadvertent War in Europe: Crisis Simulation*, a Special Report of the Center for International Security and Arms Control, Stanford University, June 1985.

2 This rationale and approach characterize the Harvard "Project on Avoiding Nuclear War," funded by The Carnegie Corporation of New York as part of a broader program for examining the danger of nuclear war. The first major publication of the Harvard project is Graham T. Allison, Albert Carnesale, and Joseph S. Nye, Jr., *Hawks, Doves, Owls: An Agenda for Avoiding Nuclear War* (New York: W. W. Norton and Co., 1985).

3 See, for example, John Steinbruner, "Launch Under Attack," *Scientific American*, 250, No. 1 (1984) and "Nuclear Decapitation," *Foreign Policy* 45 (1981); Paul Bracken, *The Command and Control of Nuclear Forces* (New Haven: Yale University Press, 1983); Richard K. Betts, "Surprise

Attack and Preemption," in *Hawks, Doves, Owls*, pp. 54-79; Bruce G. Blair, *Strategic Command and Control: Redefining the Nuclear Threat* (Washington, D.C.: The Brookings Institution, 1985); and Daniel Ford, *The Button* (N.Y.: Simon & Schuster, 1985).

4 For a brief summary of Soviet commentaries, see Douglas M. Hart, "Soviet Approaches to Crisis Management: The Military Dimension," *SURVIVAL* 26, No. 5 (1984), pp. 220-223.

5 This point is made by Douglas Hart, op. cit.

6 The broader political aspect of the Soviet military doctrine attempts to balance this technical military concern regarding the need for pre-emption by placing an even greater emphasis on deterring war. For a thorough analysis of Soviet military doctrine, see David Holloway, *The Soviet Union and the Arms Race* (New Haven: Yale University Press, 1983); chapter 3. See also Stephen M. Meyer, "Soviet Perspectives on the Paths to Nuclear War" in *Hawks, Doves, Owls*, pp. 167-205.

7 Steinbruner, "Launch Under Attack," p. 47.

8 On this and various other possible "paths" to nuclear war see, for example, Allison, et al. *Hawks, Doves, Owls*. See also Hilliard Roderick (ed.), *Avoiding Inadvertent War: Crisis Management* (Austin: Lyndon B. Johnson School of Public Affairs, The University of Texas at Austin, 1983). Thomas Schelling has discussed variables affecting crisis stability in a number of his writings; see, for example, "The Dynamics of Mutual Alarm," chapter 6 in his *Arms and Influence* (New Haven: Yale University Press, 1966); pp. 221-259.

9 It should be noted that Kennedy did *not* believe that his choice was restricted to initiating a pre-emptive first-strike himself or accepting Soviet pre-emption; therefore, the belief that there was a premium on going first did not come into play. Nor is it by any means certain that had Khrushchev rejected the ultimatum Kennedy would have immediately authorized air strikes.

10 I draw for this purpose on chapter 1 of *Inadvertent War in Europe: Crisis Simulation*. For a more detailed discussion see A. L. George, "Crisis Management: The Interaction of Political and Military Considerations," *SURVIVAL*, 26, No. 5 (1984), pp. 223-234.

11 This principle of crisis management is an important corollary to the basic rule of prudence alluded to in John Gaddis's chapter, namely that neither superpower should initiate military action against the forces of the other superpower. While both sides evidently understand very well the necessity to avoid any kind of shooting war, they have not always followed the corollary, which is not to exploit one's advantages in a crisis to the point of confronting the opponent with the fateful choice of either backing down and accepting a humiliating setback or initiating force.

12 This question is of considerable concern to thoughtful, well-informed analysts and was the focus of a conference on crisis management sponsored by the International Institute of Strategic Studies (London) in April 1984.

13 See, for example, the discussion in Bracken, op. cit.

14 John Steinbruner, "An Assessment of Nuclear Crises," in Franklyn Griffiths and John C. Polanyi (eds.), *The Dangers of Nuclear War* (Toronto:

University of Toronto Press, 1979); pp. 39, 40 (italics added). See also Scott Sagan, "Nuclear Alerts and Crisis Management," *International Security* 9, No. 4 (1985), pp. 99-139; and the detailed discussion by Desmond Ball of the special problems of controlling strategic nuclear submarines at sea, "Nuclear War at Sea," paper presented at the Conference sponsored by the Institute on Global Conflict and Cooperation at U.C.L.A. on April 26, 1985.

For Soviet commentaries expressing concern over top-level US political authorities' ability to maintain control during a crisis over forward-based elements of their strategic nuclear forces, see Hart, op. cit., and Alexei Vasilyev, "Stability—or Nevertheless Destabilization?" a paper written for the Soviet Scientists Committee for Peace, Against the Nuclear Threat (no date).

15 For a detailed summary of what is known about the effects of stress on performance of the kinds of cognitive tasks policy-makers must perform in dealing with intense diplomatic crises see Ole R. Holsti and Alexander L. George, "The Effects of Stress on the Performance of Foreign Policy-makers," in Cornelius Cotter (ed.) *Political Science Annual* 6 (1975) (Indianapolis: Bobbs-Merrill, 1976), pp. 255-319. For a more general treatment see Irving L. Janis and Leon Mann, *Decision Making: A Psychological Analysis of Conflict, Choice, and Commitment* (New York: Free Press, 1977). Noteworthy is the important collaborative research project on International Crisis Behavior, under the direction of Michael Brecher, that is evaluating the effects of crisis-inducted stress on the quality of decision-making in a large number of historical cases. The first volume in the series is by Michael Brecher and Benjamin Geist, *Decisions in Crisis: Israel, 1967 and 1973* (Berkeley: University of California Press, 1980). Additional volumes published thus far are by Avi Shlaim, *The United States and the Berlin Blockade, 1948-1949*; Alan Dowty, *Middle East Crisis: U.S. Decisionmaking in 1958, 1970 and 1973*; and Karen Dawisha, *The Kremlin and the Prague Spring*, also published by the University of California Press in 1983, 1984 and 1985 respectively.

Earlier, pioneering research on the stress-inducing effects of international crises was done by Robert North and his associates at Stanford University. A useful formulation of the findings of the Stanford project is provided by Ole R. Holsti, *Crisis, Escalation, War* (Montreal: McGill-Queen's University Press, 1972). Important contributions to this literature also appear in several publications by Charles F. Hermann, *Crises in Foreign Policy* (Indianapolis: Bobbs-Merrill, 1969) and *International Crises: Insights from Behavioral Research* (New York: Free Press, 1972).

16 Sorensen, *Decision-Making in the White House* (New York: Columbia University Press, 1964), p. 76.

17 "That kind of crisis-induced pressure does strange things to a human being, even to brilliant, self-confident, mature, experienced men. For some it brings out characteristics and strengths that perhaps even they never knew they had, and for others the pressure is too overwhelming." (*Thirteen Days*, New York: W. W. Norton, 1969; p. 22).

18 In *Crisis, Escalation, War* Ole Holsti cites historical evidence of these

effects of stress on policy-makers in the events leading to the outbreak of the First World War.

In an important theoretical-empirical contribution to the literature, Irving Janis has noted that crisis-induced stress can adversely affect the performance of decision-making tasks in a small, highly cohesive group by encouraging its members to resort to "concurrence-seeking" within the group in order to avoid and cope with anxiety-arousing emotions generated by having to make important value-laden decisions under conditions of risk and uncertainty. See particularly Janis's analysis of US decision-making in the Bay of Pigs case in his *Victims of Groupthink*, 2nd ed. (Boston: Houghton Mifflin Co., 1985).

19 Some of the difficulties of identifying reliable and valid behavioral indicators of undue stress are discussed by Margaret G. Hermann and Charles F. Hermann, "Maintaining the Quality of Decision-making in Foreign Policy Crises: A Proposal," in Alexander L. George, et al., *Towards A More Soundly Based Foreign Policy: Making Better Use of Information*. Vol. 2, Appendices, Commission on the Organization of the Government for the Conduct of Foreign Policy, June 1975 (Washington, D.C.: US Government Printing Office, 1976).

20 A substantial literature has developed discussing the idea of a joint US-Soviet crisis control center put forward some years ago by Senators Nunn and Jackson. Ideas of this kind need careful analysis if they are not to remain in the limbo of gimmicks and panaceas. Before the Nunn-Jackson proposal could be evaluated, conceptual analysis was needed that would consider what such a center would be charged with doing, what would be needed to enable it to perform its assigned tasks, how it should be staffed and where it should be located in order to perform those tasks, and—of particular importance—how it would be linked with the national infrastructures for crisis avoidance and crisis mangement already existing in the US and Soviet governments. Only through detailed, well-informed conceptual analysis of this kind can one hope to transform the general idea of a joint center into a more specific design concept that can then be assessed by the two governments with reference to whether it was needed, could perform useful functions, and was feasible.

Dr. Barry Blechman and his colleagues have played a major role in refining the original proposal and moving it in this direction. His paper, "U.S.-Soviet Nuclear Risk Management Centers" (in Roderick, ed., *Avoiding Nuclear War*, pp. 78-87, and 96-104) provided essential conceptual analysis. A similar contribution in defining and delimiting the concept of a crisis control center is made in John W. Lewis and Coit D. Blacker (eds.), *Next Steps in the Creation of An Accidental Nuclear War Prevention Center*, a special report of the Center for International Security and Arms Control, Stanford University, 1983. See also Dale M. Landi et al., "Improving the Means for Intergovernmental Communications in Crisis", R-3157-FF, The RAND Corporation, Santa Monica, California (June 1984); published under the same title also in *Survival*, 36, No. 5 (September/October 1984), pp. 200-214 and the arguments put forward opposing a joint crisis control center in Caspar W. Weinberger, *Report to the Congress on Direct Commu-*

nications Links and Other Measures to Enhance Stability (Washington, D.C.: U.S. Department of Defense, April 11, 1983). For a useful discussion of a variety of ways in which the United States and the Soviet Union might cooperate to reduce the danger of war, see William L. Ury and Richard Smoke, *Beyond the Hotline* (Cambridge: Harvard Law School, 1984).

21 Breslauer's interpretation appears as chapter 13, "Why Détente Failed", in Alexander L. George, *Managing U.S.-Soviet Rivalry: Problems of Crisis Prevention* (Boulder: Westview Press, 1983, pp. 319-340). For additional discussion of the flaws in conceptualization and implemention of détente see chapters 1 and 2 by George in the same volume.

22 For an important theoretical discussion of this problem see Robert Jervis, "Cooperation Under the Security Dilemma", *World Politics* 30, No. 2 (1978). The origins of the First World War have been viewed from this perspective by several analysts in a special issue of *International Security* (Vol. 9, No. 1, Summer 1984): Stephen Van Evera, "The Cult of the Offensive and the Origins of the First World War," pp. 58-107; Jack Snyder, "Civil-military Relations and the Cult of the Offensive: 1914 and 1984," pp. 108-146; Richard Ned Lebow, "Windows of Opportunity—Do States Jump Through Them?", pp. 147-186. See also Patrick Morgan, *Deterrence: A Conceptual Analysis* (Beverly Hills: SAGE, 1977); and the forthcoming book by Richard Ned Lebow, Robert Jervis, and Janice Gross Stein (editors), *Psychology and Deterrence* (Baltimore: Johns Hopkins Press, 1985).

23 Thus, a recent RAND Corporation study notes that while confidence-building measures that imposed restrictions on strategic nuclear force deployments and operations could contribute to reducing crisis instability, some of these measures undertaken to reassure the Soviets that crisis or conflict need not escalate might undermine an important dimension of the current American deterrence concept. Continuing, the RAND report observes that "There may be a fundamental inconsistency between current Western deterrence doctrine and the commonly accepted notion of strategic confidence building. The NATO extended deterrence concept—the link between the American strategic umbrella and Europe—as codified in the NATO strategy of flexible response is predicated on maintaining uncertainty in the mind of Soviet leaders about the possibility that a conventional war could escalate to strategic nuclear war." Alan J. Vick and James A. Thomson, "The Military Significance of Restrictions on Strategic Nuclear Force Operations," RAND N-2113-FF, April 1984.

24 Axelrod, *The Evolution of Cooperation* (New York: Basic Books, 1984). For an important conceptual analysis of "reciprocity", which plays a central role in Axelrod's tit-for-tat solution to the prisoner's dilemma and in many other analyses of the basis for developing cooperative relations, see Robert O. Keohane, "Reciprocity As A Principle of Governance in International Relations," ms. January 1985.

25 See in particular Jervis's "Cooperation Under the Security Dilemma," and the special October 1985 issue of *World Politics*, "Cooperation Under Anarchy," edited by Kenneth Oye.

26 See, for example, Robert Jervis, "Security Regimes," *International Organization*, Spring 1972; and his recent article "From Balance to Concert: A Study of International Security Cooperation," *World Politics*, October 1985.

27 On the conceptualization and empirical analysis of regimes see Stephen Krasner (ed.), *International Regimes* a special issue of *International Organization* 36, No. 2 (Spring 1982).

28 The present author is collaborating with Alexander Dallin and Philip Farley in organizing a study of this kind. A broad analytical framework is being developed which will be utilized by a large number of collaborators in doing case studies of successful and unsuccessful efforts to develop cooperative US-Soviet arrangements for dealing with specific security-related problems.

For a broader discussion of US-Soviet cooperation in non-security dimensions of their relationship and whether this can facilitate cooperation in security matters, see Nish Jamgotch, Jr. (ed.), *Sectors of Mutual Benefit in U.S.-Soviet Relations* (Durham: Duke University Press, 1985).

29 The list includes the Allied agreement during the Second World War providing for the occupation and administration of post-war Germany; the Austrian State Treaty of 1955 creating a neutral Austria; the Laos neutralization agreement of 1962; the Partial Test Ban Treaty in 1963; the Hotline Agreement of 1963 and its updating in 1971; the 1967 treaty banning stationing or orbiting of weapons of mass destruction in outer space; the Nuclear Nonproliferation treaty of 1968; the 1971 agreement on measures to reduce the risk of accidental war; the 1971 Quadripartite agreement on Berlin; the ABM and SALT-I agreements in 1972; the Incidents at Sea Agrement in 1972; the 1974 treaty on limitation of underground nuclear weapons tests; the Helsinki Accord of 1975; the SALT-II Agreement of 1979.

30 For a fuller description of the evolution of a satellite reconnaissance regime see the chapter by John Lewis Gaddis.

31 Types of partisan mutual adjustment are discussed in Lindblom, *The Intelligence of Democracy; Decision-Making Through Mutual Adjustment* (Englewood Cliffs: Prentice-Hall, 1968).

32 The American Committee's proposal would prohibit either superpower from direct or indirect use of their combat forces in the Middle East, Southwest Asia, Africa, the Indian Subcontinent, and Southeast Asia. The prohibition would also forbid "covert, paramilitary, or so-called 'volunteer' combat forces," and neither superpower would be entitled to intervene in these areas with its combat forces even if "invited" to do so. A brief statement of the proposal appears in the American Committee's *Basic Positions* (1982) and it is described in more detail by one of the Committee's members, Arthur Macy Cox, in his *Russian Roulette* (N.Y.: Times Books, 1982).

For a critical discussion of the proposal's feasibility see *Managing U.S.-Soviet Rivalry*, pp. 379-381.

33 For a more detailed account see articles by Harold Saunders, Evgeni M. Primakov, and Alexander L. George in the American Enterprise Institute's

Foreign Policy and Defense Review 6, No. 1 (1986).

34 For useful discussions of the variety of "rules" and "norms", other than those encompassed by international law, that serve to regulate international politics see the following: Hedley Bull, *The Anarchic Society* (London: Macmillan, 1977); Raymond Cohen, *International Politics: The Rules of the Game* (London: Longman, 1981); Joanne Gowa and Nils H. Wessell, *Ground Rules: Soviet and American Involvement in Regional Conflicts* (Philadelphia: Foreign Policy Research Institute, 1982); K. Goldmann, "International Norms and Governmental Behavior," *Cooperation and Conflict* (Vol. 3, 1969); Paul Keal, *Unspoken Rules and Superpower Dominance* (London: Macmillan, 1983); Neil Matheson, *The "Rules of the Game" of Superpower Military Intervention in the Third World* (N.Y.: University Press of America, 1982); Edward McWhinney, *Peaceful Coexistence and Soviet-Western International Law* (Leyden: A. W. Sythoff, 1964); Isaak I. Dore, *International Law and the Superpowers: Normative Order in A Divided World* (New Brunswick, N. J.: Rutgers University Press, 1984).

35 See Gloria Duffy, "Crisis Prevention in Cuba," in *Managing U.S.-Soviet Rivalry*, pp. 288-291.

36 For a more detailed account see *Managing U.S.-Soviet Rivalry*, pp. 377-378; A. L. George, "U.S.-Soviet Global Rivalry: Norms of Competition," presented at the XIIIth World Congress, International Political Science Association, Paris, July 15-20, 1985; and A. L. George's essay in the American Enterprise Institute's *Foreign Policy and Defense Review* 6, No. 1 (Summer 1985).

Other analysts of Middle East conflicts have also noted this tacit norm. See, for example, Bradford Dismukes and James M. McConnell (eds.), *Soviet Naval Diplomacy* (N.Y.: Pergamon Press, 1979), pp. 276-278; Christer Jönsson, *Superpowers: Comparing American and Soviet Foreign Policy* (London: Frances Pinter, 1984); chapter 5, "Crisis Management in the Middle East;" and Yair Evron, "Great Powers' Military Intervention in the Middle East," in Milton Leitenberg and Gabriel Sheffer (eds.) *Great Power Intervention in the Middle East* (New York: Pergamon Press, 1979); pp. 17-45.

37 For a detailed discussion see the articles by Primakov, Saunders, and George in AEI *Foreign Policy and Defense Review* 6, No. 1 (1986).

38 *New York Times*, February 13, 20, 21, 1985. Subsequently similar meetings were held on southern Africa issues and Afghanistan (*New York Times*, June 19, 1985).

39 See Ole R. Holsti and James N. Rosenau, *American Leadership in World Affairs: Vietnam and the Breakdown of Consensus* (Boston: Allen & Unwin, 1984); William Schneider, "Public Opinion," in Joseph S. Nye, Jr. (ed.), *The Making of America's Soviet Policy* (New Haven: Yale University Press, 1984); pp. 11-35.

40 See, for example, Elizabeth K. Valkenier, *The Soviet Union and the Third World: An Economic Bind* (New York: Praeger Publishers, 1983); Stephen Sestanovich, "Do the Soviets Feel Pinched by Third World Adventures?" *Washington Post*, May 20, 1984; S. Neil MacFarlane, "The Soviet Concep-

tion of Regional Security," *World Politics* 37, No. 3 (April 1985); pp. 295-317.

CHAPTER 8 (Walzer)

1 A reader comments that states do, after all, sign treaties and so limit their power (or, better, their right) to act independently. But this is a minor, and self-interested, surrender of sovereignty; reformers commonly have something much more significant in mind: more like the abolition of sovereignty by the sovereign state itself. And that is inherently unlikely.

2 Immanuel Kant, "Eternal Peace" (1795), in C. J. Friedrich (ed.), *The Philosophy of Kant* (New York: Modern Library, 1949), p. 454. But see the description of a "new world order" in Richard Falk, *This Endangered Planet: Prospects and Proposals for Human Survival* (New York: Random House, 1971) for a more optimistic view.

3 See, for example, Rajni Kothari, *Footsteps Into the Future: Diagnosis of the Present World and a Design for an Alternative* (New Delhi: Orient Longman, 1974).

4 John Locke in Patrick Romanell (ed.), *A Letter Concerning Toleration* (Indianapolis: Bobbs-Merrill, 1950), pp. 52, 54.

5 Michael W. Doyle, "Kant, Liberal Legacies, and Foreign Affairs", in 12 *Philosophy and Public Affairs* 3 and 4 (Summer and Fall, 1983).

6 Hedley Bull, *The Anarchical Society: A Study of Order in World Politics* (London: Macmillan, 1977), pp. 264 ff.

7 Kothari, *Footsteps*, op. cit., which defends regionalism in order to enhance the strength of Third World states.

8 Bull, *Anarchical Society*, p. 255.

List of Participants

Blackaby, Frank, Director, Stockholm International Peace Research Institute.
Deutsch, Karl, W., Professor, International Institute for Comparative Social Research, Berlin.
Freedman, Lawrence, Professor, King's College, London.
Gaddis, John L., Professor, Ohio University.
George, Alexander, L., Professor, Stanford University, California.
Goldmann, Kjell, Professor, University of Stockholm.
Hassner, Pierre, Professor, Fondation Nationale des Sciences Politiques, Paris.
Heradstveit, Daniel, Director of Research, Norsk utenrikspolitisk institutt, Oslo.
Hinsley, F. H., Professor, St John's College, Cambridge.
Holst, Johan J., Director, Norsk utenrikspolitisk institutt, Oslo.
Howard, Michael, Professor, University of Oxford.
Lundestad, Geir, Professor, University of Tromsø.
Malnes, Raino, Ass. Professor, University of Oslo.
Midgaard, Knut, Professor, University of Oslo.
Pharo, Helge, Ass. Professor, University of Oslo.
Ramphal, Shridath, Professor, Commonwealth Secretariat, London.
Riste, Olav, Professor, Research Centre for Defence History, Oslo.
Saeki, Kiichi, Dr., Nomura Research Institute, Japan.
Schelling, Thomas C., Professor, Harvard University, Massachusetts.
Sejersted, Francis, Professor, University of Oslo, Member of the Norwegian Nobel Committee.
Singer, J. David, Professor, University of Michigan.
Soedjatmoko, Director, The United Nations University, Tokyo.
Subrahmanyam, K., Professor, The Institute for Defence Studies and Analyses, New Dehli.
Sverdrup, Jakob, Professor, Director, Nobel Institute, Oslo.
Thee, Marek, Research Fellow, International Peace Research Institute, Oslo.
Väyrynen, Raimo, Professor, University of Helsinki.
Waltz, Kenneth N., Professor, University of California.
Walzer, Michael, Professor, Princeton University, New Jersey.
Watt, David C., Professor, Royal Institute of International Affairs, London.
Williams, Phil, Professor, Royal Institute of International Affairs, London.
Zinnes, Dina, Professor, University of Illinois at Urbana-Champaign.
Østerud, Øyvind, Professor, University of Oslo.

Detailed Table of Contents